FREEDOM WAS NEVER
LIKE THIS

FREEDOM WAS NEVER LIKE THIS

A Winter's Journey in East Germany

Dan van der Vat

Hodder & Stoughton

LONDON SYDNEY AUCKLAND TORONTO

British Library Cataloguing in Publication Data

van der Vat, Dan
  Freedom was never like this: A winter's journey
  in East Germany.
  I. Title
  943.1087

  ISBN 0-340-55274-3

Published by Hodder and Stoughton,
a division of Hodder and Stoughton Ltd,
Mill Road, Dunton Green, Sevenoaks, Kent TN13 2YA.
Editorial Office: 47 Bedford Square, London WC1B 3DP.

Photoset by Rowland Phototypesetting Ltd,
Bury St Edmunds, Suffolk
Printed in Great Britain by
St Edmundsbury Press Ltd, Bury St Edmunds, Suffolk

In memoriam
Norman Crossland
1928–1991

Contents

Abbreviations

AG   *Aktiengesellschaft* (joint stock company)

BASF Badische Anilin-und Sodafabrik (a chemical company)

CDU   Christlich-Demokratische Union (Christian Democratic Union party)

CSU   Christlich-Soziale Union (Bavarian sister-party of CDU)

DB   Deutsche Bundesbahn (West German Railways)

DBD   Demokratische Bauernpartei Deutschlands (German Farmers' Party)

DEFA Deutsche Film-Aktiengesellschaft (German Film Company)

DFF   Deutsche Funk und Fernsehen (GDR Radio and TV)

DR   Deutsche Reichsbahn (GDR Railways)

FDGB Freier Deutscher Gewerkschaftsbund (Free German Trade Union Federation of the GDR)

FDJ   Freie Deutsche Jugend (Free German Youth of the GDR)

FDP   Freie Demokratische Partei (West German Liberals)

FNL   Fünf Neue Länder (five new federal states from ex-GDR)

FRG   Federal Republic of Germany (West Germany until 3 October 1990; all Germany thereafter)

GDP   Gross Domestic Product

GDR   German Democratic Republic (East Germany until 3 October 1990)

GmbH *Gesellschaft mit begrenzter Haftung* (limited company)

KPD   Kommunistische Partei Deutschlands (Communist Party of Germany 1919–1946)

LDPD Liberal-Demokratische Partei Deutschlands (Liberal Democratic Party of Germany in the GDR)

LPG   *Landwirtschaftsproduktionsgenossenschaft* (GDR cooperative farm)

MWP   Mecklenburg-West Pomerania

NDPD National-Demokratische Partei Deutschlands (GDR National-Liberal party)

NVA   Nationale Volksarmee (GDR defence forces)

ÖTV   Öffentliche Dienste, Transport und Verkehr (FRG public service, transport and traffic union)

PDS   Partei des Demokratischen Sozialismus (Party of Democratic Socialism – post-union successor to SED)

RAF   Rote Armee Fraktion (Red Army Faction of West German terrorists); Royal Air Force

SED   Sozialistische Einheitspartei Deutschlands (Socialist Unity Party of Germany – GDR's Communists)

SMA   Soviet Military Administration (of East Germany)

SPD   Sozialdemokratische Partei Deutschlands (Social Democratic Party of Germany)

Stasi Staatssicherheit (State Security – GDR secret police)

VEB   *Volkseigene Betrieb* (GDR people's or state enterprise)

VK   Volkskammer (GDR legislature)

PROLOGUE

Cabaret – opportunity knocks – three Reichs – two Germanys – Wall falls – analogies – kill the patient – "Socialism" – hangover, then party – two into one – train with a view – sump of Europe – caveats

Prologue

"A hearty welcome to the BDBZ!" proclaimed Frau Doktor Gisela Oechelhaeuser. She was speaking to a full house from the stage of Die Distel (the thistle), the political revue at the Friedrichstrasse railway station in east Berlin. In the so recently bygone days when East Germany was the German Democratic Republic (GDR), the resident company acquired through its revues a reputation for political brinkmanship and artistic licence second to none in the entire Communist bloc. Dr Oechelhaeuser must be the world's only cabaret commère with a doctorate (which is wonderfully German, but no more bizarre than watching Dame Judi Dench playing Bertolt Brecht's *Mother Courage* – or Sir Alastair Burnet reading the football results on television). The doctor is the actor-manager of the Berlin Cabaret Theatre, as it is formally known, and she also directed the show running there over the turn of the year 1990–91, my winter in the east of the new united Germany.

Her opening sally reflected both the German appetite for initials and acronyms, which is insatiable, and an east German attitude to the unification of the two German states on 3 October 1990, which I found to be commonplace on my travels round the former GDR. There had been a lively but inconclusive debate in Germany about how to refer to the erstwhile republic now in dissolution: east Germany, said the pragmatists; middle Germany, said the irredentists, who wanted half of modern Poland as well; the FNL (five new *Länder*), said the bureaucrats in Bonn; BDBZ, said the Distel's principal. What did BDBZ mean? Why, the *Bundes-deutsche Besatzungs-Zone*, she said, the Federal (i.e. West) German Occupation Zone . . .

This drew much applause as well as the first of many annoying "oohs"

3

from a Hooray Heinrich somewhere behind me. He reacted to each political joke as if dapper little Erich Honecker and his Stasi agents were yet at the height of their power and the Distel company was still prancing delicately through the no-man's-land between licensed jesting and *lèse-majesté*. This element of walking through a political minefield lent their pre-unification shows a unique piquancy and gave their audiences a delicious *frisson* of shared danger in the bad old days. This was essentially spurious, because the GDR, a state which manipulated its citizens as no other, clearly regarded the Distel as a useful piece of libertarian window-dressing, a cultural figleaf and an intellectual safety-valve; otherwise it would promptly have been shut down. But the Distel earned an honoured place in Berlin's post-imperial tradition of cabaret *à l'outrance*, as so vividly portrayed by Liza Minnelli and Joel Grey in Bob Fosse's film of 1972.

My Distel evening, which unoriginally included a pastiche of *Cabaret*'s superb "Money, Money, Money" number, was robust, full of disrespectful jokes about Dr Helmut Kohl, the Chancellor of unification and therefore, on 2 December 1990, hands-down victor in the first democratic, all-German poll in fifty-eight years. One of the best of the Kohl jokes making the rounds in all the media was an uncaptioned cartoon showing him holding up a herring: Bismarck, the Iron Chancellor who united Germany in 1871, was inordinately fond of the fish, known to this day as a *Bismarckhering*. The Distel jibes relied heavily on the multiple meanings of the German word *gross*, which can be used for any of these English words: great, grand, fat, large, tall and even gross. Unification had made Helmut Kohl (objectively massive) *grosser* than ever, said Dr Gisela. But, although the show was highly professional and provided an enjoyable couple of hours, inevitably it lacked bite. The enlarged Federal Republic of Germany has made political cabaret safe for democracy and thus taken away its edge – a sad fact, but a small price, one might say, to pay for liberty. Or, more precisely, a small part of the unexpectedly large price the east Germans were made to pay for a free-market economy, whose instantaneous and overwhelming take-over of the GDR prompted Gisela Oechelhaeuser's opening line.

This book describes an exploration of east Germany at the time of the demolition of the German Democratic Republic, the Communist state which ruled the area from 7 October 1949 to 3 October 1990. At that time

East Germany with a capital "E" ceased to be the informal synonym for the GDR and became a geographical expression, east Germany with a small "e". Events during and after my winter there, however, soon showed that the region would retain its separate identity for a long time to come, regardless of the political fact of union.

Before the historic and delirious moment of the opening of the Berlin Wall on 9 November 1989 visitors to the GDR needed a visa, which entailed a long wait, and even then one's time and movements were restricted. The Communists, for all their talk of (east) Berlin as "capital of the GDR", did not dare to abrogate the postwar, four-power status of Berlin as a whole, whereby sovereignty over the former capital of the Reich belonged to the victorious wartime Allies (America, Britain, France and Russia). So one could always go to East Berlin. One could also obtain a quick visa to visit the twice-yearly Leipzig industrial fair in March or September, or a very slow one for some other trip not related to news-events. This meant that when I was the Bonn Correspondent of *The Times* in the 1970s I hardly got to know the GDR. I could never get an instant visa to cover an event outside the divided city or count on being free to go to the GDR when the authorities condescended to supply one. I had been to Leipzig and was a member of the first group of British journalists to be invited to examine the GDR's new tourist facilities in 1986 (even then the visa took three weeks), but the GDR was for me, East Berlin apart, mostly *Germania incognita*.

My journey was thus a unique opportunity: to visit east Germany without travel restrictions, but with the GDR's doomed institutions still in place. The Unification Treaty of 31 August 1990 consigned the GDR's ship of state to the scrapyard – with no serious thought for saving what was socially worth keeping. It proved to be, in large part, a voyage back in time to a Germany remarkably similar to the one in the west which I began to know as a schoolboy in the 1950s. Here was an eerie time-warp where streets were still cobbled and the lights glowed dim in the smog; antiquated cars belched fumes, battered trams rattled and the air was thick with the raw tang of burning coal; houses were heartbreakingly dilapidated; ancient, stinking industrial plants seemed still to be struggling to get started forty-five years after the war, without regard to the environment. There were villages of neglected wattle-and-daub in which not a soul was abroad from one hour to the next. Grey streets lined with crumbling grey buildings dripping in acid rain under a grey winter sky with no other colour to be seen, not even a lit-up advertisement or a

5

cheery shop window, were a powerful stimulus to depression, relieved only by the remarkable resilience of many of the people who live and work behind the drab façades of the erstwhile GDR. A veritable abomination of desolation in many places – but much natural and man-made beauty in many others.

The long and immensely complex history of "Germany" shows that political division was the norm until modern times, specifically until Bismarck united it as the Second Reich in 1871 under Kaiser (Emperor or Caesar) Wilhelm I. The Emperor Charlemagne briefly united it in AD 800; the Emperor Otto I reunited it in 962 as the Holy Roman Empire of the German Nation. But in 1250 this "first Reich", which had stretched from Holland to Sicily and from the Baltic to the Pyrenees, broke into an ever-shifting pattern of autonomous parts which paid lip-service to the Emperor but went their own ways. Some, such as France, Switzerland and the Netherlands, sooner or later broke away altogether. "Germany" was frequently at war with itself, most notably and horrifically during the Thirty Years' War from 1618 to 1648, when at least one third of the population died – a catastrophe unmatched even by the mechanised massacres of the twentieth century.

Ironically it was Napoleon who provided the first great impetus towards modern unification by reducing the hundreds of mostly tiny political units of the Holy Roman Empire, formally abolished in 1806, to some three dozen states – ironic because this tidying up of a messy map ensured the permanent eclipse of France by Germany soon afterwards as the strongest European power. After the Congress of Vienna in 1815 carried his work forward, there came the climax of a long struggle for domination of the whole of Germany between the Habsburgs of Austria and the Hohenzollerns of Prussia. After a series of border wars with Denmark, Austria and France, Bismarck imposed his settlement of "the German Question", which had plagued Europe in its ever varying forms for a millennium, in 1871. Austria with its mostly non-Germanic territories became a wholly separate empire and Prussia ruled "Germany proper", dominating north and central Europe.

But France disputed a "German answer" which robbed it of Alsace-Lorraine, one of the main causes of the First World War. After the defeat of the second Reich and the Kaiser's abdication in 1918, the first German republic was declared, eventually known as the Weimar Republic after the town where its constitution was drawn up. The Treaty of Versailles in 1919 gave West Prussia to Warsaw as the Polish Corridor to the Baltic and returned Alsace-Lorraine to the French. But the universal sense of grievance in Germany against this treaty, especially the swingeing reparations it imposed, combined with a worldwide economic collapse to cause general political and social unrest. This eventually gave Hitler and Nazism their opportunity for an entirely constitutional take-over of power on 30 January 1933. Germany's revived territorial ambitions in Austria, Czechoslovakia, Poland and, above all, in the Soviet Union led to the Second World War in 1939 – the fifth and by far the largest war launched by the Germans in Europe in seventy-five years.

The result of Hitler's defeat in 1945 was twofold. First, Germany was further truncated, with the northern half of East Prussia going to the Soviet Union and the southern half, plus the provinces of Silesia and eastern Pomerania, to Poland. In effect Germany was compressed westward, behind the line formed by the Oder and Neisse rivers. Second, what was left was divided into four zones by the victorious Allies. The ensuing Cold War between the West and the Soviet Union led, in 1949, to the creation of two separate German states: one consisted of the American, British and French zones, which became known as the Federal Republic of Germany (West Germany), the other of the Soviet zone, formally entitled the German Democratic Republic (East Germany). Only in 1990, amid a general collapse of the Soviet Communist system throughout eastern Europe, including East Germany and the Soviet Union itself, could residual Germany be united and a formal settlement of the Second World War agreed.

The unification made possible by Mikhail Gorbachev, demanded by the east Germans themselves and delivered with political panache by Helmut Kohl was greeted with very mixed feelings, not always concealed, by the French, the Dutch, the Poles, the Russians and the British, to name but five. Only the Americans showed no reserve in welcoming unification; but experience has led me to conclude that the Americans are anglophone Germans anyway – the kaleidoscope of other peoples who contributed to the US genetic stock being mere camouflage! I soon discovered that the purported beneficiaries of unification, the benighted east Germans, freed from fifty-seven years of continuous totalitarian misrule by the Nazis and then by the Communists, had decidedly mixed feelings themselves.

The Wall round West Berlin and the fearsome fence between the GDR and West Germany were at once the *sine qua non* of the GDR's existence and the essential symbol of its identity – and its failure. Less than eleven months elapsed between their opening and the unification of the two German states in an expanded Federal Republic of Germany (FRG) on 3 October 1990. This stupendous event, combined with the steep decline of the Soviet Union which made it possible, represented the biggest shift in the balance of power in Europe since the Russian Revolution, if not since Bismarck's unification in 1871 (what is more, it was united Germany's simultaneous political machinations and defeat of the Tsar's army in 1917 which provoked that revolution).

Because some twelve million people from past or present German territory east of the pre-1990 FRG had settled in West Germany after 1945, I did not expect to encounter a completely alien race or society between the Elbe and Oder rivers. Nor did I – indeed I was soon struck by how swiftly the patina of four decades of Communist repression was being wiped away. But in many ways the journey was also and very much a new experience. In order to come to terms with such a phenomenon it is customary to look for parallels, whether in personal experience or in history.

I had the honour (words not idly chosen) to witness the transformation of Rhodesia into Zimbabwe in 1980. That however was not only a different continent and a completely different context but also gave the world a new state in old borders and the United Nations a new member, as did the independence of Namibia (once German South-West Africa), another old haunt of mine, ten years later. But unifying Germany actually and uniquely reduced the membership of the UN by one. It cut the number of states at the second Conference on Security and Cooperation in Europe by one to thirty-four, in time for the signature in November 1990 of the Paris Charter officially ending the Cold War, which had both engendered the GDR and formalised the division of Germany (and Europe) in the first place.

Jerusalem is another great city which was long divided like Berlin, but its reunification was by conquest and it is still dominated by racial and religious as well as political and social tension. Nicosia remains divided, but the division of Cyprus is ethnic as well as political; so is the division of Ireland, however much it may come across as a religious phenomenon. The Korean peninsula still accommodates two bitterly opposed states, one Communist and the other capitalist, yet is inhabited by the same *Volk*, and is thus the closest parallel to the postwar division of Germany. But the analogy which finally suggested itself (obviously with many reservations) as I explored east Germany was the reabsorption into the United States of the southern Confederacy after the Civil War of 1861–65.

Comparisons are odious and analogies can easily be overstretched; this one may seem far-fetched, especially since Germany was spared a civil war over the Iron Curtain (which would surely have meant curtains for the whole of Europe and beyond). Nevertheless the Cold War was no less divisive in and of Germany, and the demands the Soviet Union made of the GDR in many respects held it back in the conditions found throughout the territory of the former Reich in the immediate aftermath of the Second World War. Chancellor Kohl compared east Germany in 1990 with west Germany in 1952–3. The latter half of 1990 brought a devastated east Germany an obvious element of liberation from servitude with the triumph of a far stronger economy and currency, plus a freer society, over a much weaker rival. There was also a reassertion of federalism. And these changes are being followed by a reconstruction which already seems to be doing rather less for the liberated than for the legions of carpetbaggers coming from the triumphant west in search of bargains, quick profit and power. Mistrust and misunderstanding be-tween rich *Westler* or *Wessis* and poor *Ostler* or *Ossis* (the new inter-German jargon) seemed well set to survive the Cold War just as they did between "Yankees" and "Rebs" after 1865. To this day the American South is largely, in social and economic terms, a USA second class; and the German East has a similar status in the expanded FRG.

The fusion of the two German states is described in the unification treaty of 31 August 1990 as the "accession" (*Beitritt*) of the five recon-stituted east German federal states (*Länder*) and east Berlin to the FRG. They did not unite: West Germany simply annexed East Germany. Of this interpretation the text and workings of the Unification Treaty leave no room for doubt. Now that I have seen the east German past I can attest that, in general, it did not work. Yet, although the GDR was misruled by a repugnant and rotten regime, by no means everything in it was bad. A conservative Federal Government in Bonn took the view, however, that in order to cure this patient, a society diagnosed as terminally ill with "Socialism", it was necessary to kill it. Many east Germans un-metaphorically and spontaneously described the ensuing process to me as an occupation. Many others made a comparison, sometimes positively, sometimes negatively, with the immediate postwar period.

9

One of the saddest aspects of the transformation of eastern Europe, of which German unification is such a crucial part, is that conservatives and others in the West and the vast majority of east Germans and eastern Europeans have concluded that Socialism is dead and has nothing to offer. What is dead is Soviet Communism, specifically Stalinism and the Marxism-Leninism from which it was distortedly derived. The fatal flaw in the Soviet model (which the east Germans operated more efficiently than their mentors or anyone else) is that it was a dictatorship of the proletariat. The phrase is not used here in the way Karl Marx intended, but conversely, because that seems so much closer to the truth: the proletariat was *subjected* to a totalitarian dictatorship which was not answerable to the people and therefore sank into a mire of complacency and corruption. What "democratic centralism", the tyrannical euphemism at the heart of the failed system, has to do with democratic socialism has never been explained. The triumphalist Right, which seeks to throw out the Socialist baby with the Soviet-Communist bathwater, is about as closely connected with Nazism as Willy Brandt's Social Democratic Party, trounced in the first free all-German election for fifty-eight years in December 1990, is with Stalin. I take no sides here: I merely take exception to the linguistic tarbrush with which many western conservatives have smeared everyone to their left, with the same mindless dogmatism they condemn in others as well as with brazen intellectual dishonesty. Yet even Helmut Kohl speaks with pride of the "social" market economy which he is busy conveying to the bemused east Germans.

Certainly Unification Day on 3 October 1990 is the only celebration I have ever attended – I was in the streets of Berlin, platonically accompanied by a lady anarchist of the non-violent persuasion at the time – where the hangover preceded the party. It was a binge too far after the heady celebration of the breaching of the Wall and then New Year's Eve 1989–90. My subsequent journey, in four parts separated by brief intervals, took place over three months and the turn of the year 1990–91, when the process of dismantling all the institutions of the GDR was already cutting deep and hard at astonishing and alarming speed. It was a curious, split-level journey, involving not only sightseeing but also exploration of political, economic and social phenomena – a tour of a society in flux as well as of a country which was and remains quintessentially German in every way.

When I flew to Bonn on 26 September 1990 there were two Germanys; when I returned from Frankfurt on October 6 there was one. I had gone to visit friends, to arrange the research for another book and to take in the Frankfurt Book Fair, which I had never visited. It seemed only natural to include Berlin as well in good time for zero hour on October 3 when unification was to be officially consummated. This was surely one of the most historic moments in my lifetime, a significant proportion of which has been spent in or concerned with Germany. Having been unable to get to the city in time for the opening of the Wall, I was determined not to miss the consequence. The complications of the trip led me to travel on from Bonn by train, which gave me my umpteenth chance to view the unlovely panorama beside the tracks of the Deutsche Reichsbahn (DR), the GDR railway, on the route which linked West Germany with Berlin via Marienborn. But this was as nothing to what I saw when I travelled south-westward from Berlin to Frankfurt-on-Main via Gerstungen on a line I had never used before. Since this experience had a lot to do with the genesis of this book, a short description now follows.

The republic whose train I boarded had ceased to exist just a few hours before I squeezed my way into an already overcrowded carriage at the Zoo station in west Berlin. The train had started from the oft-restyled Berlin-Hauptbahnhof (main station, previously Berlin-East, previously Silesia station) in the east of the city and picked up more passengers at Friedrichstrasse, also in the east. There was a collective hangover on board after the overnight celebrations in the streets. A few travellers were keeping down the blood-level in their alcohol by drip-feed from cans of beer. The drunks on view were of the morose rather than the boisterous school. A couple of them listlessly held black, red and gold tricolours, doubtless waved wildly the night before; but this was the morning after and it was time to go home. I was resigned to lurching about on one of those fold-up seats considerably but obstructively provided in the corridors of German trains when somebody beckoned me into a smoking compartment which was doing just that – smoking furiously. As several people had tetchily objected to my presence across their path and driven their point home by ostentatiously climbing over me, I put a rest for my back above the risk to my lungs.

I had enough time as we dawdled out of west Berlin's pretty south-western suburbs to reflect on the familiar irony of finding myself borne along the worn tracks of the DR in a carriage owned by the DB (Deutsche Bundesbahn, the Federal German railway) and pulled by a Soviet-made diesel locomotive. This pragmatic arrangement had been one of the few bonds between the two German states and was now a harbinger of the realisation of union, even if the administrative and technical reunification of the two heavily used German railway networks was going to take at least two years. This was not the last time I was to ask myself why the two states were given no such opportunity for a planned amalgamation. Both networks are state-owned: the sparkling clean DB's accumulated deficit is so vast that privatisation is out of the question. The same applies to the grimy DR because of its state of advanced decay, reversible only by stupendous investment on a scale beyond the means and/or the will of private investors. Weeds grow between the DR tracks, even on quite heavily used stretches. Abandoned rolling-stock rusts away in half-disused marshalling yards. The stations are usually prewar and unspeakably desolate.

The first stretch of the run west took us through the Wall on the edge of west Berlin, via an engineering detour round handsome Potsdam, through some of the wonderful forests of Brandenburg (which, as I would later discover, concealed such depressing manifestations of *Realpolitik* as sprawling Soviet military encampments and vast opencast lignite mines). A visibly depressed open landscape followed, with few villages or towns, as we crossed into Saxony-Anhalt, passing through what the battered station nameplates proudly proclaimed to be "Luther-town Wittenberg" – the place where the herald of Protestantism is supposed (on shaky historical grounds) to have nailed his diatribe against ecclesiastical corruption to the door of the castle church, though he certainly lived and preached the Reformation there. The Elbe looked foul with oil as we passed over it, the banks seemingly lined with sludge. I appeared to be the only person in the compartment who was interested in the passing scene, which admittedly went from bad to worse and then on to the outlandishly horrible. The others were asleep or attending to a baby.

The unforgettable part of the journey began at well-named Bitterfeld, some thirty-five kilometres south-west of Luther's town. This place and its larger neighbour, Wolfen, are not so much dominated by a chemical works as enveloped in it. The train ran past, under or alongside mile after mile of palpably degenerating and mysterious tubes leaking dense vapour. (I hoped this was nothing more menacing than steam from one of those long-distance piped-heating networks in use in many parts of the GDR and west Berlin, a gargantuan central-heating system whose ducts snake incongruously across open country, up and over obstacles.) There were chimneys short and tall, fat and thin, belching nameless smoke and fumes into the thick smog, chemical pipelines horribly discoloured and looking alarmingly neglected, storage tanks, furnaces and enormous buildings of unidentifiable function. Cheek by jowl with all this one could make out grimy houses with off-white chemical dust on their roofs. How could anyone live in such a place? How could any government allow such a swamp of pollution to build up for so long in such a concentrated area? Indeed; but who had enjoyed the potential influence to stop it? Obviously not the locals. And that was only the beginning. The railway follows the valley of the Saale, the river whose existence in the midst of historically rich deposits of many different minerals helps to explain the siting of the chain of chemical plants all the way from the city of Halle, the only official stop on the journey, past Schkopau, Merseburg and Leuna some thirty kilometres to the south.

The tracks go this way so as to be able to supply the plants through which they pass and to take away what they produce: here was once the heartland of IG Farben, the chemical cartel which made artificial rubber and petrol for Hitler (and also poison gas). All this was the great sump of East Germany, the region where the GDR's "rust belt" of old industries was at its rustiest, reputedly the most concentratedly polluted area of the country and probably of the entire continent, the dirtiest blot on the face of Europe. I had read about this region, of which some pretty strong language has been used; I had even seen some television footage on the GDR's greatest pollution problem. None of this prepared me for the sheer scale of the elongated disaster, as I told my publisher when I fortuitously ran into him at Frankfurt: this book arose out of the ensuing conversation.

The task of cleaning it up, as promised by the new Federal and state governments, was surely one of the most daunting in the world, I thought. But shutting it all down would surely add a substantial six-figure number to the already high total of unemployed in the ex-GDR. The money needed was presumably of the mind-boggling variety, one of those "telephone numbers" which the ordinary, semi-numerate human mind cannot encompass.

It was more than merely astonishing to pass almost immediately from this industrial disaster into a wine-growing area: I had forgotten that the GDR had a small but viable wine industry producing quite passable vintages. Next we crossed into Thuringia with its wooded hills and its historic cities of Weimar, Erfurt and Gotha, all looking pretty seedy from the train (as do most urban areas touched by a railway, a historic cause of permanent blight on all adjacent buildings). Finally there was Eisenach, overlooked by the Wartburg fortress where Luther took refuge and dashed off his vernacular New Testament, shaping the modern High German language as he worked. After that, darkness mercifully fell and we crossed the intra-German border, still marked by its tall but now deserted watchtowers with their sinister, one-way glass.

I got out at Darmstadt, Hesse, the nearest town to Frankfurt with a bed to spare in Book Fair week. Its railway station was surprisingly old (and thus similar to many of east Germany's) and it is not much of a town, even by the brutalist standards of so many completely rebuilt West German cities. How clean it looked.

It cannot be emphasised too strongly that what follows is mainly a series of snapshots of what I observed at the time I observed it. Some personal and institutional crises have meanwhile been resolved for better or worse; new ones have arisen; some, which were expected have not come to pass; some, which were not, have. The upheaval involved in reshaping the ex-GDR looked set, in and after the winter of 1990–91, to last for a decade. Sad to say, by no means everything the demolition teams are uprooting and destroying is bad, and the price millions are being made to pay for liberty is much higher than they thought. The "free" in free market does not mean free of charge and never did.

At time of writing the very rough monetary rule of thumb is DM3 = $1.70 = £1. One kilometre is five-eighths of a mile; I notched up over 7,740 of them in the driving-seat in my short climatic and economic winter in the German east, and was driven quite a few more in trains, buses and trams. I do not claim to know it all; but I managed to see more than most have had the chance to do. My only regrets are that I was alone, and that it was winter.

-I-

THE GERMAN
DEMOCRATIC
REPUBLIC

Shotgun wedding – workers and peasants – SED *rules – Nazi aliens – Iron Curtain – revolt – Berlin crisis – miracle and misery – the Wall –* JFK's *doughnut –* Ostpolitik *– recognition – Kohl – dissidents – Gorbachev – two Berlins – loopholes – protests – Honecker quits – Wall opens –* SED *falls – Stasi – union –* DM *– laissez faire – Treuhand – logistics*

– I –

The German Democratic Republic

In April 1946, at the Hotel Hamburger Hof in Meissen, Saxony, there took place the Unification Party Congress of the Sozialistische Einheitspartei Deutschlands, the SED or Socialist Unity Party of Germany. The resolution passed on the 22nd proclaimed the foundation of the party which ruled the GDR for forty years. It was described as a merger of the Soviet-Zone Communist and Socialist parties, the KPD and SPD; in fact it was a shotgun wedding. The Soviet Union immediately after the war seemed intent on making its zone of Germany a model society which the proletariat in the three western zones would envy; but everything was provisional, pending the eventual reunification envisaged by the victorious powers. On the very day of Hitler's suicide in his Berlin bunker on 30 April 1945, eight days before the surrender, Walter Ulbricht, a German Communist who had spent the war in Moscow, arrived with other German anti-Nazis to help the Russians run their zone. The KPD produced a manifesto as early as June 11, five weeks before the Allied Potsdam Conference; the SPD published one four days after the Communists and the Christian Democratic Union (CDU) in the Soviet Zone on the 26th; on July 5 the Liberal Democratic Party of Germany (LDPD) followed suit. All this, and the United Front of Anti-Fascist Parties proclaimed on July 14, was orchestrated by the Soviet Military Administration or SMA.

The fusion of KPD and SPD looked like a correction of the disastrous error which split the Weimar Left and let the Nazis in. However, it was based on cynical *Realpolitik*: the KPD alone could not hope for a majority. The SPD in the west reasonably saw it as a coup; and the new SED tilted the nature of the United Front from democratic anti-Fascism to a political

17

monopoly dedicated to the development of a Marxist-Leninist social order in the Soviet Zone. The Front was widened to increase this bias even further by the admission of the Free German Trade Union Federation (FDGB), the Free German Youth (FDJ), the Cultural League (Kulturbund) and the new Democratic Farmers' and National Democratic (middle-class) parties (DBD and NDPD), all Communist-dominated. In September 1945 the revolution from above truly began with the great land reform which dispossessed all private landowners of more than 100 hectares without compensation. In the following month similar treatment was given to private industry, or what was left of it after the SMA's dismantling activities, including bodily removal of entire plants to the Soviet Union. Both fundamental reforms enjoyed widespread popular support. When economic central planning was imposed in June 1948, the die was cast: the social order in the Soviet Zone was now irreconcilable with the politically pluralistic, mixed economy being established in the western zones. The currency reform (the introduction of the *Deutsche Mark*) accompanying the latter prompted Stalin to blockade Berlin in June 1948, in a bid to dislodge the western powers. But they stood firm and beat the blockade with the Berlin airlift. The Russians backed down in May 1949.

The SED had invited all political parties and mass organisations throughout Germany to attend a German People's Congress in December 1947. Although more than a quarter of the delegates were from the western zones, neither the western Allies nor the nascent institutions in their zones attended. The Congress eventually chose a People's Council of 400 members which, on 7 October 1949, transmogrified itself into the provisional Volkskammer (people's chamber) under the constitution promulgated on the same day. The leader of the subsumed east-SPD, Otto Grotewohl, soon received his reward by becoming the first prime minister of the new state. The constitution was a close imitation of the Weimar Republic's, which was no bad thing; but it took no account of the fact that the real power in the land lay not with people or parliament but with the Party, as in the Soviet Union (which also enjoyed a model constitution under Lenin). The constitution was rewritten in 1968 and 1974, signalling the abandonment of German unification and enshrining Socialism, the supremacy of the SED and the Soviet alliance as fundamental to the state – and abolishing the right to strike, to leave the country at will or to enjoy many other freedoms taken for granted in the West. The GDR was solemnly classified as a "workers' and peasants' state". In reality it was run by a self-perpetuating Party elite answerable to nobody but itself and its patron, the Soviet Union. It is Socialism's misfortune that not only the regimes of the former Soviet bloc but also their western ideological opponents found it convenient to use the name as a label for Stalin's perversion of it, to the apparently permanent disadvantage of decent, democratic Socialists.

The membership of the first Volkskammer (VK), the "parliament" of the GDR, was 25% SED, 15% each from CDU and LDPD, 7.5% each from NDPD and DBD, 10% FDGB and 5% each from FDJ and Cultural Federation, with the balance from other Communist-controlled mass organisations. In other words the Communists directly controlled all the seats except those of the CDU and LDPD, whose independence was purely notional anyway. The electorate had been invited in May 1949 to vote Yes or No for the entire membership list and for the programme drawn up by the Congress: the Yes vote amounted to 62% in the Zone and 52% in East Berlin – probably genuine and not unimpressive results.

The first election after the foundation of the GDR took place on 15 October 1950. Once again the electorate could say Yes or No to a unified list of candidates: 99.7% were reported to have said Yes. Until the first pluralistic elections forty years later, similar insults to the intelligence were presented at regular intervals, without trace of smile or shame, as "election results" by the regime. The various organisations wrangled over the number of seats allocated to each, which did vary slightly, but it was a private fight which always ended to the satisfaction of the SED, officially a Marxist-Leninist party since 28 January 1949.

The new state was recognised by its mentor, the Soviet Union, on 15 October 1949. The VK functioned as both legislature and executive, appointing the Council of State, whose chairman was head of state, the Chairman of the Council of Ministers (prime minister) and the leading administrative officials of other executive and judicial organs. Fifteen VK committees supervised the work of the main government departments; the Party through its Politburo also shadowed the ministries as well as exerting Party discipline over the vast majority of VK deputies and officials. The SED applied Lenin's system of "democratic centralism" making the Politburo the true source of power in all parts of the state apparatus, which was largely overlapped by the Party's anyway.

The key posts in the GDR were, therefore, the first and general secretaryships of the SED, and only two men ever held them: Walter Ulbricht became General Secretary in 1950 and First Secretary as well in

1953; Erich Honecker became First Secretary on Ulbricht's resignation in 1971 and General Secretary as well in 1976. Both leaders also came to serve as Chairman of the Council of State (i.e. president), but never as prime minister, a post of responsibility without power. In the GDR the state was officially subordinate to the Party.

This meant that it was not possible to make progress in a wide spectrum of careers, most obviously the public service as broadly defined, without being in the SED, which thus had a total membership of more than one in seven of the population. While Army officers and police had little choice (except to choose another career), the ambitious in other fields needed SED membership rather more than talent to get on. Belonging to one of the four other "bloc parties" in the Front of National Unity was not as good, but satisfactory for most purposes. If one chose to damage one's prospects by electing to be "partyless", the minimum one could get away with to avoid being constantly passed over or worse was to join the German-Soviet Friendship Society, which thus enjoyed the mostly nominal allegiance of six million GDR citizens, or more than one in three. It was difficult to avoid joining the Pioneers, the Party organisation for children up to fourteen, or the FDJ thereafter, just as their members' parents and grandparents had been members of the Hitler Youth or the German Girls' League under the Nazis.

The Ministry for State Security (Staatssicherheit or "Stasi", the GDR's KGB, of which much more anon) held a "cadre file" on every citizen over eighteen in which detailed notes were kept of the subject's "life in society" – not just his or her qualifications, military service record, career and references but also contributions or lack of them to the various mass organisations, such as attendance at meetings, voluntary work, donations to "Socialist Solidarity" funds for political causes and the like. When the Honecker regime collapsed these dossiers were thrown open and people were free to turn them into ordinary personnel files by removing all documents they felt should not be there.

Meanwhile the fledgling western Federal Republic successfully laid claim to the right to speak for all Germans, as set out in the Basic Law. West Germany established itself as the mainstream German state, the *de facto* successor to the Second and Third reichs – and acknowledged its historical guilt by, *inter alia*, paying compensation to Israel, a moral debt the GDR never acknowledged until its dying days. Prior to the general East-West settlement of the early 1970s produced by détente, the GDR was diplomatically recognised only by the Soviet bloc and its closest sympathisers round the world. For a quarter of a century, with increasing success as its "economic miracle" took hold, Bonn operated what became known as the "Hallstein doctrine": the isolation of the GDR by forcing third-party states to choose between relations with Bonn or East Berlin.

On the other hand, the GDR was rather more assiduous than the West in rooting out ex-Nazis, scoring many a propaganda point by naming people with murky pasts in western public posts (in the USA too) and publishing its "Brown Book" of former Nazi officials. But the East German regime chose a different method of coming to terms domestically with the shared German past. While the West Germans were forced by their own democratic system to face up to it, however slowly and reluctantly in many cases, but far more than the Japanese, the East Germans raised "anti-Fascism" to the status of a governing principle of their state. In so doing, however, they were subtly fudging; Nazism, a term never officially used in the GDR, is not synonymous with Fascism, but many degrees worse and exclusively German. The ideologists in East Berlin seized on the Soviet usage which, for example, called the wartime alliance the "Anti-Fascist Coalition". This enabled them to describe what looked in the West like nothing less than the smashing defeat of Nazi Germany by the Allies as a "liberation" of Germany from "the Fascists" by the Red Army. The West Germans spoke euphemistically, and still do, of Hitler's *Machtergreifung* – a "seizure" of the power which was offered to him constitutionally and on a plate; but the East Germans treated the "Fascists" as if they had been brownshirted aliens who descended on the Fatherland from outer space. That the Nazis were the largest party in the democratically elected Reichstag in 1933 was suppressed in the east as assiduously as the Nazi-Soviet Pact; at the same time the efforts of the undoubtedly brave, but embarrassingly small, German resistance to Hitler were not only seriously exaggerated but also ascribed almost exclusively to Communists (who had merrily gone along with Hitler until he invaded the Soviet Union in 1941).

The final catharsis in West Germany came more than a generation after the defeat of Hitler with the showing in the late seventies of the voyeuristic American television serial *Holocaust* – an inadequate piece of faction which nevertheless struck a powerful sentimental chord by retelling the Nazi horror as a human-interest story through a cast of identifiable characters. Younger West Germans rounded on their elders and demanded to know why they had not been told at school or at home. There seemed to be no other topic of conversation for weeks on end. *Holocaust* was the biggest West German media event between 1945 and the opening of the Berlin Wall in 1989. Many East Germans saw the show because West German television was already watched widely (and illegally until the regime gave up the fight). But it was the West, not the East, German state which was, however reluctantly, associated with the programme by virtue of its dissemination through a public institution – a state-licensed broadcasting corporation run by a board on which all the main political and social strands were represented. Whatever the private and individual reaction may have been in the east, there was no debate in the GDR, where all western publications were strictly forbidden until 1989. And when freedom of speech finally arrived, most east Germans were naturally preoccupied with getting over the forty-five years of Communist dictatorship looming between them and any recollection of the rather worse Nazi one which led up to it.

In 1950 the new East German state lost no time in regulating relations with its Communist-ruled neighbours, Czechoslovakia and Poland, where Stalin had also engineered Moscow-oriented governments. The GDR recognised the postwar expulsion of the Sudeten German minority from western Czechoslovakia as permanent and renounced all territorial claims (the presence of this minority had given Hitler his "excuse" for annexation). On July 6 the Oder-Neisse line was recognised by the GDR as Poland's western frontier; Bonn formally rejected any such recognition as "null and void".

In August the League of Expellees (Germans displaced from eastern Europe) drew up its charter, disingenuously renouncing revanchism and calling for a free, united Europe – in which of course Germany would be free to reunite, preferably in its 1937 borders.

By 1952 West Germany's first Chancellor, Dr Konrad Adenauer, was well on the way to implementing his policy of anchoring the Federal Republic in the West. The "Germany Treaty" (signed in May 1953) was to stabilise its relations with the western Allies and bring broad sovereignty to Bonn. In April West Germany was one of the six western European states which signed the European Coal and Steel Community Treaty – the first step towards today's European Community. Bonn joined the Council of Europe in May 1952 and two months later the western Allies formally terminated their state of war with Germany.

Stalin's startling proposal in March 1952 of a neutralised and demili-tarised Germany reunited within the Potsdam boundaries came too late to reverse the trend. So in May the GDR dug a ditch from north to south across Germany, the first move towards what soon became the most fearsome frontier in the world: the intra-German border, the Iron Curtain transformed from metaphor to reality, the front line in the Cold War. In Berlin border-control posts went up between the Soviet Sector and the West as roads, railways, telephone lines and other links were cut.

On July 23 the five *Länder* (states) in the GDR were dissolved and replaced by fifteen *Bezirke* (districts), another fundamental break with the shared German past. With the death of Stalin early in 1953 reunification of Germany, even on Soviet terms, became a dead letter in Moscow for thirty-five years. The long overdue disappearance from the scene of the only man who ever managed to challenge Hitler as a mass-murderer should have brought as much relief to the GDR as to the rest of the Soviet bloc; Moscow promulgated an easing of "socialisation" and of the ideological slanging-match with the West, a thaw in the Cold War.

The Ulbricht regime was reluctant to follow suit, having just raised prices and the work norm by ten per cent across the board. Moscow leaned a little harder and Ulbricht duly announced a "new course", acknowledging "serious errors". The price increases were cancelled, but not the new norm. So the workers went on strike, first in East Berlin and soon in many other places. Their protest became a campaign for free elections and German unification, and on 17 June 1953 the SED lost control. In the ensuing state of emergency martial law was declared across most of the country and the Red Army restored order by a brutal show of force. Tanks were deployed in the heart of Berlin and all the major cities. The death-toll in this first of an irregular series of eastern European anti-Communist risings is unknown. It was all "a Fascist provocation", said the regime. Ulbricht's reward was to be promoted from General to First Secretary of the SED; and on New Year's Day 1954 Moscow cancelled all its outstanding demands for war reparations from the GDR (a burden not imposed on West Germany, which received Marshall Aid instead). One year later the Russians terminated their state of war with Germany.

Also in 1955, the Germany Treaty and the Paris treaties which made West Germany a member of Nato and the Western European Union came into force. So the GDR and the other east European satellites joined the Soviet Union in the Warsaw Pact, formalising the massive armed confrontation across the intra-German border which set the tone for

East-West relations for the next three and a half decades. Both German states were permitted to rearm.

The brief thaw in East-West relations which set in when Khrushchev took over as Soviet leader was gone by 1956, despite his monumental debunking of Stalin. At the end of 1958 there was another crisis over Berlin when Moscow unilaterally "cancelled'" the four-power status of the city as a whole and the residual four-power responsibility for all Germany. The "Berlin Ultimatum" required West Berlin to be demili-tarised and classified as an "independent political unit". The West stood firm. The crisis fizzled out at an inconclusive "four-plus-two" conference (the four wartime victors and the two Germanys) in Geneva in summer 1959. Thirty years later the same constellation of powers was to agree upon German unification. Inside the GDR the regime imposed by draconian measures a new agricultural system abolishing all remaining private farms in favour of big cooperatives on the Soviet model, known from their German initials as LPGs. The churches put their heads above the parapet and protested, not for the first time in Communist East Germany and certainly not the last. The SED did all it could to undermine and constrict the mainly Protestant (Evangelical Lutheran) Christian Church, but never risked an all-out confrontation.

Life in the GDR remained grim, and thousands upon thousands continued to vote with their feet by travelling to East Berlin and crossing to West Berlin by the underground or elevated railways (U-bahn and S-bahn) or other loopholes, en route to West Germany. In the first dozen years of the short history of the GDR two million people are thought to have done so. In 1961 the West German economic miracle, boosted by new labour from the GDR, was plain for all to see as conditions grew tougher in the East. The westward flow became a haemorrhage of skilled young people threatening the very survival of the GDR's economy, warped as it was by enforced membership of Comecon, the Soviet-dominated Council for Mutual Economic Cooperation. Moscow treated the GDR partly as a colonial economy, to be exploited as necessary, and partly as a source first of manufacturing plant and subsequently of technological products which may not have been as modern as West German ones but were usually better than any others in the Soviet bloc.

In the light of all this, of the reparations exacted by Moscow and of the absence of Marshall Aid, the fact that the GDR became the eleventh (some say the tenth, a few even say the seventh) largest industrial economy in the world may be seen as the real German economic miracle. We have already noted the great political flaw in the GDR: the lack of accountability of the leadership. The great economic flaw was that the East Germans got little or nothing extra, and almost all the environmental disadvantages, from the labours which made their state the most successful exponent of Soviet command economics. In fact the two great shortcomings of the system boiled down to one and the same: lack of choice.

On 15 July 1961 Walter Ulbricht, head of the East German Party and state, told a press conference that: "Nobody has the intention of building a wall." On August 11 his deputy, Willi Stoph, told the Volkskammer that there would shortly be "measures against traffic in people, wooing away and sabotage", a reference to the economic siren-call of the West German boom. That week, a British officer told me years later, the tension in Berlin was palpable and it was the Soviet Commandant's turn to host the regular military dinner which was one of the already very few surviving institutions of the city's four-power status. The Briton asked a senior Soviet colleague what was going on and was told: "I am not at liberty to tell you anything, but I can assure you that whatever happens will be in all our best interests." At midnight that night, Saturday-Sunday, 12–13 August 1961, thousands of East German troops, police and labourers began to erect a 165-kilometre barrier (barbed wire first, later concrete) round West Berlin. In charge was that promising young member of the Central Committee of the SED and of the National Defence Council of the GDR, Erich Honecker. The idea was Ulbricht's, but the impulse came from Khrushchev; Moscow was alarmed by the mass exodus. Soon afterwards the entire intra-German border was closed to all GDR citizens. The division of Germany was now to be literally set in concrete; the wall round West Berlin was in reality a wall round East Germany turned inside out.

Historically it is too soon to say whether the Russian officer quoted above was right to assume that the entrenched division of Germany was in everybody's best interests, but the reaction of the West, even the West Germans in the middle of a federal election campaign, was oddly muted. There had been fears of another blockade, which would almost certainly have prompted the new young American President, John F. Kennedy, to go to the brink; but the Russians ostentatiously kept all access routes open. Vice-President Lyndon Johnson came over within a week to declare solidarity and renew US guarantees. When the "Berlin crisis" turned out not to be "worst case" there was almost relief, except of course in Berlin. The general rising which might have provoked an armed confrontation

25

did not happen, and the West had been handed a huge propaganda victory by this Communist *de facto* declaration of a permanent state of siege, no matter how loudly the regime and Moscow blamed "western sabotage" for their own panic measure. Some 200 people were to die trying to escape across the Wall and the intra-German border, seventy-eight in Berlin alone; Honecker's "shoot to kill" order to the border troops was the basis for his prosecution for alleged complicity in murder after his resignation in 1989. Otherwise life went on; the Wall became an attraction for western VIPs and tourists.

In June 1963 Kennedy came and wowed the West Berliners with a speech in which he declared in German, a language of which he knew nothing, "*Ich bin ein Berliner*". Unfortunately this means "I am a doughnut" (there is a type of doughnut which the Germans call a *Berliner*). In order to say what he meant, he should have used the phrase, *ich bin Berliner*. Similarly, *ich bin Hamburger* declares you to be a citizen of Hamburg whereas *ich bin ein Hamburger* means that you believe you are a chopped steak in a bun. Such are the vagaries of the German language; but the West Berliners knew what he meant and cheered him to the echo.

As the years wore on the GDR kept its citizens under psychological lock and key. Pensioners were cynically allowed to join their families in the West (so that Bonn had to pay their pensions). Every now and again a small travel concession was made, but anyone who went West for whatever reason or had any other kind of contact, including by post or by telephone, became an object of interest and not infrequently of harassment on the part of the Stasi, the Ministry for State Security run for decades by Erich Mielke. The first great sea-change in inter-German relations came with the general election in West Germany in September 1969. For the first time since the Weimar Republic, the Social Democrats, in coalition with the Liberal FDP, formed a government; Willy Brandt (SPD), Governing Mayor of Berlin when the Wall was built, became Chancellor. The previous government had paved the way for this shift in the balance of power in 1966, when the FDP withdrew from its coalition with the CDU, which was then obliged to take the SPD into a "grand coalition" as junior partner, making Brandt Vice-Chancellor and Foreign Minister. In this role Brandt began to put out the feelers towards eastern Europe which flowered into the full-blown policy of *Ostpolitik* during his chancellorship.

Thus on 19 March 1970 Willy Brandt went to the East German city of Erfurt for a historic, if not immediately productive, meeting with Willi

Stoph, GDR premier since 1964. A large crowd gathered in front of the hotel where Brandt was staying and chanted, "Will-ee, Will-ee," as the two men appeared on the balcony. No prizes were offered for guessing the true addressee of this phonetically convenient *double entendre* since no East German politician had ever had such an obviously rapturous and spontaneous reception in the history of the republic. The two leaders met again on the other side of the border in Kassel in May.

Twelve months later Ulbricht resigned from the SED leadership on grounds of age, an idea he got at dictation-speed from Moscow, which was displeased with his political arterio-sclerosis; as in 1953, he was too set in his harsh ways to bend with the new wind of détente blowing from the east. Erich Honecker replaced him. Meanwhile Brandt was mending fences with the Poles and the Russians, while the four wartime Allies came together to sort out a new arrangement for Berlin. The package, including a transit-agreement between the two Germanys, their first treaty, was ready by autumn 1971. Brandt's tiny parliamentary majority began to erode under the strain of recognising all existing borders in Europe. It has never been proved, but I was in Bonn throughout that frenetic time and I was not the only one who concluded that one or two votes were bought. Even so, Brandt survived by two votes a CDU attempt to unseat him. The Moscow, Warsaw and transit treaties went through. Nevertheless Brandt found it necessary to engineer the first premature election in West German history and was triumphantly vindicated in November, when the SPD became the strongest party in the Bundestag, the Bonn parliament, for the first time. The coalition with the FDP was resoundingly revived and with it *Ostpolitik*.

By the end of the year the two German states had thrashed out the text of a "Basic Relations Treaty" between them, ratified in the summer of 1973, when the Federal Constitutional Court threw out a plea of unconstitutionality against it lodged by Bavaria. They were to exchange "permanent representations", rather than embassies, a nod in the direction of abandoned hope for unification; but they effectively recognised each other as foreign states, even though the West German constitution continued to regard all Germans as *de jure* citizens of the Federal Republic, a fact which made it necessary for the East Germans to keep the Berlin Wall. But the GDR lost its pariah status in the West, was universally recognised and joined the United Nations at the same time as West Germany. To round off all the good news in 1973, Ulbricht died on August 1. But in May 1974 the discovery of an East German spy, Günter

Guillaume, in his private office led Brandt to resign – or else it was an excuse for a man who was tired, depressed and disillusioned to make way for Helmut Schmidt (SPD), arguably the most efficient head of government anywhere since the Second World War. *Ostpolitik* continued (as did Stasi spying in the Chancellery until at least 1984, as was revealed in spring 1991).

In a new treaty with the Soviet Union in 1975 the GDR and Moscow pronounced the German Question solved. But the GDR continued to take a hard line internally against dissidents, especially intellectuals who demanded reform. Wolf Biermann, the Hamburg lyricist and singer who had chosen to live in the East, was "decitizenised" (*ausgebürgert*, a singularly horrible and untranslatable German word) while on a tour of West Germany in November 1976. Two months earlier a priest had burned himself to death in Zeitz, near Halle, in protest against persecution of the Church. Many writers and artists left the GDR to live in exile, mostly voluntarily but sometimes not. West German journalists were thrown out from time to time. A sinister trade developed between the two Germanys in which the GDR's political prisoners – usually people who tried to "flee the republic" – were released for hard currency, about DM10,000 a head as was frequently reported. Spies commanded a higher price. Every now and again the GDR made a concession on transport, visas and other "humanitarian easements". Money played a role here too.

Schmidt fell out with the FDP over economic policy at the end of 1982 (and with his own SPD on defence policy). The FDP switched allegiance back to the CDU for the first time since 1966 and in a "constructive vote of no confidence" Schmidt was ousted and Helmut Kohl (CDU) elected in his place. Kohl won a sweeping election victory in March 1983.

In the following month the planned first visit to West Germany by an East German leader (Honecker) was called off because of two more deaths on the fortified GDR frontier. This did not stop a DM1 billion credit from Bonn to East Berlin going through in June. The *quid pro quo* included the dismantling of the sinister, self-activating blunderbusses built into the border fence to be set off by would-be escapers stumbling across the trip-mechanism; and children under fourteen were no longer required to change DM30 into GDR marks at the ludicrously extortionate rate of 1 : 1 for each day of a stay in East Germany. The deal was arranged by Franz Josef Strauss, chief minister of Bavaria and leader of the Christian Social Union, the CDU's ultra-conservative Bavarian sister party, on a visit to East Berlin. Much astonishment and not a little embarrassment, not least to Kohl and his cabinet, were caused by the nature of the deal and its provenance; but it was a sign of economic desperation in the GDR, always thirsty for hard currency. Another straw in the wind was the sale by the GDR railway, the Deutsche Reichsbahn, of the western section of the Berlin s-bahn to the West Berlin transport authority in February 1984; the East Germans had operated the elevated railway throughout the city since partition.

In March the regime was uniquely embarrassed by the arrival at the West German embassy in Prague of Frau Ingrid Berg, a GDR citizen, with her husband, his mother and their two children, all seeking a new home in West Germany. There was nothing new in their initiative because eighteen East Germans had taken refuge in the American and West German missions in East Berlin in January with the same motive; Wolfgang Vogel, the East German lawyer at the centre of so many "people for hard cash" deals, had negotiated their passage west for a generous consideration in D-marks. Frau Berg, however, was the niece of no less a personality than Willi Stoph, Prime Minister of the GDR and number two in the state power structure. As uncle Willi seethed, Herr Vogel negotiated the Berg family's return home in exchange for a promise to let them emigrate later in the year (and, of course, for an undisclosed sum from Bonn – worth every pfennig for such a propaganda coup, one would think). In June the West Germans were obliged to close their "permanent representation" (quasi-embassy) in East Berlin, it being full of more East Germans wanting to go west.

It was a tense summer and in September Honecker once again indefinitely postponed his visit to West Germany. Mikhail Gorbachev, appointed General Secretary of the Soviet Communist Party in March 1985, came to the SED's Party congress in April with a proposal for conventional arms reductions in Europe, the first of a spectacular series of offers.

Despite this, inter-German tension remained high as the GDR authorities mischievously allowed thousands of refugees from the Sri Lankan civil war to land at Schönefeld airport in East Berlin and pass unhindered to seek asylum in West Germany via West Berlin. A uniquely generous West German refugee law (more narrowly interpreted since) effectively obliged Bonn to accept them. But on October 1 the East Germans agreed to stop the flow by refusing a transit visa to anyone who did not have advance proof of acceptance by another country.

Even so the two German states were pursuing their own mini-détente throughout the year, apparently defying the postwar "rule" that there could be no improvement in inter-German relations without a general East-West thaw. Hindsight shows that this cautious warming fore-shadowed Gorbachev's initiatives, which were to lead to an unpre-cedented *rapprochement* between the superpowers. The President of the Volkskammer visited West Germany and the first of many twinning arrangements was concluded between East and West German towns, followed by a cultural agreement between the two states after twelve years of desultory talks. The SED and the West German SPD held long conversations from 1985 onwards.

1987 saw two major demonstrations in East Berlin against the Wall, which did not prevent the regime from abolishing the death penalty and extending a broad amnesty to political prisoners. The summer ended with a remarkable public admission by Erich Honecker that the intra-German border was "not as it ought to be". He was in West Germany at the time (early September) for the oft-deferred state visit, during which he was able to return briefly to his native Saarland for the first time since the 1930s.

Two steps forward, one step back. In October Berlin marked its 750th anniversary – twice over. The two halves of the city organised entirely separate, "back to back" celebrations. In East Berlin a burst of restoration activity for the occasion led to the spectacular reappearance in pristine condition of a series of public buildings neglected since the war. It had always been interesting before the jubilee to visit East Berlin at intervals of a year or so because every time one went a "new" building restoration would have been completed. The effect in 1988 was stunning. At the last minute the two mayors agreed to exchange celebratory visits. President Ronald Reagan of the United States visited West Berlin and challenged Mr Gorbachev to prove his sincerity by pulling down the Berlin Wall. He received the biggest round of applause since Kennedy's speech in 1963. Yet in 1988 the East German regime found the new Soviet leader's headlong rush for a new and deeper détente too strong for their taste.

Chancellor Kohl had long discussions with Gorbachev about "the German Question" in October; but one month later the East Germans took the unheard-of step of banning a Soviet publication, *Sputnik*, by then full of enthusiastic articles about political and economic reform. Gor-bachev was already a hero and a beacon of hope for many East Germans, who longed for *glasnost* and *perestroika* to spill over the Soviet border in their direction.

It is not difficult to understand the regime's point of view: thaws in Moscow had happened before, only to go into reverse after an unpredictable interval, leaving satellite regimes which had followed suit high and dry. Honecker, now in his mid-seventies, was not about to deviate from the orthodoxy of the past forty years just because an updated Khrushchev with a flashy wife had come to power in Moscow. As far as he was concerned, the "Brezhnev doctrine" limiting the sovereignty of the satellites (as in Czechoslovakia in 1968) was still in force. In suppressing the Prague Spring the Russians had mobilised token contingents from the other satellites, including, with supreme callousness only thirty years after Munich, a small contingent of the East German National People's Army (there was a persistent rumour that when the train carrying this unit passed one ferrying Polish troops, the Poles opened fire on it). Honecker could also remember the 1953 revolt in East Germany and the Hungarian uprising of 1956: he was not about to make another deployment of Soviet tanks necessary by lifting the lid off a cauldron of simmering discontent. (Like all modern tyrannies, the SED kept watch on the real mood of the public through secret opinion polls done by the Stasi; it knew that people were fed up with the persistent shortages of consumer goods, with the harsh travel restrictions and nannyish censorship – in spite, or perhaps because, of the almost universal availability of West German television signals.)

The great irony is that the SED regime was absolutely correct in its instinctive analysis that *glasnost* (openness) could not last and *perestroika* (reform) would fail in the Soviet Union, and that a cyclical repression was bound to follow; many western analysts came to a similar conclusion. The East Berlin Politburo was right about the long and even the medium term; what it failed hopelessly to get right was the short term – a just, if also unconscionably long-delayed, come-uppance for forty years of not answering to the people. And it was just at this psychological moment that the gut-instinct politician Helmut Kohl woke up to the political possibilities which Gorbachev had created for Germany. The Chancellor saw the "window of opportunity" and reached the high point of his career by smartly jumping through it.

In immediate terms the skids were put under the SED regime by the Hungarians, who had been quietly pursuing their own path to a social market economy before Gorbachev came to power – much more quietly and successfully than the Poles, who had been locked in confrontation with their Communist government since 1980. On or about May 1 the Hungarian government decided to open its border with neutral Austria; at any rate, the next day, border troops started to dismantle the barbed-wire fence and take it away. It did not take long for the significance of this modest easement – intended for Hungary's own citizens – to become obvious in the GDR. Hitherto East Germans had been restricted to the territory of their Warsaw Pact allies for foreign holidays: the Romanian and Bulgarian Black Sea resorts, Poland, Czechoslovakia, the Soviet Union itself – or of course Hungary. Yugoslavia had been struck off the list when it opened its borders completely to western tourism, but not a few East Germans had managed to go there and move on to West Germany before the loophole was sealed. The opening of Hungary's borders to Austria provided a new route west for East Germans in a position to take advantage of it.

Meanwhile, in the GDR, five days after the Hungarian move, municipal elections were held with the usual insulting "result": 98.85% in favour of the SED's consolidated list of candidates. The difference this time was that many ordinary citizens were morally certain that the figures must have been even more crudely faked than usual because they knew so many people who had spoiled their papers or even voted No. They also judged that under Gorbachev the regime's ultimate sanction against protest – Russian tanks – was no longer available. The murderous repression of the peaceful reformist protest in Tienanmen Square, Peking, in the first week of June 1989 gave people pause, especially when the SED regime was the only member of the Warsaw Pact to congratulate the Chinese comrades: Egon Krenz, Politburo member and trusted lieutenant of Honecker, flew to Peking with the message. But private confidence was boosted on July 7, when the Warsaw Pact meeting in Bucharest formally distanced itself from the interventionist Brezhnev Doctrine. Even if it had not fully understood the change in climate before, the SED knew by this time that if there was trouble in the GDR, it was on its own. One day earlier Gorbachev had told the European Assembly in Strasbourg of his vision of "a common European home"; one day later Honecker was officially reported to be suffering from an acute gall-bladder complaint. He certainly looked sick on his now rare public appearances.

From mid-July a trickle of East Germans used the Hungarian loophole to defect to West Germany via Austria. The stream became a river and then a flood as the summer wore on; hundreds, then thousands besieged

Bonn's embassy in Budapest; fields filled with abandoned East German cars; the Hungarians opened camps to accommodate those queuing to cross into Austria. In August East German runaways overran the West German embassy in Prague, which was forced to close. Evacuations by special trains were negotiated by Bonn diplomats with the GDR and its immediate neighbours. There were wildly emotional scenes as the defectors arrived in West German stations. These were shown on West German television, which was even more widely watched than ever in the GDR and doubtless encouraged many others to take the same step. The regime had at last shown itself to be susceptible to pressure; the long-sought Achilles' heel had been exposed. The defectors left behind growing numbers of people who now seriously began to hope for the first time that the GDR regime might be driven to slow down the desertion rate by radical reform, Hungarian style. But the bandwagon was running out of control. On September 11 the Hungarians admitted defeat in their effort to staunch the flow and, in defiance of long-standing agreements with the GDR, threw open their borders to all GDR residents. About 15,000 went over in the first three days; by the end of October 50,000 had passed through Austria. Yet on 7 October 1989 the regime, led by Honecker and in the presence of Gorbachev, celebrated the fortieth anniversary of the foundation of the GDR with the usual pomp, as if nothing had happened. Gorbachev delivered another of his *bons mots*: "Life punishes those who come too late." That night East Berlin erupted in large and spontaneous demonstrations for basic freedoms.

In Leipzig, the GDR's second city, such protests had for some time been taking place each Monday, after the weekly prayers for peace conducted with the grudging approval of the regime in the main churches of this and many another town since the early 1980s. A gentle tradition which had previously drawn a dozen or two each week now attracted first hundreds, then thousands, then tens and finally hundreds of thousands as the discontent mounted in autumn 1989. The regime initially tried to deter these mass demonstrations by surrounding the heart of the city with police, Stasi and troops, who proved none too gentle in their treatment of protesters on the edge of the crowd. The security forces were ordered by Honecker to break up the numerically unprecedented demonstration expected on Monday October 9 at any cost. Would Karl-Marx-Platz in Leipzig become another Tienanmen Square?

Kurt Masur, musical director of the city's renowned Gewandhaus Orchestra, whose building is on the Platz, played a central mediating role in ensuring that it did not. An appeal for restraint on both sides enabled the demonstration – the largest recorded outside Berlin, involving hundreds of thousands – to pass off peacefully. Local security commanders decided on their own initiative not to shoot. The people of Leipzig had issued the ultimate, gentle but thundering, rebuke to the tottering and utterly bewildered regime: "*Wir sind das Volk* – we are the people." It was an all too brief moment of glory for New Forum, Democracy Now and the other citizens' initiatives and groups which had sprung up all over East Germany in September to demand basic human rights. As the West German SPD floundered in indecision about what line to follow over these sensational events in the east, some brave spirits in the GDR refounded the "SPD-East" at a secret meeting north of Berlin on October 8.

Ten days later Honecker, after eighteen years as party leader, was forced by the SED Central Committee to resign in favour of the oleaginous Egon Krenz. But even this did not stop the rot. As the first non-Communist premier took office in Poland and the Hungarian Communist Party dissolved itself, GDR citizens continued to vote with their feet in their tens of thousands by going to Poland, Hungary and even Czechoslovakia (where the police were still beating up anti-government demonstrators) in order to transfer by special train to West Germany. The embattled Prague regime grew angry with its Warsaw Pact ally and told East Berlin that, if it was not going to stop the flow of emigrants from the GDR, would it at least mind letting them go directly to the west instead of pointlessly diverting the stream through Czechoslovakia? Visa-free travel from the GDR to Czechoslovakia was halted for a few days. Once it was restored, on November 4, 10,000 people a day took advantage of it – until the SED regime conceded the principle of free travel.

By this time Günter Schabowski, SED boss in East Berlin and a member of the revamped Politburo, had become spokesman for the Krenz regime (officially Information Secretary of the Central Committee) and took to the job as if he were one of nature's public relations officers. He gave another of his press conferences, so new-fangled in the east, on the evening of Thursday, November 9, announcing amid various other statements that, "in order to relieve friendly states" stressed by the continuing wave of emigration from the GDR, GDR citizens would be allowed to cross directly into West Berlin and West Germany, whether for short trips or for good. He read this in a monotone from a piece of paper extracted as if by afterthought from his pile of documents. The reporters seemed almost to miss it; after a comical "double take" they realised the import of what he had said and swarmed all over him. "From when?" they shouted. "If I'm correctly informed, this regulation is valid immediately," an impassive Schabowski said to camera. There it was: by a decision of the Council of Ministers of the German Democratic Republic, all official crossing-points in the Berlin Wall and the border with the Federal Republic would open at once. As the electronic media spread the news, tens of thousands of dazed, jubilant, tearful people came onto the streets of Berlin to pour through the Wall in both directions amid scenes beamed live by television round the world. The border guards were not fore-warned; they were soon overwhelmed by the crowds and the spirit of the occasion. On production of passport or identity card East Germans could now travel to and fro; over the ensuing weekend millions did so, causing unprecedented jams on the roads.

The termination of the Wall's role as barrier and symbol of both the harshness and the failure of the GDR's (and the Soviet Union's) Com-munist system was followed at bewildering speed by a chain of momen-tous events. The Politburo, which had purged itself of hardliners the day before the Wall opened, appointed Hans Modrow, an SED moderate, as Prime Minister on November 13. Although he promised democratisation and proposed closer relations between the two German states by means of a new treaty, the demonstrations continued, without violence – but the noble cry, "*Wir sind das Volk*", was now being displaced by "*Wir sind* EIN *Volk*" – "We are one nation" (the word *Volk* translates as either "people" or "nation" depending on context; the Germans refer to the League of Nations of the inter-war years as the *Völkerbund*, but also speak of China as a *Volksrepublik* – a people's republic). What may look like a minor shift of meaning marked a fundamental change of mood as the demand for reform in the GDR was superseded by a surge of support for unification, which had seemed inconceivable only days before.

As if by instinct people knew that the breaching of the Wall heralded the dissolution of the state which had found it necessary to immure itself against the lure of the West, the *Drang nach Westen* sustained by television. It was less a resurgence of German nationalism, which understandably remains the stuff of nightmares for Germany's neighbours, than a heartfelt cry for a share in the material wellbeing so long taken for granted in the West, and constantly seen on television. The East Germans were dumping dialectical materialism in favour of consumer materialism: Deutschmarks, not Karl Marx. How were they to know that conspicuous prosperity of the West German variety came only at a high price? Any doubts they might have had were drowned by the blandishments and opportunism of the ruling centre-right coalition in Bonn, which was determined to go all out for unification.

Now a new sound could soon be heard day and night throughout the heart of Berlin: the clink of hammer and chisel as people hacked pieces of concrete from the hated Wall as souvenirs. On December 1 the Volkskammer cancelled the constitutional supremacy of the SED, and three days later the Central Committee expelled Honecker and his cronies from the Party; Krenz resigned as head of state on the 6th and on the 7th the "Round Table" of Church, Party, citizens' and government representatives in east Berlin called free elections for 6 May 1990; similar round tables sat in all the main centres to reorganise and democratise local government. The state prosecutor opened investigations into alleged abuse of office and other offences by Honecker and others.

The SED regime was doomed as soon as it surrendered its impotent virility symbol, the infamous Berlin Wall, in a desperate last bid to get ahead of the demands of public opinion. Had events permitted a pause for breath at this historic moment, the German Democratic Republic might yet have survived as a separate state, perhaps a second Austria living amicably alongside its bigger Germanic neighbour. This is what those brave souls in the GDR citizens' movements which were in the forefront of the victorious moral challenge to the regime had been hoping for: an alternative Germany, free to regenerate itself and democratically find its own way at last. There was and remains no reason to doubt that a majority of GDR citizens would, on reflection, have settled for that quite happily. Many told me as much, as disillusion and uncertainty set in.

But no time was allowed for reflection, still less for the formation of credible, homegrown political alternatives to the SED, as the pressure from within and without mounted on a morally and monetarily bankrupt regime. The SED transformed itself into the Party of Democratic Socialism (PDS) and chose Gregor Gysi, a personable and highly intelligent young lawyer, as chairman. The eastern SPD came out of its closet, the LDPD moved to join up with the West German Liberals in the FDP, and the eastern CDU, its independence from the old "bloc" restored, chose another lawyer, Lothar de Maizière, deputy Prime Minister, as its chairman; all three reconstituted parties were soon to fuse with their western counterparts as the well-oiled wheels of the Bonn party-system rolled over the land. Only the SED-turned-PDS, with its untold millions filched from the people and stashed away, proved surprisingly capable of survival against the mechanised razzmatazz of the bourgeois western parties with their pork-barrel politics, their famous leaders (as seen on western television) and their free handouts funded by western taxpayers' money. All this machinery was in place and working before unification, by which time the idealistic voices of reason and concern from New Forum and the other grassroots movements which had paved the way for this smooth political hijack had already been all but shouted down.

Well-placed sources say that the awesome political possibilities in this rapidly changing scene in the GDR really dawned on Helmut Kohl when he met Hans Modrow in Dresden on 19 December 1989. They agreed on a closer relationship between the two German states, to be enshrined in new treaties, and the cancellation by Christmas of all remaining travel restrictions in both directions. The crowd once again yelled, "*Wir sind ein Volk,*" and, "*Deutschland, einig Vaterland* – Germany, united fatherland." One of the Chancellor's closest advisers said Dr Kohl thenceforward was "like a sleepwalker" instinctively feeling his way forward. He had already put up a ten-point programme for a new relationship on November 28 – in short, a confederation of the two states anchored in a uniting Europe. Barely concealed distrust, not to say horror, was the first reaction in Moscow, Paris, London, Warsaw, The Hague, Oslo and other places with vivid wartime memories. Only Washington was unaffectedly enthusiastic for German unity; western commitment to the goal of eventual German unification otherwise proved to be confined to that tomorrow which never comes. On 22 December 1989 the Brandenburg Gate in the centre of Berlin, symbol of division and unity past and future, was opened by the East Germans and the biggest street party in history began: perhaps a million, perhaps two million people turned out on New Year's Eve. By that time mostly peaceful revolutions had toppled the Communist regimes in Czechoslovakia and Bulgaria – and a bloody one had half-destroyed the horrific Ceausescu dictatorship in Romania.

Early in the New Year a mob burst into the vast national headquarters of the Stasi in Lichtenberg, Berlin; this had already happened in Erfurt, the Thuringian capital, and was soon to be imitated in Leipzig, Dresden and other places where the Stasi had a fortified local base. Many of the estimated six million personal files covering more than one in three of the population had already been destroyed by the secret police; some people managed to get hold of their own dossiers (one writer has already turned his into a book). This soon proved to be a mixed blessing as a few made sickening discoveries of the names of those "friends", colleagues and neighbours who had informed on them. But a witch-hunt was prevented by denying general access to private files, which were eventually to be consigned to the care of the Federal Archive in Koblenz, west Germany, and locked away for thirty years. Limited access was granted to lawyers preparing cases against the major infringers of human rights in the GDR; and, quite clearly, selected "sensitive" dossiers were spirited away by ex-Stasi operatives for possible later use. The Stasi has a historical claim to be the nosiest secret police in history; neither the Nazi SS nor the Soviet KGB kept such a high proportion of their respective populations under surveillance as did the perfectionist Ministry for State Security, which thoroughly earned its nickname "the kraken".

The Stasi, for which more than 100,000 people worked full time and countless others were coaxed or conned, bribed or blackmailed into providing information, was a state within a state, perhaps the strongest argument for the abolition of the regime which unleashed it and of the state in which it did its repugnant work. Sadly, many of the west Germans who moved into the administration of the ex-GDR seemed to have forgotten the lessons of their own recent history and inclined towards the kind of general witch-hunt carefully avoided in the post-Nazi period. Major criminals apart (and by no means all of those), people were not punished for membership of the Nazi Party, which passed seven million or one in ten, or for having been *Spitzel* (informers). However, when the Federal Republic took over the GDR there were no foreign victors to supervise a "decommunisation" procedure analogous to denazification – just Germans moving in on other Germans. In addition, unlike in 1945, there was no shortage of labour in the east to encourage mercy – except in the demoralised public service in general and law enforcement in particular, which were soon on the brink of collapse. But where after a revolution do you find a trained policeman to keep the peace except at a police station? And what do you do if ninety per cent of the police were, on grounds of self-protection if not ambition, members of the SED? Thousands upon thousands resigned from the force after unification over low pay and loss of status (they were all put on probation with no guarantee of permanent re-employment). Judges and prosecutors, who need years of training, presented an even knottier problem, because most of them had also been involved in enforcing unjust laws and jailing people for transgressions not recognised as such in western democracies.

The only reason east Germany did not sink into complete anarchy by the end of 1990 must be the passion for order of the vast majority of Germans, a trait immortalised by Lenin's scathing claim that German revolutionaries intent on storming a railway station would first buy platform tickets. Yet, in the evanescent GDR, there was one carbon-copy bank theft after another as safes full of the mighty new Deutschmarks drew armed robbers to ill-defended buildings, a crime all but unheard of under "Socialism" – where the money was hardly worth stealing.

The first free election in the GDR was brought forward to 18 March 1990, by which time the Stasi was at last officially wound up. Bundnis 90 (Alliance 90), representing the citizens' movements including New Forum, won just 2.9% of the vote, compared with 47.7% for the CDU and its conservative allies. The SPD got only 21.8%, while the PDS (ex SED) managed a remarkable 16.3%. The Liberals took 5.3%, about half what they usually won in the west, in this first pluralist ballot for the last Volkskammer. The result forced the resignation of Hans Modrow (SED) and made Lothar de Maizière (CDU), as leader of the largest party, the last Prime Minister of the GDR. He took office at the head of a grand coalition with the SPD and all other parties with just two exceptions: the SED, which was only to be expected, and Bundnis 90, which was sad. The key provision of the hard-won coalition agreement was the decision to unite Germany under Article 23 of the West German Basic Law. East Germany was to accede to the Federal Republic lock, stock and barrel by virtue of an agreement between the heads of the Bonn CDU and its new eastern branch, who conveniently happened also to be heading the two German governments. On May 6 the East Germans elected new communal councils, sustaining the CDU as strongest party; the SPD and SED more or less held their own. Twelve days later the two German governments signed a treaty providing for monetary, economic and social union on 1 July 1990.

Under this, to the chagrin of Karl Otto Pöhl, President of the West German Bundesbank and *ex officio* defender of the D-mark, the first few thousand marks of each East German's private savings (precisely how much depended on the age of the depositor) were to be converted to DM at the highly generous rate of 1 : 1 and all other deposits, private or public, at 2 : 1. Entrepreneurs had already made instant fortunes when the special pre-union rate of 3 : 1 governed payments in east-marks for West German goods and services. Such moneys had to be deposited in non-convertible accounts pending union, but not a few swindlers exploited the fact that they could get 7 : 1 on the black market: if the east-marks thus acquired managed to find their way into one of these special trading accounts, their value rose by an instant 133%! Not less than DM500 million was thought to have been creamed off in this way.

Parallel to the inter-German negotiations, the four wartime allies engaged in "four-plus-two talks" with the two Germanys to smooth the path to unification by winding up their residual postwar responsibilities in Germany. These talks went well largely because Gorbachev, hemmed in by growing economic and political problems at home, was anxious to secure aid from the West. He made one concession after another, dispensing first with the formal peace treaty the Soviet Union had demanded and finally allowing a united Germany to be part of Nato, a truly amazing concession to Helmut Kohl, who went to see him at his holiday *dacha* in the Caucasus in mid-July. The "four plus two" were thus able to sign the new Germany Treaty in Moscow on September 13. The price was DM12 billion in aid and DM3 billion in loans from Bonn to resettle the 380,000 Soviet troops who were to return home from East Germany by 1994.

Economic and social union was duly declared on July 1. A Volkskammer resolution restoring the five *Länder* abolished by the Communists in 1952 was wildly popular, to judge by the epidemic of car-stickers, old state flags (and boundary disputes) which erupted after the decision. This powerful resurgence of regional patriotism only goes to show how mean and arrogant the SED had been to abolish the *Länder*. East Berlin was to remain a separate administrative unit for the time being, though collaborating closely with the west Berlin Senate, but the "five new *Länder*" were to choose their state parliaments on October 14 – the third election in the GDR in seven months. The fourth and last was to be on 2 December 1990, when what was originally going to be the twelfth west German election became the first free all-German Federal election in fifty-eight years (and also the first ballot for an all-Berlin government: we should not forget that the "five new *Länder*" are actually five and a half). The Volkskammer formally decided on accession to the Federal Republic on August 23 and the Treaty of Union between the two states was signed in east Berlin on the last day of the month. Chancellor Kohl was determined to prevent the GDR reaching its forty-first anniversary on October 7: the treaty therefore set the astonishingly early date of October 3 as unification day, which was to be an all-German public holiday, 297 days after the

Berlin Wall succumbed to the will of the people. Both parliaments completed ratification of the treaty on September 20.

Helmut Kohl was undoubtedly right to seize the shining hour as he did. Subsequent events in the Soviet Union entirely vindicated his instinct that everything that was on offer or could be won from Mikhail Gorbachev had to be taken at once, even on a basis of live now, pay later. The Chancellor's ambition to be the first leader of a united Germany since the 1945 defeat, conceived as a realistic possibility before the end of 1989, made a statesman of him, if one accepts the definition of such a person as one whose personal objectives coincide with those of his country. As a supreme exponent of party politics he was already a practitioner of the art of the possible and an instinctive opportunist. He obviously shared Gorbachev's belief that life punishes those who come too late, so much so that he temporarily abandoned his habit of sitting out crises until they went away (which worked surprisingly often). He will therefore go down in history as he wished, even if his other ambition, the unification of Europe round a united Germany, does not work out as planned in his term of office.

All Kohl actually needed was Gorbachev's signature on the "Treaty on the Concluding Arrangements in Relation to Germany" as the four-plus-two pact is called. The rest – the reckless, if not disastrous, gallop to economic and then political union – was internal electoral politics. Kohl wanted to go to the country on 2 December 1990 as "the Chancellor of Unification", while voters in east and west alike were still too dazzled by the stunning pace of spectacular events to notice the arrival of the first of many huge bills. He recklessly promised that there would be no tax increases to finance union and that nobody would be worse off because of it. He left opponents such as the SPD and doubters including Bundnis 90 and the environmentalist Greens to choose between trailing in his wake or sounding like killjoys. Indeed Oskar Lafontaine, hippy throwback and SPD challenger for the Chancellorship, proved to be totally out of tune with the public mood in east or west. But within weeks of the election the victorious coalition proved him right by admitting that the cost of union was much greater than they had said – a classic demonstration of the Russian saying that a pessimist is a well-informed optimist. Lafontaine's credibility had been destroyed when the SPD voted No to the various stages of unification in the Bundestag, where the party was safely outnumbered, but Yes in the Bundesrat, the upper house representing the *Länder* governments, where the SPD had a majority until October 1990. The fact that the warnings from the left – about chaos and confusion, exploitation and soaring costs, unemployment and social deprivation – were generally justified makes the SPD's abject performance look all the more unfortunate because they obviously found no way of persuading the public to listen.

It has to be added for fairness' sake that the majority of east Germans obviously wanted instant consumer access to the free market: it was probably beyond the wit of anyone to hold them back with sober reminders that the West German prosperity they longed to share had been painstakingly built up over forty-five years and would have to be paid for. The obverse of this childlike separation of cause and effect was the frequently heard and singularly uncomprehending *Wessi* observation that "we only had DM40 each when we started" (a reference to how the Deutschmark was introduced in 1948 with magical effect) – a remark often accompanied by risible complaints that "the *Ossis* are simply buying up everything". The instant conversion to D-marks of a few thousand in savings hardly made up for forty years of repression; but, as the previously dreary shops became glittering branches of Cornucopia plc, the east German voters gave Kohl a thumping 'Chancellor-bonus', which he had never won in the west.

That any incumbent would almost certainly have benefited in this way was shown seven short weeks after the federal "unification poll", when the West German *Land* of Hesse threw out its CDU State government, giving the battered SPD and the Greens a much-needed and powerful boost. This marked a return to the political pattern of the days before autumn 1989, when the Bonn coalition of CDU, CSU and FDP seemed inert and uninspired, and the CDU in particular was punished at each regional election for an inactivity which was far from masterly. In Hesse the voters seemed to be rebuking Kohl for fudging the financing of unification and for doing as little as possible about the Gulf War, whose outbreak in January 1991 caused more protest in Germany, west or east, than anywhere else in the West (I was struck by how fast unity had been achieved between east and west in the sphere of demonstrations, slogans and graffiti – even the handwriting looked the same). That Hesse was no temporary blip in the coalition's fortunes was shown by one opinion poll after another in the succeeding months – and by massive protests and demonstrations in the east against unemployment and rocketing prices, accompanied by complaints in the west against the sharp tax increases introduced on 1 July 1991 and the incessant demands from the east. An even greater humiliation for Kohl was the SPD's defeat of the CDU for the first time ever in Rhineland-Palatinate in April 1991, when a new state legislature was elected. Kohl was chief minister of this, his native *Land*, for nine years before he went into Federal politics. Six short months after his unification triumph, his days in politics seemed to be numbered.

Kohl, meanwhile, had blithely left investment and redevelopment in the new Federal German east as far as possible to the private sector which, as it always does, took an interest only in the best parts – and then only if it did not have to take on any old burdens, including debts, pollution and inflated workforces. There need be no surprise or even criticism over this attitude: companies exist to make profits for their owners, and long ex-perience of the "social market economy" proves that they show responsi-bility to society only if they are made to by law (the odd philanthropic donation and public relations exercise always excepted – but these by definition cannot be counted upon). Kohl was quite right to assume, whether for reasons of blind dogma or not, that centralised economic planning had been the curse of the ex-GDR. Yet that does not prove economic planning *per se* to be bad, but only the inept, Soviet and GDR or Leninist-Stalinist variety. Even the most besotted devotee of free enterprise would hardly leave such an important business matter as a corporate take-over (or a personal event such as a daughter's wedding) to the free play of market forces: he would make a detailed plan. This makes leaving a merger of two entire countries to take care of itself look all the more irresponsible. Many observers and Dr Kohl's critics said loudly and often beforehand that this attitude would be a disaster and cannot be accused of hindsight now that they have been proved completely right by events.

One adverse result among many from his *laissez-faire* approach (which in Kohl's case has at least as much to do with personal psychology and style as with policy and economic theory) is the fact that the GDR was the first territory to join the European Community without an elaborate transitional arrangement lasting several years. Community law came into effect overnight with Federal German law on 3 October 1990; only in a few areas, mainly concerned with social policy, was a little grace allowed by both codes for adjustment to generally radical changes of procedure. East Germany was not adopting the free market: the free market was swallowing East Germany in a single gulp.

Kohl's original proposal for a confederation in which the GDR could have been given time to converge with West Germany, or, as New Forum and others wanted, to seek a third way, would surely have been more merciful as well as more prudent. The outsider does wonder what the point can be of a federal system which requires all its components to conform in almost all political, economic and social respects with all the others. The admirable constitutional requirements of equal rights and opportunities across the country surely ought to leave room for social experiment, especially since the GDR, as will be shown, had a few good institutions that might have been worth testing in democratic conditions (and with a better budget). This eagerness in Bonn to have the new states conform to the western model virtually at once was not matched by similar zeal to equalise wages between east and west. All the time in the world was allowed for transition there (although the incoming western trade unions soon began to fight for a much shorter time-scale), even though the easterners had lost much of the "social wage" which went a long way towards supplementing their low pay.

Like the DM5 banknote, which enjoyed a revival to help meet the smaller spending capacity of the easterners, certain barely translatable German words experienced a new vogue after union. *Anpassung* – adaptation to conform – was an obvious one (I also heard *Gleichschaltung*, the specifically Nazi term for forcing institutions and people into line, used in this context). Many people I met ruefully conceded without being asked that *Anpassung* was something Germans were only too good at. *Abwicklung* (dismantling or winding up) was applied to some institutions, notably outmoded ones such as university departments of Marxist-Leninist philosophy and the like: it seemed to be a euphemism for total suppression in many cases.

Even so, consumer demand in the east, despite spiralling unemployment, produced a boom for the lucky *Wessis* as the *Ossis* blew their savings on cars and other smart western products; the labour-intensive western construction industry won fat contracts to rebuild eastern Germany. Unification soon seemed set fair not only to insulate the Federal economy from a deepening world recession but also to impose a form of Keynesian anti-slump economics on monetarist Bonn, which readily plunged into unprecedented debt – DM70 billion in year one of union – to finance the take-over of the ex-GDR. This soon began to look remarkably like spending one's way out of a depression. The Bundesbank, the German central bank which enjoys independence from the Bonn government, was appalled and its President, Dr Karl-Otto Pöhl, publicly attacked Dr Kohl in a speech at Brussels in March 1991 for mishandling economic union as the east Germans took to the streets again just as they had done in autumn 1989.

Meanwhile the institution funded by Bonn and set up by the late Volkskammer to privatise east Germany's 8,000-plus *Volkseigene Betriebe* (VEBs or "enterprises owned by the people"), the Treuhandanstalt or Trust Corporation, became the world's largest holding company, legally owning the bulk of east German industry. By spring 1991 it was in imminent danger of going down in history as the world's greatest asset-stripper: huge companies were allowed to go to the wall with the loss of countless thousands of jobs. Worse still, five *Ossi* executives with the Treuhand were accused in April of selling off businesses very cheaply to friends who had managed them under the old regime. The trust's task is to privatise everything it possibly can, to dispose of all nationalised assets by selling off, amalgamating, dismembering, reorganising, restructuring, salvaging or, in the worst cases, *Abwicklung* or just shutting down the nationalised concerns left behind by the SED regime. The big enterprises regained their capitalist status as an AG–*Aktiengesellschaft*, a joint stock company; the smaller ones became a GmbH, a limited company.

Because east German undertakings were often hugely overstaffed and had very broad social responsibilities thrust upon them by the old regime, the future of millions of workers came to depend on the Treuhand. Once the glamour of being free to spend hard currency on the bewildering new display of goods wore off, countless east Germans were plunged into prolonged economic uncertainty, unaccustomed as they were to taking decisions on a wide range of social matters which the defunct nanny-state used to take for them from cradle to grave. These included guaranteeing everybody, even ex-convicts, a wage and a place to live, free medical care, a crèche, holidays and massive subvention of essentials from rent and energy to bread and public transport – and much more besides. This was the not unbenevolent other side of the coin of lack of individual choice. It was as paternalist in motive as Bismarck's revolutionary social security system (the basis of the west German model imposed on the east), but was much broader and entirely state-run. "All you needed in the GDR," said one citizen to me, "was 5,000 marks in savings and you never needed to worry about money for the rest of your life." Provided of course that one did not criticise the system out loud . . .

I had decided to proceed round the territory of the former GDR in an orderly manner, starting in the south to forestall the first winter snow which usually falls there, and working my way round the *Länder* clockwise – Saxony, Thuringia, Saxony-Anhalt, Mecklenburg-West Pomerania, Brandenburg and finally Berlin. I therefore resolved to fly to Tegel, west Berlin's airport and eastern Germany's only readily usable one, spend a few days in the city arranging the later instalments of my journey, then hire a car and drive to Dresden, the Saxon capital. Hindsight makes all this seem very naive: I was behaving like a westerner, fondly imagining that the customer was always right, even in the GDR now that it had embraced free enterprise (or vice versa). The alert reader will have observed, however, that the next chapter is headed Thuringia, and will soon discover that my first base was its capital, Erfurt, a city some 200 kilometres due west of my original target. All this was the result of my first defeat at the hands of the unfortunately still extant (but disintegrating) GDR tourist system, which eventually forced me to start in Thuringia and proceed anti-clockwise to Saxony, Brandenburg, Mecklenburg and Anhalt (which route served just as well).

Still functioning in London, at any rate when I was hastily making my plans, was Berolina Travel, the GDR agency. I asked them for a list of east German hotels, which to my astonishment arrived overnight. It contained a list of the main towns of the ex-GDR with hotels, their addresses and prices (steep) – but no telephone numbers or other details, which struck me as less than helpful. I therefore rang Berolina again and persuaded them to supply a few numbers for hotels in east Berlin. Hotels being places which tend to be open round the clock, I rang these numbers that very evening. Over a frustrating period of several hours, during which the invention of the push-button telephone with memory was triumphantly vindicated, only one of them answered, even though I checked all the numbers with international directory inquiries. The exception, a very large and expensive hotel in the centre of the city, asked me to call back between 9 am and 5 pm the next day, when the reservation desk would be open. On doing so, however, I was told none too politely that the hotel was booked out. Fortunately my wife was already in Berlin with a group of her students, and she managed to find me a room in a modest pension in the west. By dint of hard work on the telex my Twickenham travel agent, challenged to get me a room ten days hence anywhere in southern east Germany, found me one in Erfurt – at seventy per cent more than I wanted to pay. I surrendered and took it.

From west Berlin I took the elevated s-bahn railway straight through to Alexanderplatz in the east – the "Alex" which had been the heart of old united Berlin and was now at the hollow geographical centre of the reuniting city. This was an experience in itself; in the old days one travelled no further than the Friedrichstrasse (where, as if out of habit, I half-stood to get out this time too). Below the tracks there used to be a huge immigration hall through which foreigners were slowly filtered into "the capital of the GDR" by the Volkspolizei, the "people's police", who knew all there was to know about the insolence of office. After that tedious process you were free to continue your journey without a visa so long as you exchanged DM30 for unreconvertible east-marks and stayed within the east Berlin boundary. Coasting straight through to the Alex was, therefore, my first palpable sign of *die Wende*, the change, the revolution of a year before. On the Alex is the Reisebüro of the GDR, the state travel agency through which one is obliged (or was – the system was already breaking up as hotels went for independence) to book rooms: even Berolina and my own agency had to work through them. I was eventually offered a room in Dresden for DM280 a night, which was not much different from offering a hitchhiker a suite at the Ritz. In the end the nearest I could get to elusive Dresden was Meissen, twenty-five kilometres along the Elbe to the north-west. Having recovered from these labours and having refamiliarised myself with east Berlin over a couple of days, I collected my car and took to the autobahn, route E51.

Work had already begun on upgrading east Germany's battered roads (as I soon discovered to my cost). On an unimproved one, all but the biggest cars feel as though they have four flat tyres as they bump over the slabs of disintegrating concrete (or even cobbles in a few places – just imagine a cobbled motorway) at the maximum permitted 100 kilometres per hour. Neglect and Soviet tanks had wrought havoc with the network and unfortunately when I drove along this part of it, on a Sunday when there were mercifully few trucks about, I got into the world's longest contraflow, almost 100 kilometres of repair-work, which seemed to be contracted to a Bavarian (i.e. western) company. There would have been riots on England's M1, I'm sure. I never thought I would be quite so delighted to see Erfurt – after five hours rather than the three I had expected to spend on 270 kilometres of autobahn all the way. Filling stations were as few and far between as ever, but no longer run by Intertank, the state concern which took only D-marks from foreigners and also laid on an "Intershop" at service areas – also a place where only

hard currency was accepted. These *"valuta"* or real-money-only estab-
lishments were a feature of life all over eastern Europe, including the
Soviet Union, and represented an unforgivable disgrace to the name of
Socialism: only foreigners or the privileged with access to hard currency
could use them, and they were the sole source of goods simply unavailable
to people with nothing but east-marks to their name.

My hotel in Erfurt would have had at least three stars in the west and
proved to be the most comfortable of my entire four-part expedition
round the German east. It was also where Willy Brandt stayed on his
historic first visit by a West German leader to the GDR in 1970 and was
cheered by a delirious crowd when he appeared on his balcony. It seemed
a propitious place from which to start my exploration of east Germany, in
a winter which was to prove rather longer and much chillier economically
than climatically.

– II –

THURINGIA

Geography – history – Erfurt – schools – two ladies – property problem I – city spokesman – street names – the mayor – pastor of peace – Church and tax – artisans – Gotha – Eichsfeld – Red Army – police – back to school – daily life in GDR – clinic doctor – life in a bottle – Wartburg – Luther and Goethe – Buchenwald – Weimar – collective farm – defecting boar – Carl Zeiss

– II –

Thuringia

Thuringia has two and a half million people living in 15,500 square kilometres of rolling country, forest and hills. It is bounded to the north-west, west and south by the west German *Länder* of Lower Saxony, Hesse and Bavaria respectively. To the north it touches the foothills of the Harz mountains, to the south-west it has the elevated Thuringian Forest and to the north-east and east it borders on the east German states of Saxony-Anhalt and Saxony. Now it lies again at the heart of a united Germany, an ancient Germanic tribal kingdom which has managed to retain its regional identity despite a long history of divisions and sub-divisions from the Dark Ages through the feudal period, when it mostly belonged to fissiparous Saxony. Several smaller political units were briefly united into an approximation of the newly reconstituted state in 1920, when the Coburg area was lost to Bavaria. The GDR divided Thuringia into the three *Bezirke* (administrative districts) of Erfurt, Suhl and Gera, which, like all such districts, bore the name of their own capitals.

The main artery of the region was an ancient east-west trading-route, now represented by the B7 road (B stands for *Bundesstrasse* or Federal highway; the GDR called it the F7, for *Fernstrasse* or long route; before the war it was the *Reichsstrasse*, R7). Along it stand the venerable cities of, from east to west, Gera, Jena, Weimar, Erfurt, Gotha and Eisenach, all of them steeped in history and all served by route E40 from Poland to the old intra-German border.

Luther's stay at the Wartburg fortress in Eisenach has already been mentioned; Johann Sebastian Bach was born in the town and in 1817 nationalist students opened their German unification campaign at the Wartburg. Weimar was where Goethe and Schiller flourished (as, briefly, did Germany's first attempt at democracy), Jena a famous seat of learning, Gera an early industrial town, Gotha and Erfurt ancient centres of culture and of the organisation of labour and the SPD in the last quarter of the nineteenth century. Thomas Müntzer, revolutionary theologian and leader of the Peasants' Revolt (of which Thuringia was the epicentre) and latter-day hero of the GDR regime, based himself at Mühlhausen, twenty-five kilometres north of Eisenach.

With its relative lack of heavy industry, its varied and afforested landscape, its collection of small towns and its extraordinarily varied history, Thuringia is the most consistently attractive of the "new" *Länder*. As it wakes up in the heart of the new Germany from its erstwhile status as a backwater of the GDR it should have little difficulty regaining its old place as one of the most popular tourist regions in the country.

The capital, Erfurt, has a population of 217,000, but seems much bigger because its centre is so grand. The entire core of the city is under a preservation order, the biggest urban area so protected in the whole of Germany. Built on a bend in the Gera river, it was established as seat of a bishopric by St Boniface in AD 742; to this day its oldest monument is the Scots Church (because Celtic monks founded it before 1150). It has an enormous Cathedral Square dominated by two of the most unusual Gothic churches in Germany: the cathedral itself, dedicated to St Mary, which appears amazingly tall because its crypt stands above ground in front of the Cathedral Hill; and the church of St Severus next door, with its three tall steeples. The square looks capable of accommodating the entire population; and it came close to doing so during the demonstrations in autumn 1989 which led to the fall of the SED regime. What Leipzig did every Monday – a "demo" after prayers for peace – Erfurt did every Thursday. In March 1991 the demonstrators were at it again, demanding jobs and protesting against escalating prices. Erfurt was the first city in the GDR to experience the storming of its Stasi headquarters (a red-brick fortress just off the square) by the citizenry, who were rather proud of themselves for having set such a record.

In earlier times the city was a major trading centre which hosted important church synods and sometimes the original Reichstag, the Diet of the Holy Roman Empire. Napoleon liked the place enough to accept the homage of the German princes there in 1808, and in 1838 it provided the site for the first garden show, as it continued to do during the lifetime of the GDR. Luther lived in Erfurt for ten years from 1501, as a student and also as a monk in the Augustinian monastery still to be seen (the Prussians closed the university in 1816). The parliament of the shortlived German Union (the association of states, including Austria, set up after the nationalist revolution of 1848) met in the city in 1850; in 1891 the SPD met there to draw up its seminal "Erfurt Programme". The city got off lightly during the Second World War and its centre boasts acres of magnificent public buildings and houses from the "foundation period" (of the Second Reich in the 1870s) all the way back to the Middle Ages.

As was soon to become familiar in the ex-GDR, the restoration work had been painstaking and of high quality, but the budget for such work was squeezed hard by the overriding demands of East Berlin. (The capital had the biggest buildings which were, therefore, the most expensive to restore, depriving even the rest of East Berlin of funds so that it was mostly shabby and dilapidated except in the centre. Next in line for refurbishment money, apart from jewels such as Weimar and other unique monuments, were *Bezirk* capitals like Erfurt, where the local administration often took the lion's share before handing on the rest to lesser places.) Further, the universal atmospheric pollution, caused largely by burning lignite (brown or soft coal universally available in the GDR), began to undo the limited good work even before it was finished. Behind the meticulously restored main streets and squares, buildings in imminent danger of collapse were all too readily found, their fabric crumbling into potholed streets and with no prospect even of a lick of paint. It soon became clear that the building stock of the ex-GDR would take decades to rescue, restore or replace and would almost certainly be the last task to be completed of all the work involved in raising the quality of life in the east to western standards. The unimaginable sum of DM550 billion has been mentioned as the likely total cost.

Nevertheless Erfurt has an exceptional collection of remarkable buildings, including not only a whole range of old churches but also the unique Krämerbrücke (bridge of small traders), built in wood early in the twelfth century and rebuilt in stone 225 years later after a fire. The bridge is so closed in (you enter through an archway behind the imposing *Rathaus* – town hall – from the western end) that you have no inkling you are crossing the river Gera. The eastern end is closed off by a church, and the thirty-three buildings, all from the fourteenth century and including a little museum about the bridge, are in excellent condition. I saw no finer city in the east.

I came to know Erfurt well by walking round it, since traffic was excluded from much of the generously defined centre (the *Wessis* having nothing to teach the *Ossis* about pedestrian precincts). But before becoming familiar with the place I had to make a start on the non-touristic side of my enterprise: I was not there just to see the sights, but to take the measure of the country and the people as their former state went into dissolution. It seemed a good idea to start with people on the threshold of their own lives as their homeland embarked on a new course – senior schoolchildren, the more intelligent and talkative the better. I therefore located an "Extended Upper School" as the GDR called it – a place for sixteen-to-nineteen-year-olds going on to higher education, a kind of *lycée* or sixth-form college unknown in west Germany. The Humboldt School, named after one or other or both of the polymath scholar brothers of the German Enlightenment, was somewhere off the Juri-Gagarin-Ring (good name for a road orbiting the city centre; abject souvenir of past crawling to the Russians). When I missed my way, a young man with a beard did not just correct me but, as Germans often do, actually led me to where I needed to be.

He was just recovering from the shock of discovering that in order to achieve his ambition of qualifying to teach under the new political dispensation, he was going to have to do two more years instead of one, a total of five. "I still don't understand why," he said. "You'd think four years were enough, and it's all theory and little or no practice anyway." I could only admire his sense of vocation to a profession in which there was notable unemployment in west Germany and soon to be more in the east, as the services of countless teachers of Russian were about to be dispensed with and cash shortages in regional governments threatened many other posts. "I expect bigger classes, fewer schools and fewer teachers," he said. We passed another school which was likely to close because the original owners of the site and building wanted to charge the city five times more rent than it had been paying. This was a first brush with the knottiest legal and social problem to arise from the *Wende*, as the 1989 revolution is now universally known in Germany: the ownership of property seized, borrowed, stolen, expropriated or otherwise sequestered by the defunct state.

Walking into the Humboldt unannounced, I found the school secretary and made my pitch for the first time: *Guten Tag*, from England, researching book about the *Wende*, telephoning didn't work, decided to risk walking in, *entschuldigen Sie bitte die Störung* (please excuse the interruption) and so on. The secretary disappeared and returned with a neat and competent-looking, lively woman with dark curly hair and in her late thirties. Frau Doktor Renate Meyer, a mathematician and physicist by qualification, turned out to be the Principal, a post she had held for less than eight weeks; she was elected to it by her colleagues – her reward for remaining *parteilos* (refusing to join the SED or any of the bloc parties) under the old regime. She promised to introduce me to one or two of her students later in the week.

Having broken the ice, I decided to celebrate with a coffee in the centre of town before descending on the obvious fount of local wisdom, the *Rathaus* (town hall). Finding a large, thronged café on a busy square, the Anger (meadow or village green originally, but now paved, pedestrian-ised, yet criss-crossed with tramlines), I took an empty table and immedi-ately fell victim for the second time to the universal east German custom of *Zusitzen* – table-sharing. The first time had been over the previous night's hamburger, which turned out to be the fag-end of my hotel's "American Week" in more ways than one: I was promptly joined by three heavy smokers who had no objection to my eating as they puffed away – no environmentalist awareness there. At the café it happened twice; a white-haired, elderly woman, Frau W, asked if she could join me, and no sooner had she given her order to a waiter apparently supplied by Monty Python's Ministry of Silly Walks than a second woman about twenty years younger did likewise, just as I was striking up a conversation with the first: from England, book on *Wende*, excuse my asking, how have the changes affected you?

"What I didn't like about the old days was the lousy little potatoes which were all you could get after queuing for hours," said Frau W, who had just been doing her daily shop. "You used to have to throw two thirds of them away – and you should have seen the carrots. As for the fruit – they should have been punished for daring to sell it."

The younger lady had hair swept up into a doughnut on top of her head and had just been to her hairdresser for elaborate maintenance work: Frau D. "That's right," she chipped in, "I always thought the people who produced the food were keeping it, but they couldn't possibly have eaten it all or put it on the black market."

I suggested that the real reason for such shortages had been the GDR's desperate need for hard currency, causing it to sell all such produce it could to the European Community via West Germany (thus giving the lie to the general assumption after the *Wende* that GDR produce was inferior just because it was crudely packed).

Frau D agreed: "The fields weren't even properly harvested in many places this autumn. It all had to be ploughed in, given to the animals, destroyed or left to rot. Meanwhile all the shops have filled up with food from the west. You can get anything you want with D-marks."

Frau W now waxed indignant about something I had already noticed in walking across the Anger, which, like the central square in any east German town had several *Imbiss-Stuben* (snack stalls), always a notable feature of German life and an obvious source of many American fast-food ideas. The elegant German phrase for what Britons call carrying coals to Newcastle translates as "taking owls to Athens". I was prompted to invent another: bringing sausages to Thuringia. Long before this, my first visit to the region, I knew of the existence and popularity all over Germany of the Thuringian fried sausage, which is imitated and sold everywhere. All German sausages differ from the British banger in being made almost exclusively of meat – even their frankfurters (which, confusingly, they call *Wiener*, or Viennese) and their massive cousin, the *Bockwurst*. Be that as it may, the Anger reeked of a mixture of burning coal (a smell I had not experienced since I lived in the North-East of England twenty-five years before) and griddled sausages. But half the stalls selling "Thuringian sausages" sported western number-plates: they had brought the salsician impostors from places as far away as Cologne and Hanover. A measure of indignation inspired by local patriotism seemed entirely justified as a reaction to the intrusion of these carpetbangers.

"The *Wessis* come here with their vanloads of goods at 5.30 in the morning," said Frau W. "They get the best positions on the Cathedral Square and other places. A lot of what they're selling is rubbish – we've been overwhelmed. At the moment people seem prepared to buy anything because they're still not used to all this choice. There used to be a black market based on west-marks before the *Wende*, which meant you couldn't get a lot of things which were supposed to be generally available unless you could get hold of some D-marks. But every day the prices are going up, catching up with the west, which doesn't mean wages or pensions are going to do the same: that would be too good to be true!"

Fully aware of what was coming on New Year's Day 1991 – the removal of subsidies on water, gas and electricity entailing a trebling of charges, soon to be followed by a huge jump in rents and western rates for insurance of everything from health to cars – Frau W thought it was going to be tough for young families in particular. "I'm seventy-four and I can live pretty cheaply. I don't want much and I'm not going to wallow in materialistic luxury in my old age. But it's going to be very hard for the youngsters." She picked up a bread roll left over from her "second breakfast" and said: "The price of this for the whole time of the GDR – forty years – was five pfennigs. Now it's twenty."

After describing how to regenerate a stale one by sprinkling a few drops of water on it before putting it in the oven, she conceded that such economies had become worthwhile, not only because of the huge increase in the price of bread but also the great leap in its quality. German free-market bread is one of those humble wonders of the world on which I had grown overweight in my years of living in West Germany. The East German roll, staple of the national breakfast, had degenerated to a nasty grey pellet because of the artificial price restraint maintained by the SED after the abortive attempt to raise the cost of essentials led to the East German workers' rising of 17 June 1953. To keep such prices down, state subsidies had risen over the years to as much as eighty per cent. But once the price of bread was deregulated, the frustrated master-bakers of the ex-GDR rediscovered their suppressed art overnight and began to pro-duce the great variety of bread which west Germans were long since wont to consume in startling quantities. Frau W's parting word on getting up to go and meet her daughter was: "But I think unification is smashing."

Now assured of my undivided attention, Frau D got down to some more basic economics. She said the interest rate on her mortgage had jumped from an artificially restrained four per cent to a free-market nine (still a rate for a British home-owner to drool over), which was costing her headmaster husband and her an extra 250 marks a month. Frau D confided that she had been registered as sick and had not had a job for twenty-five years; she did not say what her illness was and certainly looked both fit and a lot younger than her age – fifty-six. She volunteered a précis of her life history – dramatic, but far from unusual in Germany east or west – with minimal prompting.

Aged eleven when the war ended, she and her family were expelled from Königsberg (once capital of vanished East Prussia, now Soviet Kaliningrad) when she was fifteen, ending up in Erfurt. "We lost everything, but we had some relatives in Erfurt or else we might have gone even further west, out of the Russian zone. Nobody knew what would become of Germany in those days." Now she felt threatened again, by the fact that someone who had managed to get to the west had laid claim to the ground on which her house stood. "It was farmland when we got it; we built the house ourselves and we laid on the services, like electricity, water and drainage. It's terrible to think that we might lose everything again."

I could offer nothing but sympathy because at that early stage of my travels I was unaware of the fact that no such cruelties were intended under the union treaties and related legislation (much of it still to be passed at time of writing). Some 200 pages of amendments and qualifications to the property arrangements were proposed by the Bonn government at the beginning of 1991. Legal owners of abandoned or sequestered land would not simply be allowed to cash in on such added value; sitting tenants were likely to be offered compensation instead, to minimise dispossession and disruption. But Bonn appeared unaccountably reluctant to ease anxiety (and desperately needed investment) by substituting compensation for restitution as its guiding principle in property issues – no doubt because the former would entail much greater expenditure by the state. This struck many observers as one more opportunity among many missed or ignored on unification. Compensation for lost assets, without which the dispossessed had survived perhaps for decades, seemed not just fair but a positive windfall for those who had regarded their property as lost forever until the *Wende*. Restitution threatens tenants and discourages investors; the only business it is good for is the practice of law. The prevailing uncertainty threatened a lot of small businesses and was deterring people from setting up a new home or a workshop. I had come up against the east Germans' second-greatest anxiety (after unemployment) – property claims from the west.

Frau D's not untypical story was a reminder of the vast upheavals the Germans, so unlike the Anglo-Saxons in this respect, have experienced this century: the 1918 defeat, including revolution, reparations and loss of territory; the Great Inflation of 1923; Hitler's accession in 1933; the second defeat in 1945, followed by massive migration, more loss of territory and the division of the residual Fatherland in 1949; and now 1989 and its aftermath. Frau W was just old enough to have lived through them all; Frau D could remember three.

She was also worried about her son, who had recently married someone Frau D described as "money-oriented". At the moment they were paying just over thirty marks a month as a controlled rent for a miserable flat with three rooms, no bath and a shared shower and WC. This admittedly risible sum would go up enormously in 1991; nobody knew by how much.

"Mind you, the low rents meant no landlord, public or private, could afford to keep the places up; a lot of owners gave tenanted houses to the local council in the end for this reason, but the council often didn't have the money either."

Here was one obvious explanation for the abysmal state of so much of the ex-GDR's housing stock.

The holder of the proud new post of spokesman for the city council of Erfurt (the largest town parliament in Germany for reasons which will become clear) rejoices in the surname Meinung (the word means "opinion") and was more than ready to live up to his name What was the council's biggest problem, I asked him?

"Property claims. We had to employ six people just to open all the letters which arrived here by the deadline for claims [13 October 1990]," he said. "There were more than 10,000 just for Erfurt and they came by the sackload, day in, day out. It's going to take years to sort it all out; a lawyer's beanfeast."

Two years ago the owner of the house in which Michael Meinung then rented a ludicrously cheap flat wanted to make him a present of it because he could not afford the upkeep from the controlled rents. "Now he wants three million for it because it's right in the town centre," he said. "It's in a shocking state but it's a prime site. The city wanted to buy it but didn't have the money. In the end some kind of deal has been done in which a private company will give him DM680,000 towards jointly developing the site."

According to Herr Meinung, a member of the CDU and a former journalist in his early thirties, Erfurt escaped wartime damage almost completely "only to be destroyed by the GDR". Its splendid collection of old buildings had been deliberately neglected in favour of constructing huge, soulless, ugly estates on the outskirts (not an exclusively east German or Communist phenomenon, we may agree). The other big problem was unemployment. Erfurt was the GDR's leading centre for microelectronics, an industry which employed 8,000; but nobody is interested now in east German electronics. Although by far the best in the old Soviet bloc, they were ten years behind the west in an industry where a week seems rather longer even than in politics. As an example (from elsewhere), an East German concern borrowed four million east-marks to buy its computer system just before the *Wende*. When the Treuhand moved in and took it over, there was some good news and some bad. The good was that the 2:1 rate of exchange had reduced the debt to DM2 million; the bad news was that the firm could have bought a computer of similar capacity off the shelf in the West – for DM10,000! One or two of the plants involved have found partners in west German industry, which seemed likely to set up branch factories assembling their own products for the local market. The outlook for other local industries including telephones, shoes, textiles, typewriters and other light industry was poor to indifferent.

"More than 6,000 people want to start a business here," said Herr Meinung, "but we can't get them the premises or the land. We can't respond fast enough because of the uncertain legal situation. It can take five years to work out a proper land-use plan, but we haven't got that kind of time. We are drafting a provisional one without legal force in the hope of being able to create some space for development."

At least all land and property in the hands of local and state Governments and not the subject of a restitution claim by October 13 remain public.

Our session was interrupted by a telephone call. "That was a factory which was demanding to know its own address!" said Meinung. One of the many administrative problems was the need, widely felt as urgent all over the GDR, of changing street names. The first five to be consigned to the dustbin of history in Erfurt were Leninstrasse, Karl-Marx-Allee, Klement-Gottwald-Strasse, Hermann-Jahn-Strasse and the Square of the Paris Commune; all these Socialist bywords were replaced by the old bourgeois names like Magdeburgerstrasse and Leipzigerplatz, as per council resolution number 56 of 19 September 1990. Many more were due to follow; a pressing candidate was Wilhelm-Pieck-Strasse, named after the first President of the GDR, a luminary who has whole gazetteers of streets and even a town named after him – I soon wished I had DM1 for every Wilhelm-Pieck-Strasse on which I lost my bearings.

Also seriously over-represented were Friedrich Engels, Rosa Luxemburg, Wilhelm Liebknecht, Georgi Dimitroff, Dr Richard Sorge, Friedrich Ebert, Fritz Reuter, Ernst Thälmann, Clara Zetkin, Geschwister Scholl (all Socialist, Communist or anti-Nazi), Moscow, the Young Pioneers, Liberation, Unity, Solidarity (no relation to Poland), Friendship among Peoples, Peace, Red October, Socialism and German-Soviet Friendship, to name but twenty. On a bad day it was difficult to work out which town one was in. I was astonished, however, to find Clausewitz, Scharnhorst and Gneisenau in the Erfurt gazetteer after all the old regime's strictures against German militarism. Obviously the SED saw street names as a cheap and easy way of hammering home the anti-Fascist, pro-Soviet-Communist message of the regime. More subtly, the German names chosen reflected a desire to oversell the German resistance to Hitler as well as the suppressed nationalism also attested by the belated rediscovery of such non-Communist heroes as Luther.

The story of Erfurt during the revolution which ended Communist rule threw up some distinguished local candidates for commemorative streets in due course. One could be the first mayor of the city since the *Wende* – Manfred Ruge, aged forty-five, a Catholic electrician with a large family. He had attracted official displeasure by starting campaigns to aid Armenian earthquake victims in 1988 (such things were supposed to be covered by "Socialist Solidarity", private initiative being automatically suspect) and Romanian orphans in 1989. He had been a member of the "bloc CDU", but when tension rose in summer 1989 he thought the party's reaction much too slow and started the local New Forum in his own home – two doors away from a Stasi "conspiratorial residence", as the secret police's ubiquitous local monitoring centres were called. He also founded the Citizens' Committee which, on 4 December 1989, led the storming of the local Stasi headquarters before Leipzig or Berlin got around to such liberating acts. He was elected mayor in May 1990 by 160 out of 167 councillors, with seven abstentions and none against, not even the PDS. There are so many seats because it was decided to do everything possible to keep up representation of the citizens' groups as well as the conventional parties. Ruge, still in the CDU, formed a grand coalition administration supported mainly by CDU and SPD. When I was in town he was abroad, getting himself elected as vice-president of a worldwide organisation of municipalities.

Before leaving, on the instruction of the council he gave the city's "Prize of Honour" to the Reverend Helmut Hartmann, head of the Evangelical Lutheran City Mission. The prize marked the anniversary of the initial "round table" session in the town hall between the local SED administration and the citizens' movements; Herr Hartmann more than anyone else saw to it that the confrontation between *Volk* and state did not lead to violence between the ever-larger crowds of protesters and the badly rattled security forces. What Kurt Masur did for Leipzig, the rather more self-effacing Helmut Hartmann did for Erfurt. So I went to see him, in his office in a restored parish building on a narrow street close to St Michael's Church in the city centre. His Mission runs a wide range of services for the physically and mentally sick and handicapped, addicts, ex-convicts and others in need of care and counsel. In this respect at least the two states in divided Germany were rather similar in relying on the churches to make a major contribution to social walfare.

Almost as soon as he arrived in Erfurt from a church administration post in Halle in 1987, Herr Hartmann was confronted by the problems of dissidents. Many of them had been released unexpectedly, alongside thousands of convicted criminals, under a general amnesty when Honecker made his state visit to West Germany. Dealing with the consequences soon became a total immersion course in social problems. Hartmann put his church at the disposal of a group opposing an insane scheme to drive a four-lane road through the heart of the city; resistance was so strong that the plan was dropped.

The next local manifestation of discontent was a growing queue in 1988 of those who had applied for a permit to leave the GDR despite the disgraceful official pressure to which would-be emigrants were known to be exposed. Once again St Michael's offered counsel and comfort, even though seventy per cent of the applicants were not Christian. For the twenty months until the Wall opened, a service with discussion was held for them every Wednesday evening; up to 200 attended.

"My advice was always the same," said the vicar: "Stay, because we need you here. Be patient, look at what Gorbachev is doing, wait for things to change here too. You can imagine how depressed we all were after Tienanmen Square in June 1989 and the SED's enthusiastic reaction to it. I feared the same would happen here because discontent was obviously building up. But I still wanted them all to stay and help to make changes from within. I also wanted to keep those intent on leaving separated from the general wave of political protest."

But church activists helped to monitor the last Communist-controlled elections, the municipal poll of May 1989, an action which revealed massive fraud.

When the ecclesiastical authorities decided to throw open the churches to general protest groups like New Forum, meetings inevitably turned into quasi-political rallies amid the general ferment. But the churches played a major role in preserving calm against a backdrop of increasing general frustration with an apparently immobile regime ready to sanction lethal force against demonstrators. In autumn 1989 attendance at the ecumenical peace prayers in four local churches every Thursday evening grew from barely fifty to 50,000 and beyond in a month.

"I must say I hoped at that time, when the New Forum and others arose and the round tables began their work," Herr Hartmann said, "that a new grassroots movement would arise to offer a real alternative, not only to the SED but also to the political parties in the west, which began to intervene and take over before unification, through their revived organisations over here. I can't tell you how disappointed I was with our first democratic elections since the war. Everybody was swamped by the western parties. They staged colossal rallies and people turned out to admire such famous figures as Kohl, Brandt and Genscher. The round tables (at the time they were the secret, *de facto* government here, you know) asked the western parties to stand back but they were ignored. And the eastern SPD and CDU had no chance to establish distinct identities before being swallowed up."

Short, pale and earnest, Hartmann spoke softly in a Saxon accent strongly reminiscent of Foreign Minister Genscher, another son of Halle. He insisted he was not a pessimist despite one disappointment after another since the border opened. "Take these flying tradesmen from the west, who started coming even before monetary union. People weren't prepared for this and were swindled with awful goods. We are being used as a dump. I'm sure our economic system was unhealthy and doomed, but it was stronger at the beginning of the year [1990] than it is now. I think it was deliberately allowed to be undermined. And all this uncertainty about property! Surely it didn't have to come to that? I'm terribly worried about future social provision here, especially health, and I dread the real changes which only come next year [1991]. We have never had unemployment or homelessness here. But I'm a Christian and I try to offer hope and to arouse it in others. A lot of people who have never had to cope with this kind of uncertainty must be close to despair; many seem to have given up. It has all happened in such a rush that it seems much more like a takeover than a unification . . ."

With almost as many Catholics as Protestants, in ecclesiastical terms Erfurt is an exception in the former GDR, where Protestants outnumber Catholics by four to one overall (they are roughly equal in the west). Indeed the relatively high number of Catholics in Thuringia showed the greatest enthusiasm in the ex-GDR for the return of the carnival tradition, or *Fasching* as it is called in the German south. Forty years of SED rule seems to have left an actively Christian population of thirty per cent (though some seventy per cent were baptised), rather more than in Britain or even France, though only half the west German proportion. But, until harassed officials were obliged to turn them away, people had been queuing to deregister themselves as Christians by affidavit at Erfurt *Rathaus* in order to avoid church tax. This Bismarckian invention, retained by Bonn and extended to the ex-GDR, imposes on citizens a surcharge of nine per cent of their total income-tax liability, which is handed to the church into which they were baptised – unless they take the trouble to opt out. West Germans are apparently so used to the tax office demanding to know their religion that they see nothing odd in this intrusive arrangement, even though details of those opting out are also passed on to the churches, and they may be publicly named! As the Thuringian state government, responsible for all income-tax collection in its region on behalf of Bonn, *Land* and municipality, had not yet organised itself, there was no *Land* tax office, the proper place for Erfurters to make an official declaration.

One of the great hopes for the economic future of the east lies with the German artisan tradition (*Handwerk*), which is as strong there as in the west of the country. Independent skilled tradesmen and craftsmen are most likely to set up the small businesses which are so important to every economy (even Daimler-Benz was a small business once). In west Germany, little firms account in round figures for ninety per cent of companies, nearly seventy per cent of employment and GDP, and nearly fifty per cent of exports. In east Germany mostly artisans ran such private businesses as the SED regime allowed, with strict controls on numbers of employees. They were usually family businesses and had to contend with daunting obstructiveness from the bureaucracy and general official suspicion of *petit-bourgeois* capitalist tendencies. Private enterprises had to wait for raw materials until the state undertakings had been supplied; if items were in short supply, which was the norm, the business either did without or joined in the widespread, low-level corruption which fuelled a parallel or "black" economy. A DM100 note did wonders; some skilled workers preferred or even demanded hard currency only and used some of it to get their hands on essential supplies. Deliveries from state suppliers customarily occurred in the wrong quantity to the wrong specifications and/or at the wrong time (much too late or perhaps at a weekend; if there was nobody in to take delivery, the goods might be driven away again).

Faced with such an inadequate distribution system large enterprises, including even the People's Army, tried to make themselves as self-sufficient as possible, running their own services and making as many small items of equipment as they could. If little firms could not do this, they would sometimes barter unwanted goods or services for what they needed or else used judicious bribery to get round the restrictions. Only in the last years of the GDR did the regime begin to see that discouraging small-scale, independent economic activity was counter-productive. The rules were eased, but the relaxations were a far cry from positive encouragement.

That the spirit of private enterprise at its most important level – the independent craftsman and small business – triumphantly outlived all this frustration is shown by the fact that the Erfurt *Handwerkskammer* (Artisans' Chamber), which covered the eponymous *Bezirk* (about a third of Thuringia), had some 8,500 members when I visited its handsome headquarters on the Fishmarket for a talk with Klaus Günther, senior director. The Chamber had, like any other social organisation in the GDR, been supervised by the Party, but was now learning to act independently and in the interest of its members, like its west German counterparts. The membership was responsible for the bulk of the 6,000 approaches to the city council for facilities to set up small businesses. The artisanate was second only to big industry in the east as a contributor to the economy.

In the GDR artisans could not work according to the market. When the *Wende* came, they faced competition for the first time, without the advantages of their western opposite numbers who often live very well indeed. "Our members tend to be the kind of people who pay their own way in life and don't like borrowing," Herr Günther told me. But monetary union rewarded the profligate and punished the thrifty because at the 2:1 exchange rate any debt was halved – but so was the book value of assets. Artisans had to work in their own backyards most of the time or in cramped old premises. They had to train their apprentices as best they could because the state never provided the kind of training facilities urgently needed and commonplace in the west.

The medieval craft system survives intact in Germany, more strongly than anywhere else I know. The three grades – apprentice, journeyman, master-craftsman – flourish to this day and make a major contribution to Germany's large stock of skilled workers, many artisans with certificates of qualification being employed by industry rather than running their own businesses. The apprentice is still known in the east by his old German name of *Lehrling*; for once it is the west Germans who have adopted a bureaucratised acronym for the trainee-grade: *Azubi* – not a tribesman from the upper Nile but an *Auszubildender*, someone to be trained up. After five years he becomes a *Junggeselle* or *Handwerksgeselle*, a journey-man or fully trained worker, who may then start saving to run his own business, whereupon he becomes a *Meister* (master craftsman).

A fundamental difference between Germany and Britain is the high social status a *Meister* enjoys, usually with earnings to match. This derives not only from the long training and experience required to gain it but also from the meticulous supervision of standards by the state. Well-thumbed copies of the West German statutes governing artisans – a closely printed, large-format paperback book – were required reading at the Erfurt *Handwerkskammer*. In it, 125 artisan trades are listed with standards of work and training in what must stand as a model of German conservatism in its most positive sense, of organising ability, thoroughness and deter-mination to preserve the best traditions. In other areas (such as the rental contract, the notorious *Hausordnung*) the Germans tend to regulate themselves into a corner in an effort to cater for every conceivable contingency in advance. What Anglo-Saxons politely call Murphy's Law decrees that such efforts almost always cover every eventuality except the disruptive event which eventually eventuates. Thereupon all concerned are reduced to going to court instead of informally sorting out the problem over a drink or the garden fence. But, as the west Germans' economic performance and prosperity show, they got the education and training of their workers absolutely right, in keeping with the spirit of their con-stitution which says that the principal national resource is the people.

This is but one respect in which east Germans have much catching up to do. They lack new technology and techniques; even woodworkers have a lot to learn from the west. So do hairdressers. I read somewhere of a *Wessi* woman who was passing an *Ossi* hairdresser's open for business but devoid of customers. Three assistants were chatting and buffing their nails. So she walked in and asked for a shampoo and set. "Have you got an appointment?" she was asked. "No, but I saw you had nothing to do so I thought I would take the opportunity," she said. "We can't do your hair unless you have an appointment," said one of the girls. The bemused would-be customer told a friend afterwards that she would have gone round the corner and called for an appointment – except that the hairdressing emporium had no telephone . . .

East German tradespeople need to learn about the primacy of the customer in the free market and the infrastructure is terrible, but at least they no longer have petrol rationing to contend with. Herr Günther pointed out that many of the most enterprising *Ossis* had already gone west.

"People here are going to have to get used to the idea that the customer is supposed to be king. Too many people here used to say, 'If you don't buy from me, that's your look-out.' Rents are about to shoot up and we have to face western competition. Our role in the Chamber is to help inform our members, retrain them, tell them of new techniques and bolster their confidence for going into the market-place. We are short of master craftsmen because state control of industry left too little scope for them; and under the new [western] law you can't practise a trade without the *Handwerk* qualification – unless you work in the black economy. It's no good saying you've been doing the job for twenty years if you haven't got the paper qualification. Adapting to the new economic and social conditions is going to be pretty painful for many."

I found a general expectation that it would take the ex-GDR ten years to catch up with west German wage-levels and half that to reach the EC average. This could be pessimistic, to judge from the progress already made by the rapidly expanding western trade unions, which do not want competition from cheap labour inside their own expanded borders. If the wage gulf (roughly 2:5) remains too wide for too long, even more young people will go west looking for a better standard of living, abandoning an area of Germany which already has only three-fifths of the western population per square kilometre. Within nine months of economic union, half a million people were reported to have migrated or to be commuting westward for work, often over enormous distances.

Herr Günther was cautiously optimistic about the longer term: "People have already forgotten the terrible shortages of a year ago. We've got much more buying power now, you know, and those who complain about having less money forget they now have a good car, a good savings contract with a building society so they can have a better house in due course, and they can save up to buy whatever they like, including a luxurious foreign holiday. The economic competition is savage and unfair, but at least we're all running on the same track now. It's like a race, and we are probably going to be lapped by our western friends who are our rivals on the track; but we'll train and practise and do better in the next race, and better still in the one after that. The free market which everybody wanted brought us lots of problems, but it also brought the incentives we never had before. I've never admired the profit motive, but the desire for reward is only human, something the old bosses never admitted as they enriched themselves at our expense."

This vicarious optimism on behalf of small entrepreneurs seemed justified even in the rapidly worsening economic winter enveloping east Germany in 1991, but was demonstrably not transferable to big industry.

Herr Günther grew quite angry about the old bosses, not least because too many of them had become the new ones. "Many firms are going into partnership with western companies, and these western firms pick those people over here with the best connections and contacts and information. And who are they? They are the old bigwigs who knew where everybody and everything was!" The German for bigwig is *Bonze*, a word for a Buddhist priest taken from Japanese and now heavily overworked as the popular pejorative term for a big-shot. "The new company directors," said Klaus Günther, "are often the old State bosses. So those who fought the system in the old days, as so many of our members did, are faced with the same enemies as before, people who should have been sidelined, sacked or shot – and all this after decades of refusing to do anything for the party and being refused what they needed and deserved from the state by these same *Bonzen!*"

Every society has its share of people who always manage to survive and prosper, often at the expense of others, no matter who is in charge or what political changes are made. In German a turncoat is called, literally, a turnthroat – *Wendehals*, the name of a bird known in English as the wryneck, a relative of the woodpecker. Just as Nazis seamlessly turned into punctilious democrats, so German Communists are smoothly transforming themselves into liberal free-marketeers. The observer may recall the English archetype:

> *And this is law, I will maintain,*
> *Unto my dying day, Sir,*
> *That whatsoever King shall reign,*
> *I'll be the Vicar of Bray, Sir!*

68

Having plunged as quickly as possible into some of the largest issues raised by German unification (thus ensuring that the Thuringia chapter was larger than any other), I felt the need to go and look at some of the surrounding countryside, which my battery of guide books were unanimous in extolling. So on a public holiday morning I headed due east to Gotha, on a French-style country road lined with trees and occasionally by dull-looking villages – the B7.

Like Erfurt, Gotha (population 58,000) was first settled in the eighth century; it became the "capital" of the Landgraves (Counts) of Thuringia in the thirteenth. On the edge of the Thuringian Forest, it grew fat on wood, wheat and woad (used as blue dye until displaced by indigo in the sixteenth century) and changed ruling hands like so many other places in Germany for reasons of war and inheritance. In the sixteenth century it came under the Elector of Saxony and in the seventeenth it went to the Dukes of Saxony-Gotha. The first Duke, Ernst "the Pious", built the early baroque *Schloss* Friedenstein on the site of an older castle. This vast and splendid building, one of the biggest and best palaces in Germany, stands on a hill overlooking the late medieval town centre from the south. Gotha was a centre of the Enlightenment; Voltaire spent some time in the castle and lived to see the publication in the town of a uniform edition of his complete works, in French.

In 1825 another dynastic carve-up caused the town to pass into the hands of the new Duchy of Saxony-Coburg-Gotha, a minor house which did very well in the royal marriage industry. Prince Albert of Saxe-Coburg-Gotha gave his title to the royal house of England when he married Queen Victoria (the name was changed to Windsor only in 1914; the duchy was abolished in 1918). In 1875 the town was the venue for a meeting between the Social Democratic Workers' Party of Germany and the General German Workers' Association, leading to their merger in the SPD and the promulgation of the new party's "Gotha Programme". At the other end of the social scale, the town's name is associated with the German equivalent of Debrett's Peerage, the *Almanach de Gotha*, still minutely studied by the descendants of the aristocracy in these republican times. But this tome was not widely read in the German Democratic Republic.

I made my way upwards to the *Schloss* to admire the view of the town on a bitterly cold morning before taking refuge in the superbly restored pile, 100 metres wide with two wings of 140 metres each. It contains a chapel, a theatre, a banqueting hall, a library of half a million books and manuscripts plus several museums, including a small but exceptional art gallery. To be admired here are the first German double portrait ("the loving couple of Gotha" by an unknown master) and an amazingly complicated triptych by Heinrich Füllmaurer. Each wing has three leaves and each of those is cut in half with six self-contained pictures on each side, providing space for a total of 144 biblical themes; the central panel has another thirteen pictures. The lack of haloes and the quotations indicate an early post-Reformation date of about 1540. One wonders what Master Füllmaurer did for an encore; many artists have left fewer paintings than this single *tour de force* contains. Along the corridor is a roomful of works by Lucas Cranach the Elder, the great artist of the Reformation and admirer of Luther.

Down below, the town is well worth a stroll, slightly decrepit by western standards with many neglected old houses away from the centre, but offering a generally attractive collection of buildings from the last five centuries, notably the ochre-coloured, freestanding Renaissance *Rathaus*. Some 400-year-old houses are being restored; others simply fell down and have been replaced.

Taking the B247 north-north-west from Gotha you pass through several little towns unusually well-endowed with old, half-timbered houses, like Bad Langensalza, a county town untouched by the war, Mühlhausen with its curtain-wall and a disproportionately huge church, and Dingelstadt. You can take the sulphurous waters at Langensalza (hence its title of Bad) – and you could also read a large graffito: "Don't let them swallow YOU!" I was on my way to the Eichsfeld area, a Roman Catholic enclave of which the chief town is the suitably named Heiligenstadt (saints' town; whether this is still justified I was unable to discover). The place seems to have been a centre of Christianity since the sixth century (and centre of a major counter-reformation effort in the sixteenth) and still boasts an unusual number of churches for a town of 16,000 souls.

At one such there was a long notice explaining the workings of the church tax, introduced on monetary union at half the going rate and from 1991 at the full rate. The notice said that someone with no children earning DM800 a month would pay about DM14; someone getting DM1,800 would pay some DM96 as a childless person, but DM44 with two children and DM21 with four. The involvement of the German state in stuffing the collection plate in this way never ceases to strike me as bizarre and an inroad on personal liberty: but *autres pays, autres moeurs.*

On the wall of the pretty, white *Rathaus* is a plaque commemorating two local men murdered "by the Reaction" during the abortive, right-wing "Kapp Putsch" against the fledgling Weimar Republic in 1920. Another records how "the Fascists" assembled eighteen local men there and dragged them off to a concentration camp for resisting Hitler in 1933.

Heiligenstadt is not just a *Bad* but a *Heilbad* – a place where heart and other patients can avail themselves of that quintessentially German institution, as widespread in east as in west, the *Kur* or health cure. People go on these courtesy of their health insurance for weeks, sometimes months, at a time, to convalesce – sometimes before rather than after they are ill. Among the many refinements of this extraordinary indulgence, finely tuned to the national hypochondria, is the *Nachkur* (post-cure) one sometimes needs to get rid of the virus ailments picked up on the *Kur* proper. A West German friend told me of a teacher who got four weeks off in the middle of term to prevent her becoming ill! No wonder German health contributions are so high and that they spend so much of their GDP on them. The elaborate facilities all over the ex-GDR show that the *Ossis* are as deeply committed to the *Kur* as any *Wessis* – possibly more so because of greater need.

On a roundabout route back to Erfurt via unmemorable Sondershausen I saw plenty of evidence of the hottest trade in the country: second-hand cars. Many of these businesses, run by *Wessis* more often than not, were on borrowed land, with a tent or caravan as an office. Outside Beuren I saw so many cars in a field that I thought something unusual was going on; but the happening was the car-park itself. I would not have bought a second-hand car from any of these people, despite the solemn promises of one-year guarantees which looked less than convincing on a caravan already hooked up to a powerful towing vehicle as if poised for an instant getaway. I had already read of swindles galore, of rust-buckets held together by their paint, but with engines still powerful enough to ruin the lives of their deluded owners accustomed only to the two-stroke joke-cars made in the GDR. Just before Sondershausen, on a back road, I saw my first lignite-fired power station, a physical shock to the senses standing in lovely country all on its own, a veritable "dark, satanic mill" against a black sky, surrounded by spoil-heaps, belching smoke from tall chimneys protruding from a complex of crumbling brick buildings. These monstrosities are to be found all over the former GDR.

Nevertheless, this first foray into the country left me with an unexpectedly positive feeling. Thuringia is renowned for its beauty, so perhaps I was being spoiled. There were many boring towns and villages, but I had seen similar in west German backwaters; the only difference here was that there was not a single advertisement or cheerful shop window to add a touch of life and variety. But there are many historic towns with well-tended monuments and museums, and astonishing numbers of imposing churches. The main roads were not so bad even if many lesser ones were often (and unevenly) cobbled. There were far too many level-crossings and far too few filling-stations, all with long queues. The odd "No Tanks" sign and a few dark green trucks with Cyrillic number-plates were reminders of the usually hidden presence of Soviet troops in the most remote places. I saw a couple of miserable-looking young conscripts in filthy yellow fatigues, hands in pockets, cigarettes dangling from their mouths, wandering through Heiligenstadt and gazing in the shop windows of the little pedestrian precinct. How bored and frustrated they must be, waiting to go home and seeing this sudden new influx of glittering consumer goods. They are allowed just DM30 a month in hard currency to spend and must surely envy the people their army had once defeated and subjugated. No wonder they were selling items of uniform in the big towns and – according to rumour and report – Kalashnikov automatic rifles at DM100 apiece. On the way into Erfurt I got a good look at the vast complex of high-rise workers' flats north-east of the city, featureless buildings of the kind known to the Germans as *Wohnbaracken* (living-barracks). Closer in were their predecessors, the traditional but no more beautiful five-storey apartment blocks – all a dreary contrast with the grubby but grand city centre.

The face of the hotel receptionist fell when I asked the whereabouts of Erfurt police headquarters, which appeared on no map. "Don't worry, I'm not going to make a complaint," I said. Obviously anyone who showed the slightest sign of wanting to have anything to do with the police in these parts must be regarded as eccentric. I had already heard someone in the street muttering sarcastically to his companion about "our friend and helper" in reference to a policeman who was being officious. Our friend and helper is how German children – east as well as west, apparently – are taught to regard the boys and girls in green. Nonetheless I hoped that a voluntary visit to the Old Wilhelm down at the Erfurt nick might prove instructive.

I have long since become accustomed to the fact that the average police constable looks distressingly young. So indeed does his German opposite number, whom one addresses as *Herr Wachtmeister*. But I thought it was a bit thick when Hauptkommissar Dipl. Ing. Jakubowski looked like a student who has had to grow a moustache in order to appear older. Even so the Chief Inspector, holder of an engineer's diploma (nothing unusual among German military and senior police officers) was mustard-keen to assist me with my inquiries into the condition of the force a year after the revolution.

"The situation has changed fundamentally for us since they opened the border," he said. There had been a huge increase in traffic for one thing; people were driving much too fast. The autobahns were seriously over-loaded: "The accidents that result from people who used to potter about in a 26-horsepower Trabi racing around in an unfamiliar, 120-horsepower western car which probably hasn't been looked after properly are horrifying. We've got unheard-of parking problems as well."

At this point an officer who was reassuringly older than I staggered past the open door of the Chief Inspector's office with a huge television set. "That's our *Polizeipräsident*," said Jakubowski. The Police Chief looting his own headquarters? No: the headquarters was about to move to the glowering red fort near the cathedral previously occupied by the Stasi, and the Chief was democratically lending a hand. Were the police in the east as hopelessly overburdened as I had read in the newspapers, I asked?

"No. It's ridiculous to say that the police aren't intrinsically capable of dealing with these problems or increased crime or crowd control, even though all that is new to us. It's just that there are so many cases and we aren't equipped to deal with the avalanche." In other words, for No read Yes, even if there is nothing that retraining, better pay and conditions, a recruiting drive, faster cars, modern equipment and money cannot eventually solve. There could be no doubt that the east German police forces (each *Land* has its own) were going through a profound crisis of organisation and morale which began before I started my research and was still worsening rapidly when I finished.

The Chief Inspector said there had been three amnesties for criminals in the previous year. In autumn 1989, 24,000 prisoners convicted for acts which were not criminal under western law, such as trying to flee the republic or other "political offences", were discharged. Shortly after that the Volkskammer freed another 5,000, and in October 1990 3,200 more cases were being considered with a view to release. "There were a lot of real crooks with real records among them, no doubt about it, and a lot of them are very busy now." Under the old system released prisoners had to be given a job, a place to live and even help with basic needs like coal. All that had gone, so "these crooks are wandering about, getting little or no social benefit and they're stealing to stay alive. Thefts are rocketing up. We never used to have bank robberies, but we've got them now all right. We picked up three youngsters in a bank last night."

Many ordinary people could not cope with the new conditions, including unemployment. There were also extremists of left and right to contend with and squats full of *Autonomen* (anarchists), all apparently bent on provoking street battles. Here was the underside of free-enterprise capitalism, to be sure: the arrival of this familiar but daunting package of western social problems had obviously been as swift as the descent of the market economy upon the land. The police thought it only a matter of time, and not much of it, before the ex-GDR acquired a serious drug problem and attracted the interest of organised crime. There had been a significant increase in violence in general and also against the police.

Meanwhile, within the force, there was general uncertainty about the future. In west Germany a police officer becomes a *Beamter* – a public official – after a couple of years' satisfactory service. Such status is also conferred on civil servants, teachers and even engine-drivers, postmen and women after a similar probationary period and brings enormous privileges with it, such as a generous free pension, minimal social insurance contributions, early retirement, tenure for life and good holidays; as a *quid pro quo* they are not allowed to go on strike. This social inheritance from Bismarck's Prussia is intended to provide the state with dedicated and upright servants of high calibre, and to make the public service an attractive career. Engine-drivers and postmen were included to insulate state communications against industrial action when the workers were struggling to organise in the early days of the Second Reich. Modern Germany may have been very badly ruled for much of its history, but it has always been very well administered.

All police officers in the east were put in limbo after the *Wende*, pending a check on their records. Senior officers were sent into early retirement on the reasonable assumption that they had been obliged by virtue of rank to work closely with the Stasi, and probably to order infringements of human rights as understood in the democracies. Nine police out of ten had been in the SED; as Jakubowski pointed out, if party membership was a reason for dismissal then just about everybody would have to go. But because nobody seemed to know exactly what criteria would be used to decide

whether an officer would be re-employed in 1991 – and even then only on
two years' probation before getting security of tenure – morale had sunk
out of sight. The Stasi had maintained close relations with the detectives,
⌐ police and the document section which issued
⌐ also exercised the right to take over the
⌐es, "political" or not, including drugs and
⌐hey were interested in (like the K G B in the
⌐ detectives had been in the Stasi. The
⌐ithout the police, he said. "And if a
⌐ an informer about, say, somebody
⌐egally, and the person was caught at the
⌐he policeman sacked if they ever found out he
⌐ple who wanted to travel or to emigrate had to
⌐thered the relevant information and passed it
on ⌐ s the Stasi which said yea or nay. The Stasi would
act against police officers with contacts in the west, which they were
forbidden to have without special permission.

The police were subjected to "political education" throughout their
careers. "This made the *Wende* all the more shattering for them, when
everything collapsed. They were being told: 'You have served the wrong
system for thirty years and the law has been radically altered, but would
you mind going out on patrol tonight as usual'!" A *Wachtmeister* now
earned DM1,400 a month gross, of which DM300 was deducted – thirty-
five per cent of his western counterpart's pay. There was no clarity about
insurance against professional risks, no money to pay overtime, and too
few staff to enable time to be taken in lieu. In Erfurt, as elsewhere, the
once separate transport police had been dissolved and its 300 members
transferred to the uniformed branch; the military border police had also
been dissolved, which helped the regular force (some border police were
being absorbed into the Federal Border Guard, which is used to reinforce
the police if desired by the *Land* government). Although the Stasi was
dissolved at the end of 1989, some highly qualified technical specialists
were taken into the police: there was no alternative. Stasi agents used to
be picked out during their military service by talent-spotters and received
extra pay, privileges and study opportunities, earning 300 marks a month
more than the regular police. Jakubowski thought that between 3,500 and
5,000 Stasis had been kept on in the east, on a strictly individual basis.
"It's not so different from what happened with the SS at the end of the
war, really – a lot of them were just technicians. But I think it's right, then

as now, to get rid of anyone known to have infringed human rights," said the Chief Inspector.

When I went back to the Humboldt School to see Dr Meyer for the second time, she and a colleague, an English teacher, took me down to the basement, where there was a club-room used for extra-curricular meetings. It was 2 pm, but the school day had already ended, according to the German custom (children start at eight and work through; but the east was ahead of the west in having completely abolished Saturday school). There I met two boys who looked typically German: tall, both over 1.80 metres, both fair to blond with blue eyes and long heads and faces. Falko, eighteen, was talkative; Christian, seventeen, more reflective. We started warily, but before long my German was put to the test by the speed of their speech and some of the slang they used as they told me how the *Wende* had affected them.

"It was quite something for me to get to the Baltic in the old days, even if I couldn't cross it to Sweden," said Falko. "I went to Czechoslovakia, Poland and Kiev in the Soviet Union, but that was just educational. Now I can go anywhere I like – if I can afford it. I was in Switzerland and France, all over the place, in summer. If I was free and I had the money I'd like to travel all the time now."

Christian said how glad he was to be out of the Free German Youth (FDJ), the Party organisation for young people. Membership was not compulsory, but non-membership was a grey if not a black mark on one's record. "There was no fun in it, just duty. I was in it because if I hadn't been I would have been disadvantaged in later life. The Young Pioneers [precursor of the FDJ for children under fourteen] was OK – I liked that, and there was lots of enthusiasm. In the FDJ the minimum was to go to a monthly meeting, except for the office-holders who were the really keen types." Classes had been evaluated much more for their FDJ contribution than for their academic work. Students had had half an hour's political education every week, and there were also the German-Soviet Friendship Society and the Cultural League – if one really wanted to get serious about things like that one could spend half one's time on them. The ambitious students did just that. But because "everybody" was in the FDJ the general level was low.

Falko, unfazed by the presence of his principal as he spoke, thought some teachers were still trying to maintain the old-fashioned kind of discipline, but the school atmosphere had improved a great deal. "There used to be informers all over the school," said Christian. Falko then put his finger on the dilemma of petty authority in a social revolution. "Suddenly students found that the teacher had the same opinion as they did. Last year the teachers were always reminding us to go to the FDJ and warning us against going to New Forum and church meetings where all the protest began."

Christian added: "To hear teachers say the opposite of what they said last year, it makes you sick – they are going to find it very difficult to keep the respect of the students. We might as well import new ones wholesale from the west."

Dr Meyer chipped in: "Some old school heads got themselves re-elected by their staff, but how they can live with themselves having said all last year the opposite of what they are saying now is beyond me."

Dr Meyer, I deduced, was not seen as a "turnthroat" or they would not have spoken so bluntly in front of her.

"Those who believed in the old system were shattered," she said. "A lot of others saw it was all wrong but didn't protest because they were scared or under pressure. I myself thought nothing would change after 1961 [the Berlin Wall] and lots of people can't cope with the fact that the system collapsed almost overnight."

There it was: the morally unanswerable challenge from the innocent young, not yet disabused of their ideals: how can loyal servants of Communism change overnight into loyal democrats? Adults, who fear for their children, their parents, their jobs, their debts, their homes and their place in society know the answer: in real life heroism can damage your health and most people keep their heads down; moral courage is hard to find and even harder to sustain, so rare indeed that it cannot be demanded of anyone. People who have never lived under a dictatorship, like those younger west Germans calling for a witch-hunt in the east, should be chary of retrospectively demanding that others ought to have suffered for their principles. This issue has come to the fore in Germany for the second time in forty-five years. The transition from Nazism to democracy in the west and Communism in the east in 1945 threw up exactly the same problem, twice over and on a larger scale. For older east Germans, however, it is the second about-face in a lifetime, as difficult to handle psychologically as the first. West Germans only had the one upheaval.

To me the most staggering fact about modern Germany is that in the thirty years from 1933 to 1963 it first tested Fascism to destruction and then, reduced in size and split in two, produced the most successful democratic capitalist and Soviet-Communist economies in the world, side by side but back to back, on the territory of the former Reich. *Anpassung?* Obedience? Thoroughness? Efficiency? Amorality? Or just a fine-tuned instinct for survival in unique circumstances?

Falko repeated that the school had been riddled with informers. The English teacher confirmed this: "If a teacher said something out of line in class she would be up before the old principal the next day. That could only have been the result of denunciation by a student." No doubt this added points to the nark's FDJ record; small wonder that the Stasi never ran short of recruits. Highly reminiscent though this is of the awful stories of Hitler Youths turning in their parents, the doubly repugnant phenomenon of the child-informer can be blamed only on the older generation which got them to do it and on the system which encouraged the practice.

During this conversation, as on many other occasions, I was told that, in the days before the GDR allowed its citizens to watch West German programmes, people would inform on neighbours whose television aerials faced west; and if someone rang the bell in the evening, the television was always switched from "west" to "east" before the door was answered – even after western television was tolerated. Dr Meyer said this was an example of the universal double standards imposed by the system. "Children followed the official line at school but were different at home if their parents were easy-going; adults dissembled at work and only showed their real selves at home or among very close friends. We all led double lives; we all spoke with forked tongues, if you like."

In the GDR, as in the Third Reich, the eleventh commandment – thou shalt not be found out – clearly prevailed. Some take the view that the most pervasive legacy of Nazism (and perhaps of Communism too) is the amorality bred by this self-preserving form of constant dissimulation, whose essentials were learned in the kindergarten.

Falko came up with another poser, the great political irony of the *Wende*: "I think it's pretty rough that those who started it are hardly being heard from now. The citizens' movements and so on were the opposition when it started, and now it's happened they're in the opposition again. And we've got all these right-wingers on the streets as well."

The consistency between the pre- and post-revolutionary positions of New Forum and the rest surely lies in the fact that they were not a political movement, but the practical expression of a resurgent sense of social justice suppressed until Gorbachev came. The conscience of the people in 1989 still has a role in 1991 and beyond, a role which cannot be measured in votes and is more effective outside parliament than in it.

We talked a lot about personal relations between east and west Germans and restrictions on movement in divided Germany. Dr Meyer said the divide between family members in east and west had been growing deeper with the passage of time, regardless of the various visiting "concessions" made over the years. "But for the big new exodus in 1988–9, before people realised the *Wende* was coming, most such connections would have withered by 1995 or so if the change hadn't come." Her colleague said that people needed permission to visit relatives inside the GDR if they lived within five kilometres of the border (and even more so if within 500 metres). Police with dogs used to go up and down trains approaching the border questioning passengers, just as in wartime. Not many people knew that, outside the country. Sometimes permission was given to go to the border-zone – provided it was not by car. "We have a holiday place in the Harz Mountains close to the border. So we had to drop off our luggage and then park our car three kilometres further away from the border and walk or get a bus back!"

Falko told the story of a young man he knew who was first jailed for dissidence and then expelled. He spent three years in West Germany trying to find his feet. His father, a friend of Falko's family, was not allowed to visit the boy at Christmas, which was par for the GDR course in these matters. But the young man was then killed in a car crash – and the father was not even permitted to attend the funeral in the west, to which the son had been forced to emigrate. "Young people's chances were ruined, even in school, because some remote relative had applied to go west. Every member of the extended family came under suspicion," said Falko.

Freedom of speech takes some getting used to. Christian said: "You can say what you like where you like," with a sidelong glance at Dr Meyer, "or almost. Before, you used to think whether to say anything or not, and then what to say. I think people have understood pretty quickly about free speech."

His principal said that many of her colleagues still felt uneasy. "Some still say that we used to discuss things among like-minded people where everybody knew what everybody else was going to say. Now they complain that they have to work out what to say to whom. They're completely unused to spontaneous and honest debate, and they – we – badly need training in tolerance of other people's views."

I asked the boys about sport, the activity which did almost as much for the reputation of the GDR as wall-building. As usual Falko spoke fast and foremost. "They used to come round looking for volunteers for sport. Then they recruited the promising ones for intensive training. I was into football and I was chosen for special training, but my parents blocked it because I'd have had to spend my whole life at it for years. And say I'd made it all the way to a top team like Dynamo, which was made up of Stasi and Army people – there would still have been no European-level club competition." Christian said: "There was very little normal sport, sport for the fun of it – just this forcing-house atmosphere." Falko had no doubts: "All the top stars were on drugs." He added: "I like cycling, but I couldn't do it because it wasn't one of the sports the regime went for. You couldn't get a decent bike, let alone a good track to use it on."

What struck the two students most forcibly about the change through which they were living?

Christian: "We didn't have the independent politicans who could stand up to the western parties, which came here and took everything over. Otherwise a lot of people would have opted for a better GDR."

Falko said: "We need to be careful not to fall for the hand-made suits and the Mercs, which all seems pretty sterile and boring. *Nicht wie die Bundis werden!* Don't get like the Feds!"

Bundi – *Bundesdeutscher* or Federal German – is one of many east German nicknames for west Germans. The wittiest is *Besserwessi*, a pun on the besetting German sin of didacticism, of always knowing better – *Besserwisserei* – and the most common slang name for a westerner – *Wessi*. More proof, if any were needed, that the old canard "The Germans have no sense of humour" is as unjustified as the tired old sneer about their trains always being on time: they have, and they aren't. What is in short supply in Germany is a sense of irony, especially self-irony.

Walking up the street with me afterwards to do some shopping, Dr Meyer said that the SPD might well have been right to oppose instant monetary union, but "The people here definitely wanted the D-mark. They even forgot that the CDU over here had been a bloc party in cahoots with the SED, because Kohl is CDU – and it was the CDU which presided over the change. I think it's fair to say that the CDU is identified with consumerism and that's what people wanted. The SPD has never got in step on this, and the Bonn coalition has simply swallowed up the programmes of New Forum and Democratic Breakthrough. But I can't see consumerism lasting four years [until the next scheduled federal election]. There is simply too much western goods, too much of every-thing all at once, including a flood of pornography at DM25 for a video film. I never realised that this was what they meant when they said there would be lots of meat on the shelves!"

I was particularly keen to check on the condition of one GDR institution which was condemned to death like so many others in the western take-over, but seemed to my layman's mind to be rare for having something to teach the rest of the world: the *Poliklinik*. As its name implies, this is a multiple health-centre where east Germans went (and were still going for a transitional period of five years) for all their medical and surgical treatment, except for conditions which could be handled only in hospital. The west German health service is comprehensive and generally of high quality – but very expensive. Compulsory for those earning average or lower pay, German health insurance has the merit of being funded by a separate premium, the cost of which is shared by employer and employee – and the demerit of encouraging maximum profit-taking at all levels, from the pharmacy to the posh consulting-room of a *Chefarzt* (consultant) and the operating theatre of a superbly equipped hospital. *Die Krankenkasse zahlt*, the health insurance will pay. Health care in the GDR was free of charge: the state subsidised it completely.

I returned to orbit on the Juri-Gagarin-Ring, bound for the main *Poliklinik* in Erfurt for an appointment with Herr Medizinalrat Dr (med.) Seyfarth. His wondrous title makes him a medical officer of health in British terms, roughly speaking; he is the medical director of the *Poli-klinik*, in a crumbling, rambling, but clean, late nineteenth-century public building. There is a huge notice-board inside the entrance showing the many departments on the various floors – they seem to cover every nook and cranny of the human body. There is no central reception and each section has its own waiting-room, as I discovered when I got lost looking for the doctor's office.

Dr Seyfarth, robust of build but pale of face and an enthusiastic smoker, made me dredge deep in forgotten corners of my vocabulary (English as well as German). Not only is my command of scientific terminology fragile but German also has homespun words for most of the medical terms which English, French and other languages take from Greek and Latin. Thus if you remember the "English" word "peri-tonitis" (and what it means), you then have to remember that the German is *Bauchfellentzündung* – literally, abdomen-membrane inflammation, which however, once learned, tells you a lot more than mock-Greek "peritonitis".

This linguistic nationalism (perfectly legitimate) also crops up in daily life, where television is *Fernsehen* (far see), pork is *Schweinefleisch* (swine flesh) and independence is *Unabhängigkeit* (un-offhanginghood, an exact, syllable-by-syllable translation of the original Latin). The national penchant for directness is reflected in the language or vice versa, according to choice. But modern German is taking in foreign words (mostly from English) with none of the reluctance shown by official French (which threatens to wither on the vine as a result; one of the strengths of English is its appetite for borrowings, which has given it a uniquely vast vocabulary). At the same time German has lost none of its ability to invent new "snake words" (combination words like *Kindergarten*, children's garden, or *Bundeskriminalamt*, Federal Criminal Bureau) for new concepts. As an English colleague is fond of saying, German is a Lego language. Thus east Germans worried by the shortage of public funds since unification demand a *Ressourcentransfer* from the west before everybody is reduced to *Krisenmanagementpolitik* (crisis management politics), especially in the area of *Poliklinikfinanzierung* – a word I have just invented but which any German would understand.

"We are going to get the western health system whether we like it or not," said Dr Seyfarth, who was forty-eight at the time. "And a lot of us don't like it. We suggested that doctors here should remain employees of the State with a guaranteed minimum income for minimum work, say DM1,000 [sic], and the more work they do beyond what it takes to earn that, the more they are paid."

It needs to be noted at this point that in the workers' and peasants' State of the GDR, doctors (and other people we describe as "professionals") often received little or nothing more than manual workers; a new teacher or doctor got about 1,000 marks and a senior person in either profession got around 1,600. In the GDR you really did need a vocation to be a doctor; no doubt the good ones gained job satisfaction as well, but precious little else.

"We were not able to save money or acquire our own premises," the doctor, in fact a consultant general surgeon, went on, "but we didn't need to. We were also not required to pay the kind of high insurance western doctors have to take out to cover themselves for professional error. We were covered by the State. Now we are expected to pay for that, to borrow money to set up a private practice and to encourage people to take out private health insurance [if they are not compulsorily covered already]."

The *Poliklinik* does everything for the out-patient, almost always under one roof, from consultations to X-rays, blood-tests, physiotherapy, minor operations and post-operative care. Ambulances (and a mobile doctor with a car radio on call from 7 am to 7 pm) are also attached to them for emergency house-calls.

One obvious drawback of the system is that, while such a concentration of facilities is handy for city-dwellers and for all patients once they are there, people living far from a town of reasonable size are at a considerable disadvantage. I also found people were having to wait a long time, but much of that derived from the suffocating GDR bureaucracy. A properly run reception and booking system would ease this enormously for an outlay which would swiftly be repaid in increased efficiency. Like most GDR institutions, the polyclinics were overstaffed, with many workers whose productivity was low or as near to nil as made no difference. This was due to several factors, including old-fashioned working methods; the state's commitment to the right to work, which meant everybody had to have a job even if there was too little work to go round; and the practice of continuing to "employ" people after they retired to eke out their pensions. This applied to auxiliary and non-medical staff; doctors were commonly in short supply (but the former were paid not that much less than the latter).

The long and the short of the *Wende* in the sphere of medical care is that east Germans used to have a health service in which money was not a consideration, but in its place they were getting an industry in which it is a primary one, complete with lots of scope for profit. A highly symbolic example of the change of atmosphere was supplied by the west German drug industry, whose products are generally the most expensive in the world. On monetary union these companies agreed to supply the ex-GDR at fifty-five per cent of western prices for a transitional period. But they neglected to deliver the medicines, and serious shortages of some drugs developed in the east, until Bonn was forced to make financial concessions to the firms.

The doctor blamed chronic under-investment for many of the obvious shortcomings in GDR health care, sounding even more like a defender of the British NHS in its hopeful early days when he upheld the idea of no charges for treatment at the time it is needed. The *Poliklinik* also ran all the social and home-care side of public health, such as doctors' visits to those unable to come in, health visiting, pregnancy advice, alcoholism counselling, child-care and the like. But since the average experienced doctor was earning between 1,500 and 1,700 marks a month the overheads were not enormous.

"A lot of doctors escaped from the GDR over the years. There were obvious economic reasons: look at what we can earn in the west and the working conditions! Also a lot of things were demanded of us that flew in the face of our professional principles. We were liable for compulsory call-up for military and civil defence at any time, which entailed lots of extra paperwork, abandoning patients and wasting time on exercises. We also fell further and further behind professionally in the last fifteen years. We found it harder and harder to get new equipment. And if they gave you a little extra, such as a bonus for exceeding your 'norm', the Party worker would be round asking for a special donation to Socialist Solidarity [which funded aid to North Vietnam and similar causes – to refuse was regarded as anti-social and earned a black mark in one's cadre file]. The general, all-pervading frustration affected our efficiency and our will to work," said Dr Seyfarth. "If the building needed urgent repair, as it did all the time, you could never get the money, the workers, the equipment, the supplies and the scaffolding together because central planning caused permanent shortages."

About a year before the *Wende* whole hospital departments were closing for lack of staff, including nurses and doctors who had gone west for up to ten times the money. Some nurses did not go west but left for local jobs with more pay and less stress. Wards were closing all the time (how familiar this must sound to anyone in Britain). Hospitals were even more physically neglected than polyclinics. I heard of a senior sister who was paid 300 marks a month more for a simple office job with a housing authority. Qualified nurses received more as raw trainees in Erfurt's electronics combine. The *Poliklinik* was free to give annual bonuses of up to 250 marks to auxiliary workers, but even these paltry awards caused more envy and anxiety than they were worth. Dr Seyfarth needs no conversion to the famous west German *Leistungsprinzip* (performance principle): "If you work hard, you should get paid more," he said. "A certificate honouring you as an 'Activist of Socialist Labour' is no substitute."

The union treaty allowed five years, to the end of 1995, for the winding up of the polyclinics and for doctors to go over to private practice. The resulting problems for the medical profession are formidable indeed: little or no capital, no premises, no polyclinics in which seventy per cent of doctors learned their specialisms, tiny pension entitlements with no chance to make them up unless they are young . . .

The Erfurt polyclinic (one of several in the city; big industrial plants provided their own) was once the biggest in the GDR, but became typical for the centre of a fairly large city: 410 workers, including sixty-three doctors in eighteen specialisms and eighteen dentists (services completely free). The rest were all trained auxiliary staff. Hospitals usually needed to check on their patients after treatment; otherwise everybody was treated at the *Poliklinik.* "I think it is a terrible shame that we cannot carry on, with enough money, proper equipment and the experienced people. We should have been given a chance, because I really believe we could prove that, suitably modified, it is a good system for public health, an example of centralisation at its best." As a layman and a foreign observer I can only conclude that it is a great pity a federal system like the German one cannot find the flexibility to give an obviously salvageable and improvable medical system a proper trial.

Had the doctor ever thought of going west?

"I lack the courage to move to another region," he admitted. "*Heimat* [which means so much more than such English expressions as 'homeland' or 'native heath'] is very important here, and I wouldn't want to leave mine. I thought about it, yes, but there are problems over there too, and I wouldn't want to lose touch with my roots. What I missed most was freedom of movement. Now I'd like to take my son to England and my wife to France; I'd like to drive round Austria. It's good that the shortages and the petty corruption, the payments you had to make to get anything done, have gone. There used to be ten million GDR citizens milling about every day looking for something they needed. You had to wait fifteen years for a telephone or a new car unless you knew somebody. Bribery was endemic.

"But I listen to my patients and they are already sobering up after the first bout of consumer materialism. They're all frightened of unemployment and bankruptcy, and they never had to spend a pfennig on their health before. I think there will be unrest, or tension between east and west within Germany. I fear something akin to civil-war conditions unless they show more understanding over there of the problems over here." This from a dedicated man who refused to give up his surgical work although his job was supposed to be entirely administrative, who earned half the average British industrial wage and seemed content still to drive about in a Wartburg, a car of 1960s design with a 1930s engine.

On my next day out in the Thuringian countryside I drove to the original Wartburg, a classic German castle on a high escarpment overlooking the town of Eisenach, where the eponymous vehicles were still being made pending a take-over by Opel, the west German subsidiary of General Motors of America.

But first I deliberately overshot, passing Eisenach on autobahn E40 and heading some thirty kilometres north-north-west, to Grossburschla. Two people I had met mentioned it independently as worth a detour because the place stood right on the intra-German border between Thuringia and Hesse. Some villages, though not this one, were actually cut in half by the vagaries of the fortified frontier, singularly arbitrary in this area. Grossburschla did not live up to its name (big Burschla), nor could I find a Kleinburschla (little); nor indeed did I see a soul on the cobbled streets. It was not much of a place, just a working village of unfinished-looking houses surrounded by rolling open land with some hills and trees, typically German for having no farmhouses on it (endless wars and feudalism made the German landscape radically different in this respect: the farms are all in the villages and strip-farming was commonplace until the 1950s in both Germanys). An old woman appeared briefly on the street and went into a terminal gape at my modest hired car with its Hanover number-plate (absolutely everybody is hypersensitive to cars in the ex-GDR); I feared for her health if I spoke to her.

The point about Grossburschla was the view, not of it, but from it. Whichever way one looked, between, round or even over the houses, or through them if the windows permitted, one saw the border fence. It had, of course, been largely torn down since the *Wende*, but the concrete posts were still in place, running over hills out of sight down into a valley and back again, sealing off stands of trees "over there" and enclosing the one road out of the place, which naturally ran due east. The entire wriggling line of fence, which had a sandy strip on the GDR side, was within the enclosed republic so that anyone crazed enough to cut through it could still have been shot down before reaching the west. Whoever built such a thing must have been mad. Grossburschla was said to be the most enclosed settlement in the GDR, a village in a wire bottle, the only way in or out via the neck, and every view up every side alley closed off. People with relatives there told me they were never so depressed as when they went visiting (with special permission, of course, and no car). Now the road west is open one can go five kilometres down the road to Hessian Weissenborn, where the white stucco and the roads are flawless.

This eerie detour made the view from the magnificent Wartburg (the name means 'guard-fort') seem all the more splendid. A sign at the bottom of the hill barred all traffic, so I parked like an orderly person and took a Disneyland-style, battery-powered road-train (run by *Wessis*) to the top, only to find a car-park full of west German cars and coaches. At least the locals were running minibuses up and down the long hill. From the top you could look over the town four kilometres to the north and great swathes of Thuringian Forest stretched in most other directions. The *Schloss* itself was doing a roaring trade for a cold, dark, dank Saturday at one mark for admission.

The older and more southerly half of the castle (eleventh century) includes the finest and one of the oldest profane Romanesque buildings left standing north of the Alps, once the palace of the Landgrave. On the later, northerly courtyard is the *Lutherstube*, the little apartment where the Reformer dashed off his vernacular New Testament while hiding for ten months from the Emperor Charles V after the Diet of Worms. The room is about four metres by three with a huge, green-tiled stove in one corner and a contemporary table (1521–2). The ancient wood panelling is still in place; the only movable item which may genuinely have been used by Luther is a small stool. Pilgrims stole everything else except the very walls of the castle over the years. So many people, overwhelmingly *Wessis*, wanted to see it that I came to know several of them quite intimately by the time we had shuffled through.

After several restorations, the last in the early 1980s, this part of the building, half-timbered in black and white, looks most impressive. The roofed battlements, the sloping, tiled roofs and "capped" towers make these wonderful, Grimm-grim, Gothic fairy-tale castles uniquely German. The country seems littered with them; Wartburg is unsurpassed, and I have seen quite a few, from the Middle Rhine to Liechtenstein and from Alsace to Austria. This is a connoisseur's *Burg*, even if the latest addition was completed only in 1867, and the best value for a D-mark of all my east German sightseeing.

Having had a good brush with Luther, I went in pursuit of Goethe. This entailed taking the B88 south-east from Eisenach towards the eastern Thuringian Forest, in Suhl, one of the most intensely rural and remote *Bezirke* of the GDR – now readily accessible from Bavaria and Hesse. I was going to Ilmenau, where Johann Wolfgang von Goethe, who is to German as Shakespeare is to English, frequently carried out his duties as, of all things, a tax-collector. But the young Goethe had to make a living somehow and he also had wider responsibilities, such as encouraging the flagging copper and silver mines in the area as well as other economic activity, including iron and porcelain manufacture. His employer was the remarkably enlightened Duke Karl-August of Saxony-Weimar-Eisenach (they had been carving Saxony up again). This paragon was the first ruler to present his people with a written constitution. He also recognised the multiple talents of Goethe, who became one of his most senior administrators. The writer visited Ilmenau twenty-eight times between 1776 and 1831, as recorded at the small Goethe Museum in the *Amtshaus* (the local government house, new in his day and excellently preserved and furnished). He wrote several poems and a novel here, as well as conducting scientific experiments, studying local plants and fossils and knocking up a few of his indifferent drawings (some are on display).

I could not fail to stay in Weimar, the most important place on my loose itinerary after Berlin. I would have been happy to pay through the nose, or possibly trunk, for a room at the beautiful old Hotel Haus Elephant (named after its own inn sign), but that was impossible. No matter – I got my two nights in different hotels and I was well content.

Germans prefer precise labels for places, especially when it comes to giving addresses or locations, so they do not speak, as do Anglo-Saxons, of Mayfair in London or Manhattan in New York, but rather Berlin-Lichtenberg or Bonn-Bad Godesberg. I have not been to Auschwitz-Birkenau, as it was called until 1945. But I knew there was a Weimar-Buchenwald; and even before I saw either the town or its nightmare suburb, I felt there was a fearful symmetry in this place-name. It seemed historically fitting that there should be the site of a notorious death-camp just six kilometres from the heart of Germany's cultural showpiece – a double memorial to the best and the worst in the story of a nation which has given house-room to unparalleled extremes: Marx and Nietzsche, Beethoven and Hitler, Brandt and Ulbricht, Dachau and the Lorelei.

Driving east along the B7 from Erfurt to Weimar, a short and gentle hop of some twenty kilometres early on a crisp Sunday morning, I could see for most of the distance, over to my left, what looked like a giant stump looming out of the forest covering a distant ridge. Only when I reached the western outskirts of Weimar, a town of 64,000 people, did it disappear from view. On coming to a crossroads before reaching the town centre I saw a sign pointing leftward to Buchenwald and on an impulse decided to follow it there and then. The sky had turned threatening and the forecast on the car radio was unfriendly. The minor road took me steadily uphill to the Ettersberg, a ridge 478 metres above sea-level at its highest point. The area had once been used for hunting and recreation by the local nobility and citizenry. The greasy cobbles led past depressed houses, apartment blocks and great lengths of dirty, whitewashed walls on either side of the road – a sure sign of Soviet Army quarters. Sure enough, a few disconsolate young soldiers in their hairy greatcoats and soup-plate caps came strolling downhill, their eyes on the pavement. What a posting – a dilapidated barracks in the shadow of the Buchenwald Memorial, the great stump now discernible as a huge stone cenotaph with a pillared crown. At ground-level in front of it is a montage of life-sized, free-standing statuary representing the prisoners, a parade-ground and a commemorative grove. Given that building a memorial to something so unspeakable is a task which has overawed or defeated most artists who have attempted it, the overall effect is creditable. Nor can it have been a bad thing in itself that new recruits to the NVA, the GDR's armed forces, were brought here to be sworn in.

Less appropriate, it seemed to me, is the character of the museum standing on the camp-site proper, which lies a little further along the Ettersberg ridge, completely surrounded at a distance by the beech trees (*Buchen*) which gave the place its name. Joining the few vehicles in the huge car-park outside the gates, I was slightly taken aback to see a row of half a dozen two-storey barrack blocks with red roof-tiles and yellow stuccoed walls which were obviously still in use. The woman on the gate said the residents were the personnel who looked after the site and the museum. There is a hotel, a youth hostel, a cinema which shows a half-hour documentary on the camp, and a cafeteria in the complex of buildings once occupied by the SS garrison, south of the camp and west of the remains of the railway station which was the end of the line for so many.

Written into the double, wrought-iron gate through which the prisoners passed – 56,545 of them in one direction only – was the supremely chill motto, *Jedem das Seine*, to each his own. The broad, flat site on which the long wooden huts once stood (Block 17 was for Britons and Canadians; Block 8 for children), teeming with lousy prisoners in three-tiered bunks, is paved, but otherwise empty except for a scattering of small memorials to the victims of various nationalities. It was bitterly cold and trying to snow.

To the right or north-east of the gatehouse is the crematorium block. A notice says that 8,483 Russian prisoners were executed by pistol-shot through the back of the neck. The prisoner was brought in, stripped and led to what is laconically labelled the doctor's room (if there was ever a more depraved specimen of *Homo sapiens* than the SS concentration-camp doctor, I hope never to hear of it). The victim was led to a spot on a wall where he was told to stand against what looked like a simple metric scale for measuring height. But down the middle of this is a slit, through which one of the pair of SS killers always on duty could fire his pistol from a cell hidden behind the scale. A close-up photograph from over the shoulder of one of the executioners makes it absolutely clear how it was done. The floor of the room in which the naked prisoner stood slopes from all directions down to a drain in the middle. Over that is a wooden duckboard and on a wall a tap with a hosepipe. Passing on through the ground floor, you come to the pathology department, a room lined with pale yellow, glazed tiles; the similarly covered mortuary slab in the middle with its channels and drainhole for blood was immaculate, as if last used yesterday. In a yard outside is the spot where Ernst Thälmann, leader of the KPD, the Communist party of the Weimar Republic, was "murdered by Fascism" in 1944: he is specially commemorated there. In the cellar is a room with steel hooks set in the ceiling. Their purpose is not explained. From there a hoist – death's dumb waiter – carried the corpses up to the oven-chamber, which is still horribly intact, the doors standing open.

Passing on from there to the far north-eastern corner of the site you come to the *Kommandantur*, the large, grey, three-storey block which now serves as the "resistance movement museum". The visitor's imagination is put to work by a detailed display on life and death in the camp, complete with a gallows, mock-ups of the hut interiors and the crude "equipment" used by the prisoners in their forced labour of stone-breaking and road-building. Many were worked to death in the local quarry. Tattoos, which seem to have provoked the puritanical Nazis to a singularly obsessive and prurient rage, were cut from the prisoners' skin, we are told, and made popular souvenirs. In Buchenwald they made lampshades from human parchment and shrank heads for keepsakes. Samples are on view. Interesting or particularly sound skeletons were sent to the medical schools of Goethe's fatherland for the edification of students: waste not, want not. People from thirty-five countries were brought here. Buchenwald was not an extermination camp as such (those were all out east in modern Poland), but of the 250,000 brought here, a total of about 65,000 died in or near the camp, which was opened in 1937. In 1945 General Patton's furious US troops, the first Allied force to occupy the area, drove many of the citizens of Weimar up the Ettersberg and made them walk through the camp. This macabre history lesson was filmed. Not the least shaming fact about this awful place is that Buchenwald was used as a detention camp by the Russians, who took over the area from the Americans in accordance with the carve-up of Germany agreed at Yalta.

"Get rid of the Communist propaganda" said a recent entry in English in the visitors' book, not the only such complaint to be found there. It is undeniably true that there was a considerable resistance network within the camp. Its members' desperate courage commands speechless admiration and unqualified respect. Communists were prominent, even dominant, among its members, which was not surprising as many political prisoners, including German Communists like Thälmann (but let us not forget the SPD leaders and the churchmen), as well as Russians were sent to the camp. They stole weapons and even manufactured guns in the nearby arms factory which used camp-labour, and they saved lives at incalculable risk to themselves. So it is not wrong to extol the heroism of Communist resisters in Buchenwald; on the contrary. But it is wrong to omit such phenomena as the Nazi-Soviet Pact from the history of events leading up to the establishment of the concentration camps; and it is a distortion to make no mention of the postwar Soviet use of the camp. It is also misleading to leave the untutored visitor with the impression that the camp was humming with German and other Communist resistance to the SS throughout its gruesome history by, for example, playing up the role of the camp committee at the end of the war. The last 21,000 prisoners, excluded from the horrendous evacuation death-march which preceded the arrival of the US Third Army, liberated themselves under the leadership of the camp committee on 11 April 1945; the SS garrison melted away.

The exhibition, in which the common humanity of the victims appeared to have been subordinated to the twin aims of exalting Communism and suppressing the word Nazism, seemed to me to sidestep the fact that

Buchenwald was run, not by alien Fascists, but by German Nazis. It was another reminder that the dedication of the GDR state to "anti-Fascism" (even the Berlin Wall was an "anti-Fascist" barrier) was not only a way of looking at the shared German past but also a way of looking straight past the central issue in it: that Nazism was uniquely German, that its crimes were not done "in the name of Germany" as Chancellor Kohl is fond of saying, but *by Germans*, whose victims were overwhelmingly non-German. These considerations, prompted by my first and last visit to Buchenwald, led me to the reluctant resolve to visit Ravensbrück during my explorations in Brandenburg: in one important respect that was to provide a heartening postscript to my pilgrimage into recent German history. I had got wind of a small historical revolt . . .

As far as I could establish there was no legal means of getting anywhere near the centre of Weimar by car, and its ring-road and traffic signs were so confusing that it was no less difficult to get out of the place. I was not yet accustomed to the GDR habit of sealing off entire town centres as a substitute for thought in the matter of traffic engineering (hardly necessary in most places before the *Wende*). Obviously Weimar drew and will always draw huge numbers of visitors, and an unprotected centre would soon lead to permanent traffic chaos in the tourist season. But I was not there in the tourist season: this was a wet Sunday in winter's antechamber and not even the Germans, understandably, were showing much interest in a cultural outing in such conditions. If I could only get in, I might have the town to myself, but to put a sign meaning "no traffic except residents and deliveries" at the entrance to every single street leading to the centre struck me as a mite excessive.

When I stopped to ask the way of a rare, dripping passer-by, he courteously gave me detailed directions. Unfortunately I could not understand a word because he had either a cleft palate or, more likely in the ex-GDR, uncontrollable dentures (false teeth being an area of technology in which most of the old Soviet bloc has yet to make progress). When I drew up alongside a second man, he saw what I was doing, turned expectantly towards me, stopped and waited, and, when I put my question, smiled innocently, saying: "*Nicht sprechen Deutsch*." I did not bother to ask whether he spoke English or French because I knew in my soul that he wouldn't. Two sets of intelligible directions failed to lead me to my hotel (next to the main railway station, which is not in the centre); I still believe I only ever got to bed that night because I had the luck to hail an elderly couple who lived almost next door to the place and were glad of a lift in the rain. But that frustration was still to come in the evening. Assuming I could ever get myself off the hateful orbital Friedrich-Engels-Ring, I had the best part of the day to immerse myself in this epicentre of *Kultur*. Having circled the centre two and a half times I penetrated the barrier by the simple expedient of breaking the law and ignoring a "no vehicles" sign, promptly found a legal place to park and set off in search of Goethe and friends.

Archaeological finds show that the Weimar area was already well populated in the Old Stone Age; Neanderthal remains indicate settlement up to 60,000 years ago. There was a Count of Weimar by 963 and the Emperor Otto II held court there in 975 and had a castle built. During and after the Middle Ages the town passed to and fro between local rulers in the customary German way. Lucas Cranach the Elder worked and died (1553) in Weimar; J. S. Bach (inevitably, it seems) was court organist for nine years until 1717. But it was the youthfully widowed Duchess Anna Amalia of Saxony-Weimar and her son, Karl-August, Duke from infancy, who raised the town to its pinnacle of glory in the last quarter of the eighteenth and the first of the nineteenth centuries. An ambitious ruler of a no-account, independent political entity like Saxony-Weimar-Eisenach could hardly nurture realistic territorial aspirations, but was free to seek greatness in other, less aggressive ways. Christoph Martin Wieland, poet, dramatist, linguistic stylist and novelist of the Enlightenment, was called in as the young Duke's tutor. The youthful Goethe followed him there in 1775; one year later Johann Gottfried Herder, theologian, essayist and literary critic, was appointed Moderator of the local Evangelical Church; Schiller also lived the last years of his brief life there.

Weimar became a grand duchy in 1816 and Karl-August set a precedent in Germany by giving his people a written constitution. This made it historically appropriate that the German National Assembly should sit there (at the German National Theatre) from 6 February to 21 August 1919 to draw up the constitution of the post-imperial "Weimar" republic. Writers, artists and musicians came to live in Weimar to draw inspiration until the First World War: they included Liszt and Richard Strauss. And while the Assembly was sitting, Walter Gropius founded the Bauhaus, which inspired much of the best in modern architecture, in the town (it moved to Dessau in Saxony-Anhalt in 1925). Capital of Thuringia from 1920 to 1948, when Erfurt took over, Weimar was badly damaged by

Allied bombing in February 1945, but has been triumphantly and lovingly restored.

Passing the National Theatre (where Goethe was director for twenty-six years), I noted with some scepticism that I had just missed a lecture there on the theme "Old Age has a Future", presented the previous day by a public health official from Bonn. The current production was Engelbert Humperdinck's *Hänsel und Gretel* – not a pantomime starring the hirsute pop-singer, but the original fairy-tale set to wonderful music by the rightful proprietor of the name. None the less I felt just a touch of disappointment, while freely conceding that they could hardly stage *Faust* all the time. The building was also disappointing: the baroque original (1779) was rebuilt in the German neo-classical style in 1825 after a fire; in 1907 it almost fell down and had to be completely rebuilt; in 1945 the building was burnt out a second time; by 1948 it had been restored to its present state.

Goethe's big, baroque town-house with its yellow walls and grey roof is, by contrast, entirely worthy of its fame as the home for half a century of Germany's greatest writer: he had it rebuilt in classical style after receiving it as a gift from his patron the Duke. His last surviving grandson bequeathed it to the nation in 1886 as the National Goethe Museum. It is full of his furniture, works of art, papers and personal effects, including his study and library, and the modest little bedroom where the leading figure of the German Enlightenment died in his eighty-third year, in 1832, sitting in a chair and asking for "more light". The whole building is an exemplary memorial to a unique figure.

A short walk to the north-west brings you to Schiller's rather more modest but no less well maintained house, where this army doctor turned poet, playwright, philosopher and professor of history (how versatile these stars of the Enlightenment were, all Renaissance men) died in 1805 at the age of forty-six. An expansive Schiller museum was harmoniously built on to the house in 1988.

There are houses, memorials and/or museums associated with and dedicated to Wieland, Herder, Cranach Senior, the Duchess Anna Amalia, Charlotte Baroness von Stein (Goethe's friend and inspiration) as well as several palaces and castles, including that of Grand Duke Karl-August with its important art gallery and literary research centre, to see in and around the centre of Weimar, which is also noted for its schools of architecture and music. Goethe and Schiller stand together in a sculpted memorial outside the National Theatre and also share an archive north-east of the centre and a vault in the cemetery to the south-west. All in all, a week of concentrated sightseeing would hardly have done justice to Weimar, a national cultural centre without obvious parallel anywhere, and proof positive, if any were needed, that the rulers of the GDR were not merely true Germans after all but also closet nationalists. The huge effort which went into the detailed restoration of Weimar must have made an enormous hole in their limited funds for such work.

Unfortunately I did not have a week to spend in Weimar. I had just heard that the Westhausen *Landwirtschaftsproduktionsgenossenschaft* (LPG; see what I mean about linguistic Lego) had gone bankrupt, the first collective farm in Thuringia (and, as far as I was able to establish, in the entire ex-GDR) to go into receivership. It was time to go from the sublime to the agricultural. Westhausen is a small and otherwise unremarkable village about as far west of Erfurt as the crow flies as Erfurt is of Weimar. But it lies off an unnumbered rural road and is not easy to find. Essentially it consists of two parallel, badly potholed streets and one shop, whence I was directed to the LPG office in an adapted house. In no time at all I was seated across a conference table from Karl-Heinz Kott, the elective chairman of the enterprise, as if inquisitive foreign writers arrived unannounced on the doorstep every hour on the hour.

The LPG (literally an agricultural production collective) had forty-six full-time employee-members when I called; but it had about 200 members in all, more than half of whom were eking out their pensions. Like so many other economic units in the GDR, the LPG had a grossly overlong payroll because it had its allotted part in the social security system as well as its economic function. It was not a firm with staff, but a state institution with dependents of various kinds. Such soundings as had been made of farmworkers' opinions by the time I took an interest in the issue showed that very few fancied the idea of returning to the private smallholdings of old. Since these have proved largely uneconomic in west Germany and might have gone under but for the indefensible distortions of the European Common Agricultural Policy, this instinctive scepticism seemed entirely rational. LPGs were founded at village level in the GDR from the late 1950s, when all the farms in a village were combined into one unit, which tended to specialise in one aspect of farming. Then in the mid-1970s the system was changed; big LPGs were formed by combining several small ones. Fruit and vegetable farming was organised on a regional basis for communal processing facilities and marketing. The Westhausen collective therefore encompassed four villages, each of which specialised in one main farming activity, whether in animals or crops. Westhausen itself concentrated on pigs – and the LPG fell victim to its own confidence in the future of this branch of agriculture, a sad and undeserving casualty of the *Wende*. Let Herr Kott explain.

"We invested in a big new piggery in 1985 – on GDR terms, naturally; it was all planned as usual. It was nearly finished, on schedule, and was supposed to be ready this year. If it hadn't been for outside factors, it would probably have been fully operational by the end of this year [1990]. I've no doubt at all that if we had still been the GDR, that's what would have happened. But two things went wrong: because of the *Wende*, the price we could expect for pork fell by 70% overnight on July 1 [monetary union]; and the interest we had to pay on the development loan for the piggery jumped from 1.8% under the GDR to 9.5% at the *Wende*, on an investment of a nominal DM5 million. That's what did for us."

On paper the debt had, of course, been halved by the 2:1 conversion rate from east-marks – but the interest had increased by more than five times, just as the farm income from which it was meant to be paid was divided by three by free-market forces.

"There was no point, we decided, in trying to save the situation by borrowing still more, as some people have done. Every day would have made things worse, so we decided to resort to bankruptcy. We hope the farmworkers on this land will be able to continue working and somehow make a new start with the 1,000 pigs still here and the new piggery. Meanwhile, of course, we are still looking after the animals (there are 200 cows here as well) and we are still being paid – for the moment. Maybe a meat production company could take it over, or else a few private farmers.

"We were put at a terrible disadvantage with the overnight changes in the system. People round here preferred to buy western produce when they got the chance, so we couldn't sell locally, but only to distant buyers, who naturally expected a substantial discount for taking otherwise unsaleable produce off our hands. We sat down last March and foresaw what was going to happen, and we knew we would not be able to survive unless the state cancelled our debt, as they were saying in the Volkskammer would happen, but it didn't."

In the same week of November as I met Herr Kott, Dr Roland Huttenrauch, chairman of the Stiftung Warentest (goods-testing foundation, the west German body which monitors quality), said on television that east German goods, including foods, were a lot better than their reputation and sometimes excellent (this should cause no surprise as so much east German produce found its way into the European Community via West Germany before the *Wende*: it was a principal source of much-needed hard currency for the SED regime – so much so that it starved its own people of items which were readily available at GDR farms). The products were mostly of "acceptable quality" but "lacked the western image". One serious problem was that "ugliness is hard to sell". In January 1991 the west German Central Agricultural Marketing Society also declared that east German farm produce was "much better than its reputation". The society's seal of good quality would be conferred on ten eastern agricultural enterprises in February, said its director in Berlin. But on the shelves of east German shops, eighty per cent of the goods were from the west long before Christmas. All this and the fate of the Westhausen LPG seemed to lend special significance to a discovery which was made when winter descended in earnest on central Germany. Now that the border fence has gone, the still plentiful wild boar have much more freedom of movement to follow their uncanny instinct for knowing from many miles away where the best pickings are. This winter they were all heading from east to west . . .

After Weimar any other major town in Thuringia was likely to be an anticlimax; nor was I disabused of this surmise by what I saw of the two most important, Gera and Jena. The latter, however, interested me particularly for one entirely unaesthetic reason: the presence of the GDR's most illustrious and successful industrial undertaking, the world-famous company most likely to succeed, *Wende* or no *Wende*: Carl Zeiss-Jena, manufacturer of optical instruments. Thanks, among other things, to Warsaw Pact defence contracts and work for the Soviet space pro-gramme, the firm, one of the very few Communist enterprises which has at least matched if not surpassed anything done in its field in the West, seemed likely to have little to fear on the open market. But, as I soon discovered from Herr Zuber, the information officer, things were not quite as simple as that. There was the small matter of a company called Carl Zeiss of Oberkochen, 270 kilometres to the south in Baden-Württemberg, west Germany.

This is merely the most spectacular example of the commercial schizophrenia which affected quite a few companies in divided Germany.

I once followed an unlikely byway in this area when I corresponded for *The Times* in Bonn. I was astounded to learn, on a quiet day, of a diatribe on the English-language service of Radio Moscow (of all places) castigating a West German MP for suggesting that the East Germans were trying to dump 250,000 garden gnomes on the West German market. Knowing my Germany, I assumed that there would be a garden gnome manufacturers' umbrella organisation; the only problem was how to find it. Where better to begin than at the Federal Ministry of Agriculture? But the spokeslady there was highly indignant at the idea of *The Times* Correspondent breaking into her afternoon with such an unlikely request. "But *is* there an umbrella organisation of garden gnome manufacturers?" I gently persisted. "Of course," she said, giving me the name and number of its general secretary.

This luminary worked for West Germany's largest gnome-maker and knew all about the rumour. The firm's former East German branch, a VEB, was churning out the gnarled horticultural horrors as if there were no tomorrow, he confirmed; but he wasn't worried by that kind of competition because they were using prewar moulds over there. "We're much more sophisticated; we've got the very latest technology and if it ever happens, we'll see them off." I was thus able, after exhaustive researches, to reassure a waiting world that the possibility of invasion by fifteen divisions of garden gnomes pouring over the inter-German fence was not seen as a serious threat. A week later I went to dinner with a diplomat. While I was there a gnome was stolen from a nearby garden. Somebody gave my car-number to the police, who solemnly hunted me down, first at home and then in the office. The *Herr Wachtmeister* kept his nerve and his face straight when I showed him my cutting. All became clear and I was officially removed from the list of suspects. Gnomes are not mocked, apparently . . .

Be that as it may, Zeiss of Oberkochen owes its existence to an American coup in the immediate aftermath of the war. It will be recalled that the Allied force which reached Thuringia first was Patton's Third Army, which was only later replaced by Soviet forces. The Americans took with them as many key workers from Carl Zeiss-Jena, which had had a very busy war working for the Wehrmacht, as they could find – 126 in all – and the Oberkochen company was built around them in 1948, the year in which the Jena works was nationalised as a VEB. Each firm ran an optical glass and an optical instrument subsidiary; and each company claimed to be the true heir and successor of the prewar original. Years of disputes and inconclusive court cases about trademarks and patents ensued. As usual in such circumstances, the only visible gainers from this endless bickering were the lawyers of several countries. So, for all the world as if they were a couple of squabbling states bent on improving diplomatic relations, Carl Zeiss-Jena and Carl Zeiss-Oberkochen sent top-level delegations to a neutral place – Britain – and thrashed out their London Agreement in 1971. Acknowledging that all the legal disputes were expensive and futile, they agreed to halt them and to divide the world into three zones. The Jena firm would have the political "East" (not inconsiderable because of the defence and space work mentioned above), Oberkochen would have the West (where there was much more competition); and both companies would divide the market in every other country by agreement.

The one possibility for which they had not catered was, of course, a future unification of Germany, which made another "treaty" necessary. A "declaration of intent" was signed in May, and a substantive agreement in September 1990. The three-way carve-up of the world was to continue – and united Germany was to fall into category three, where the two companies would operate alongside each other in accordance with an agreed division of markets. Both trademarks would remain. In fact, the two companies started talking in February 1990 and agreed in principle to "come together and cooperate".

A further complication was the Carl Zeiss Foundation, founded in Jena by Ernst Abbé, partner and successor of Carl Zeiss himself (who had supplied Goethe with lenses for his scientific work). The Foundation, which came to own the original company, was constitutionally incompatible with the forcibly nationalised status of Zeiss-east. Its social welfare functions were transferred to the VEB itself in 1948 – at which time Zeiss-west set up a new one in Heidenheim, Baden-Württemberg. "The humanitarian work continued uninterruptedly in the GDR," said Herr Zuber, "in the social and cultural areas, with sanatoria for sick children, holiday homes for workers, extra pensions for former workers and the like." The closure of the eastern and the opening of the western foundations was dictated by the occupying powers. Unfortunately a west German court upheld the Heidenheim foundation as the legitimate heir and successor of the original one because Zeiss-east was nationalised without compensation. Since West German law now applies in Jena as well, that was bound to complicate matters. So must the decision of the Volkskammer to hand back twenty per cent of the shares in the GDR state-owned holding company to re-establish the separate identity of the Foundation in Jena. Herr Zuber left no room for doubt that this issue was a highly sensitive one on which the two companies had decided to make no statement unless jointly agreed.

Carl Zeiss-Jena was obliged by the SED regime to become involved in other areas of the economy, notably cameras and micro-electronics, so that from 1985 until the *Wende* it was the largest undertaking in the country, with a work force of nearly 70,000 at its peak. In 1989 Zeiss-east had a turnover of 3.9 billion east-marks with an already shrinking staff of 60,000, while Zeiss-west managed DM4.5 billion with 32,000 on its payroll. But the eastern workforce was halved in 1990 and the company extricated itself from cameras (the uncompetitive Pentacon company in Dresden was closed) and electronics; the Jena glassworks with 4,500 workers was also hived off. Carl Zeiss-Jena was back where it belongs, in the optics business. The eighty per cent of Carl Zeiss-Jena GmbH remaining after the Volkskammer revived the Foundation (east) was temporarily taken over by the Treuhand, like all the other VEBs. Its future seemed secure, no matter how it adjusted itself constitutionally and/or by merger to the free market – and regardless of the fact that the company did not even expect to know what it was worth on paper until the middle of 1991. It needed to find new markets to replace those lost in eastern Europe since east Germany withdrew from Comecon, where it used to sell two-thirds of its products. But the staff at Jena were confident they had the know-how to keep abreast, if not ahead, of the competition. "We are in a position to buy any new technology that we may need, which is quite a normal procedure," said Herr Zuber.

The tentative plan was to unite the two companies, east and west, in stages over three to five years. The observer could only admire the caution, the common-sense and the pragmatism of this considered approach – and perhaps wonder why the West and East German politicians had not done likewise with the much knottier problem of merging the two macro-economies. What's good for Carl Zeiss (and the railway industry, and others) would surely have been good for Germany . . .

But it was not to be. In February 1991 Zeiss-west suddenly swallowed up Zeiss-east with the blessing of the Treuhand. Only 5,000 workers – about one in six – were to be kept on. This disaster for the town of Jena was a microcosm of the catastrophe which by this time was poised to overwhelm the ex-GDR as a whole, inspiring massive protests in the big cities and panic measures and even tax increases from Bonn, regardless of the famous election promises. Reality was beginning to intrude: the free market, left to its own devices, would not save, but only destroy the defenceless industries of east Germany. It was high time to move on to the epicentre of the threatened economy – Saxony.

– III –

SAXONY

Many Saxons – history – Meissen – Colditz – porcelain – Albrechtsburg – Dresden – bombing – restoration – city story – Augustus the Strong – ghosts – Karl May – Zwickau and Trabis – Chemnitz – Leipzig – hero city – history – Biedenkopf – how to start a government I *– labour office – professional optimist – minorities – Zittau, Bautzen, Sorbs – Saxon Switzerland – green arrow*

– III –

Saxony

With the accession of Saxony-Anhalt and Saxony proper to the Federal Republic, to which Lower Saxony already belonged, the newly united German state wears a Saxon sash which runs all the way across the body of Germany from the Netherlands on the north-west shoulder to Czechoslovakia at the waist in the south-east, encompassing the Hanseatic enclaves of Bremen and Hamburg. The Saxons were and are a mighty tribe with a strong accent and fissiparous tendencies which help to explain the fact that there are three Saxon *Länder* today. One east German in two is a Saxon. Most of Thuringia and parts of Bavaria and Brandenburg (not to mention the old kingdom of Poland) were once ruled by Saxony or offshoots of its ruling house. The *Land* which today once again proudly calls itself the Free State of Saxony (the only other German "free state" is Bavaria; the term means a former monarchy turned republic) is nearly as small as Thuringia with an area of only 17,000 square kilometres. It is, however, by a large margin the most heavily populated of the "new" *Länder* – about five million people live there, almost 300 per square kilometre, twice the GDR average and above the west German average of 250 (at the turn of the century Saxony was the most densely populated area of Europe). It also has the second, third and fourth largest cities of the ex-GDR in Leipzig, Dresden and Chemnitz (previously Karl-Marx-Stadt). It is in this Saxon triangle that east German industry was and is likely to remain most heavily concentrated. It was for all these reasons that I had wanted to start my expedition round east Germany in Saxony, but the reader is already aware that I made it only on the second attempt. As a place to stay, the Saxon capital of Dresden remained out of my reach, but I was able to commute to it from Meissen.

Meissen was the first capital of what later became the duchy and electorate (1423) and finally kingdom (1806) of Saxony. It was from there in the tenth century that Heinrich I began to push the Slavs eastward. The Elector Augustus the Strong (reigned 1694–1733; also King of Poland from 1697) turned his capital, Dresden, thrice destroyed and thrice rebuilt since, into a "Florence on the Elbe". He also founded the state porcelain factory at Meissen.

Leipzig, meanwhile, established itself as the region's chief commercial city (its industrial fair goes back to the Middle Ages and the city stands where two major ancient European trade routes crossed) and the home of German book publishing as well as a leading artistic and musical centre. After the death of Augustus the Strong Saxony grew weak, finding itself on the wrong side in the Seven Years' War (Frederick the Great's Prussia versus Austria), the Napoleonic Wars (half of Saxony was lost to Prussia in 1815) and Bismarck's war with Austria in 1866.

Chemnitz mushroomed as the regional industrial centre after unification in 1871 and Leipzig was the first home of the General German Workers' Association, a forerunner of the SPD. The left-wing tradition survived the First World War, after which the new Free State elected an SPD government, deposed by the Social Democrat President Friedrich Ebert in 1923, when it co-opted two Communist ministers. The Saxon industrial triangle was severely battered by the Anglo-American bombing campaign in the Second World War, after which, slightly expanded by the transfer to it of the Görlitz area from what is now Polish Silesia, it formed part of the Soviet Zone and hence the GDR. Leipzig with its vast demonstrations was the springboard for the 1989 revolution – the "hero city".

Four days after briefly returning home from Thuringia I was back in the ex-GDR, bound for Meissen through Saxon countryside which looked a little more prosperous and rather less beautiful. Fully accustomed by now to following the signs for *Zentrum* (east German for western *Stadtmitte*, town centre) only to be abandoned to my fate once I got there, I was entirely unsurprised to find myself lost, misled by bad signposting, one-way streets and my own famous lack of a sense of direction. A woman pulled up behind me as I once again stopped and ducked out of sight to look at a map, got out of her car into the rain and came to put me right. Eventually I found my accommodation, the Mitropa Hotel, by looking for the railway station. Mitropa (short, I believe, for *Mittel-Europa*) I knew to be the execrable catering arm of the Deutsche Reichsbahn; and sure enough my room commanded a constantly shifting view of platform one. It would have made an excellent stationmaster's office, complete with hot and cold running trains. Fortunately there were not very many; so few, indeed, that one of the two tracks on the railway bridge over the Elbe had been torn up years ago. Access to the hotel was gained through the suicidally gloomy station restaurant, also run by Mitropa, where some people were almost always to be found drinking themselves into a stupor, while others sat and ate from the tiny menu and still others just sat. The station concourse was favoured by drunks of the horizontal variety. As usual in Germany, one could not buy a bottle of alcoholic drink to take away after 6.30 pm or on Sundays except at the station. In marked contrast with the cavernous restaurant and its very limited menu was the amazing old-world courtesy of its staff, who behaved as if they were on loan from a stately home rather than serving up primitive German institutional food.

I was thus in exactly the right frame of mind when I set off first thing next morning to visit a prison (after a generous – uncooked – breakfast during which, as ever, I was didactically reminded to allow my tea to draw for a minute or two as if I'd never drunk the stuff before). I was, in fact, bound for a nondescript small town in Germany which is forever English – and virtually unknown to any Germans who do not actually live in or near it, which is to say very nearly all eighty million of them. It was a journey I felt obliged to make because many readers of this book would not have understood if I had failed to do so, even though I had been there, and even written about it, before. The town, population 7,000 or so, is notable for a large castle on top of a crag (there are any number of these in the area and this *Schloss* is not architecturally remarkable in its context). It is also justly renowned among connoisseurs for its beer (Saxony prides itself on its brews, which are a challenge to those of Dortmund and Bavaria). But it does not appear in any known German guide book, although it rates a passing mention in a book on the east German railway network, and of course a page or two in the only English language guide to the ex-GDR. Yet it has been the subject of a dozen books (in English, French and Dutch), several of which have been long-running bestsellers, a good British war film of the 1950s and a highly popular BBC television series in the 1970s. I refer, of course, to Colditz.

Getting into Colditz threatened for a while to become as difficult as it once was to get out. To the customary east German blockade of the town centre were added some radical roadworks which were being done without even the token nod to the convenience of passing humanity normally, if reluctantly, exhibited by contractors. Not only were both sides of the road blocked; they were fundamentally dug up, to such an extent that I wondered whether someone was trying to dig his way out. Only by ignoring a "no vehicles" sign could I get anywhere near the *Schloss*.

It had been just as hard for me to get to Colditz the first time I went there, in summer 1986. I was a member of a group of British journalists invited to the GDR to inspect its new tourist facilities (the hunt for hard currency had driven the SED to discard a generation's paranoid suspicion of westerners and go for tourism as a source of funds). When we arrived in Dresden, we mounted a small *démarche* and insisted on going to Colditz: our readers would not forgive us if we didn't, we said, waxing uneconomical with the truth. Our minders' revenge was to make us get up at 5 am the next day in order to fit the detour into a crowded schedule which left no time for spontaneous diversions. On my return I placed my tongue firmly in my cheek and wrote for the *Guardian* an article which should have been printed in ironic type, recommending that Colditz be turned into a holiday centre for nostalgic Britons, complete with escaper weekends, home-made glider races across the River Mulde, which the castle overlooks, and similar distractions. Imagine my amazement when just such a plan was announced by the GDR authorities a few months later – only to be withdrawn the following year for lack of funds. But after the *Wende*, when Britons and other western visitors no longer faced getting a visa and a long wait at the border in order to go to Colditz, coachloads of veterans and their families were turning up unannounced and the idea of exploiting all this thriving nostalgia was once again alive in the gloomy little town.

The castle entrance looks good with its white stucco picked out in red sandstone and adorned with a splendid coat of arms covered in gold leaf, but the rest of the building is manifestly crumbling, including the roof (which may or may not be due to the microbes introduced into its beams by prisoners of war). It is still used as a medical and social welfare centre, offering a polyclinic, homes for the mentally handicapped and old people in need of care. It would be hard to find a less suitable environment for these purposes, but the GDR was so short of funds for such facilities (and of public buildings) that someone had obviously decided a place of such size must be put to use somehow, *faute de mieux*. The GDR regime was not the first to think of this. The site was originally fortified in the eleventh century, an obvious bastion commanding the Mulde, and was rebuilt in its present form in the sixteenth century as an occasional residence of the Dukes of Saxony. The Swedes captured it in the Thirty Years' War. In the eighteenth century it was a hunting castle, but it was beginning to fall to pieces at the beginning of the last century, when it became at various times a hospital for the physically and/or mentally sick, a prison and an asylum for the violently insane.

In 1939 it was turned into a POW camp for Polish officers (*Oflag* IVc) and in 1940 it became a *Sonderlager* – special camp – for persistent would-be escapers from other POW camps all over the Reich. Hermann Göring foolishly proclaimed that it was escape-proof, a challenge to the recidivists from the American, Belgian, British, Dutch, French, Polish and other Allied forces who were eventually confined to this university of escapery. The most famous British graduates (successful escapees) were Pat Reid, who wrote the definitive books on the camp, and Airey Neave, later a Conservative MP and political intimate of Margaret Thatcher, who was eventually killed by an IRA bomb in the House of Commons garage.

The man with the hardest wartime task at Colditz was undoubtedly Hauptmann (Captain) Reinhold Eggers, the security officer responsible for preventing escapes, always portrayed as a fundamentally decent adornment to the Wehrmacht. When I was in the rather remote part of Baden-Württemberg where he and his wife had chosen to retire to a home, I called on Dr Eggers because the Colditz series was running on British television at the time and there was a feature to be done on "the real Hauptmann Eggers". He turned out to be a charming old man, born in 1890, a teacher who survived the Western Front in 1914–18 and who went home to Halle after the Second World War. He was promptly imprisoned by the Russians for ten years for having supported Fascism by serving as an officer, even though Hitler had not offered him the choice. He wrote a book on Colditz in German in 1961 (which naturally sold better in Britain in translation) and edited another, and his modest apartment was full of memorabilia, including a bulky correspondence with the late Pat Reid. He was living at Bodman on the Bodensee (Lake Constance) by the Swiss border – right across the route favoured by Colditz escapers aiming for Switzerland. "This only really struck me later, after moving here," he told me, "but I should think it is no coincidence."

The burgeoning little museum in the town now has a room devoted to the castle as POW camp, revealing the kind of ingenuity with which

Eggers had to cope – usually with success, it has to be said. Among the forgeries on view are a cardboard rifle and pistol holster, German rank badges, caps and ornamental daggers, fake documents, radio parts and the like, even a wooden sewing-machine for tailoring uniforms. During the war, the German Army used photographs of such gear and of discovered diggings in exhibitions to train troops in preventing escapes. They were taken by Moritz Lange, a local photographer, who had the wit to take two shots of everything, leaving him with a complete collection even after he had handed in his pictures and the negatives. The extra copies have been found in the west German Military Archive, and Colditz Museum is arranging to draw on them.

I was told all this by Steffen Hemper, the lean and febrile deputy head of the museum, a fast-talking chain-smoker who could not do enough for me. After showing me the museum he took me round the castle itself, which I had, reasonably, not been allowed to enter in 1986 out of consideration for the inmates. Passing from the dilapidated outer to the partly restored, partly crumbling inner courtyard, courteously greeted by a couple of residents, I was shown the recently reopened chapel (reduced to a storeroom in 1967 by a law forbidding religious facilities in state institutions). Restoration work had barely begun and the place was in a mess, but the splendid wooden galleries which had been added to it in the nineteenth century for patients were still there. There are traces of very early murals, possibly going back to the origins of the *Schloss*. The cellar under the chapel will soon accommodate the wartime exhibits from the town museum.

"We can't cope with the flood of visitors from Britain since the *Wende* because we haven't got the space or the facilities for a whole coachload," said Herr Hemper. "We are, of course, delighted to see them and we want them to keep coming because that way we stand a chance of raising the funds we need for a proper display. Lots of people and groups seem to be making a special detour to come here for a few hours. If we can get the funds, we would like to open a hotel, a restaurant and a proper museum here. The town council is all for it, but the lack of money and the bureaucracy are making it all very slow work. The majority of visitors are British, but there are also Dutch and some French veterans or relatives. We arranged to hoist an elderly Frenchman all the way to the top of the building so he could show us where they started their tunnel on the top floor!" The most elaborate tunnel in the history of the camp, the French enterprise began at the top of a sealed tower, passed under the chapel and came within inches of success before the guards found it. A British tunnel almost as long, abandoned because it failed to link up with the main drain at which it was aimed, had also just been rediscovered with the help of a visiting veteran.

What of Colditz in united Germany? Its main industry has traditionally been associated with the local china-clay deposits. The area used to deliver kaolin to Meissen and in the early nineteenth century a ceramic industry was started in Colditz itself. In mid-century, porcelain, though of a rather less refined and more robust variety than Meissen's, began to be made; it still was when I was there, though few seemed to think the plant had much chance of survival because the products were too crude and expensive. The works, which employed 1,500 people or rather more than a third of the total working population of the town, had become a GmbH owned for the time being by the Treuhand. "Everybody is on tenter-hooks," said Herr Hemper. "Everything seems to go so slowly here at the moment."

Colditz also experienced rising tension before the *Wende*. At the little church in the shadow of the *Schloss* the weekly prayers for peace which had been going on, as in most places of any size in east Germany, since 1981, began to draw bigger and bigger congregations in autumn 1989. "Then they opened the borders. That is as much as people round here wanted. They're mostly politically unaware, the type that says, 'All I want is peace and quiet'. But everybody liked the idea of having hard D-marks and what they could buy. My wife and I used to be sent a few from relatives in the west, so we could go to the Intershop and buy luxuries. But that connection put us in the Stasi's books."

Herr Hemper explained that he had come to Colditz for his own peace and quiet. A Leipziger, he had studied agriculture and done various jobs since leaving the army, before taking a correspondence course in cultural studies qualifying him for the museum post, which he had held for a year. "We came here to get the house that was not available in Leipzig, where we got married thirteen years ago. Colditz was our niche" – a reference to the *Nischengesellchaft*, the niche society which the GDR became for so many of its citizens. They cast aside ambition (hardly extraordinary in a state where pay differentials were so small and a high profile only drew the attention of the regime) and found themselves a quiet place to live and a job which did not demand too much of them, thus acquiring the niche which enabled them to live in peace for what they could make of their free time. Herr Hemper had been lucky: his hobby of dabbling in the past had become his job. Any unusual behaviour drew the attention of the narks and the snoopers. "My wife and I were invited to the west once for two family occasions, a wedding and somebody's fiftieth birthday," said Herr Hemper. "So we went to the police and applied for travel permits. And we got them, for two weeks – so long as we weren't out of the country at the same time! So she took the first week and came back, and I left the same day for the second . . ."

And what about the Stasi in a backwater like Colditz? "Those who used to inform, the petty sneaks, are known and people avoid them," Herr Hemper said. "There hasn't been any trouble, they're just cold-shouldered and there's no lynching sentiment. But they were just the small fry. The big fish, the *Bonzen*, are still running around, of course, with new jobs. The two or three conspiratorial residences [from which the Stasi used to spy on local people] were well known. Now they're empty. It's unbelievable that they bothered with a place like this, I know, but they did. It was the secret of their success, I suppose."

A financial sword of Damocles hung over the future of the "State Porcelain Manufactory, Meissen" when I went to see Bettina Schuster, head of its public affairs department and co-author of a book on the place, whose world-famous trademark is a pair of blue crossed swords (symbol of the Elector of Saxony). It was the first place in Europe to make porcelain ware, hitherto seen only as fantastically expensive imports from China and Japan, brought to Europe by the Dutch merchants who dominated the luxury goods trade with the Far East. The Elector Augustus the Strong, Saxony's homegrown Louis XIV, liked the delicate stuff which was rather out of keeping with his bull-in-a-china-shop character – so much so that when he met the alchemist Johann Friedrich Böttger, who said he could make it in Saxony, the absolute ruler decided to monopolise it. He issued a proclamation in 1710, when he was forty years old, in German, Latin, Dutch and French, warning off the rest of the world, and set up the enterprise as if it were an undercover military operation. He commandeered the disused, late Gothic castle, the Albrechtsburg, which glowers over Meissen (of which he conveniently happened to be Margrave) from a high crag where the cathedral also stands, for the factory so that its secrets could be protected by his guards. There was china-clay in the region and wood for the firing-kilns could be brought to the foot of the castle hill via the River Elbe. Other ingredients such as precious metals were close at hand in the Erzgebirge (ore mountains) along Saxony's border with Bohemia (Czechoslovakia); the region was already Europe's most advanced mining area and the contemporary bedrock of the Saxon economy.

The products were on confident display at the Leipzig autumn fair in 1710 and they have been on show at every such occasion since, the oldest continuous exhibit. The crossed-swords trademark was adopted in 1722, and the subsequent decision of the Prussian royal house to set up a state porcelain works in Berlin must rank as an outstanding example of the principle that imitation is the sincerest form of flattery. A series of talented masters, designers and artists succeeded Böttger and applied their ideas, some wonderful, some not, to the extraordinary range of objects, from plates and statuettes to a stupefyingly elaborate, white table-centrepiece over four metres high, produced in all manner of traditional and modern styles. Some look overwhelmingly ornate; others appear too delicate to touch. They are all to be seen in the works museum in the Leninstrasse (what would Augustus have had to say about that?). The factory moved from the Albrechtsburg to its present site in 1863 because a steam-engine installed in a cellar ten years earlier threatened to hurl the castle off its crag. When the Saxon royal house abdicated in 1918, the new free state took over and continued to subsidise the works. They started up again two days after the Soviet "liberation" (occupation) of Meissen in May 1945 and were already able to mount a display at the Leipzig spring fair in 1946, when they were taken over by a Soviet combine called, unpromisingly, Zement. This enterprise installed a managing director with the unforgettable, not to say addictive, name of Mikhail D. Nikotin. Comrade Nikotin gave up in 1949 on the formation of the GDR, which nationalised the plant as a VEB and thus, in a way, restored the Meissen works to its traditional status as a state-owned enterprise.

Frau Schuster took me round the works where supremely skilled artists painted pictures or designs on the porcelain, which would eventually be twice glazed and thrice fired in all. In the section where birds were painted, they actually used dead birds (found in the area or from aviaries or taxidermists) as models. They even had a *Jynx torquilla*, our friend the *Wendehals*, "turnthroat" or wryneck, apparently a very popular design – especially nowadays, they joked. It takes a fortnight to paint a small to average-sized vase. Even with GDR wages it is no wonder that the finished product costs so much.

When I was in Meissen delicate talks were going on between the

Treuhand and the new state government while investors as mighty as Mitsubishi, Japan's biggest conglomerate, were waiting in the wings. There was a possibility of turning the GmbH into a joint stock company (AG), with worker participation in the ownership. Frau Schuster said that there were 1,500 jobs and 200 apprenticeships at stake; there were plans to shed 200 mostly administrative employees as painlessly as possible by March 1991. The Meissen works had obviously functioned like other large GDR undertakings, overstaffing and retaining on the payroll skilled service workers in order to be able to keep going amid chronic shortages. The latter were expected to become self-employed or work for specialised firms whose services could then be hired as needed in the normal, free-market manner – a development which was, however, being held up for lack of suitable premises for small workshops and the like. The company polyclinic was already being supplanted, I noticed, by doctors in private practice on the premises (I could tell from the brand-new nameplates). Frau Schuster said seventy per cent of the workforce were women, trained for a minimum of four years, and there was a crèche and a kindergarten. Wages were up to nearly sixty per cent of western levels already – unusually high and a reflection of the skills involved.

After two management studies by independent consultants the company had already cut the number of directors from eight to three, including new managing and marketing directors; a west German-style works council with "teeth" was already in operation, representing executives, workers and unions (such institutions are a key secret of west German economic success). "We are going to need some outside economic experts," said Frau Schuster. "We can't have people who used to go on about the virtues of Communism turning into credible capitalists overnight!" It was general knowledge that many ex-Communist managers, instilled with the evils of Gradgrind capitalism all their lives, seemed to be taking their free-market guidelines from Charles Dickens, illegally sacking and bullying workers as if they were serfs. This is the opposite extreme from what prevailed in the GDR, as Frau Schuster explained. "We used to have the unemployed – those who would be out of work in the West – inside the factories. Managers could do nothing about the unemployable layabouts and drunks because the regime forbade firms to put the anti-social on the streets. People from the west who have come here since the *Wende* have been amazed that we ever managed to function at all."

The obstacles the porcelain works had to overcome included the usual problems: the disastrously deficient infrastructure; social passengers on the payroll; pettifogging directives from the state to offer visitors tea rather than coffee to save foreign exchange. Like many other plants the works were ordered, after the 1973 oil crisis, to switch from oil-fired heating (crucial for their operations) to the all too easily available, homegrown brown coal. Now for environmental reasons the change would soon be reversed. The firm had managed a turnover of DM60 million a year (converted by a book transaction to four times the number of east-marks) from exports to West Germany but could not get its hands on any of the money, even for the urgent needs or obvious benefit of the business, without an enormous bureaucratic struggle. Now that oil-rationing had been abolished there would be a big switch from rail to road, Frau Schuster thought, which would not be good for the reliability of deliveries because the road system could not cope. The company had been able to handle 300,000 east German visitors a year because they had usually come in groups, but now *Wessis* were coming in their own cars on a whim and the workers could find nowhere to park.

Nevertheless the Meissen porcelain factory, famous showpiece of the GDR economy, was surely fated to survive. What did Frau Schuster hope would become of it? "I think we would all like to see the *Land* of Saxony take it over in accordance with tradition. I hope the government in Dresden has the strength to resist the foreign investors who want to buy in." Just before Christmas the state administration did exactly that, announcing the formation of a company which the Saxon government would control. It will thus revert to being the State Porcelain Manufactory, Meissen, as ever was.

It seemed logical to go next to where the factory used to be, on the fortified pinnacle overlooking the city. One glance round the walled-in clifftop, after recovery from a 184-step climb, explained why castles like Colditz, quite remarkable in themselves to a foreign eye unused to the German *Burg*, were left lying around to rot. The *Burg* at Meissen is quite magnificent, with the Albrechtsburg castle, a superb cathedral (being restored externally), a bishop's palace (now the county court) and a collection of marvellous seventeenth-century houses once occupied by factory masters, cathedral staff, officers and other worthies retained by Augustus and his heirs. The castle is in very good condition and includes a museum of art history with early Meissen ware and some magnificently fitted state-rooms (even though the place was never a royal residence).

The cathedral, however, was in a sorry state; with luck the repairs just begun will prevent it from falling down. The outside is black with pollution and the cloister attached to it is little short of devastated. The two western towers, brought down by lightning in 1547, were rebuilt only just before the First World War; it would be more than a pity if they fell down again from sheer neglect. The third church on the site, it is a late Gothic pile dating back to the thirteenth to fifteenth centuries, although the Mary Magdalen chapel, the oldest part, goes back to the twelfth. There is an unusual double entrance: once inside the door, you are faced with an elaborate, high portico crowned with bas-relief figures (this at least is in very good condition). The cathedral used to have no less than forty-five altars round its walls, but the Reformation left it with just one, the main altar. Services were held only in summer, I learned, because there was no effective heating. It is not a particularly big cathedral, but the builders created an impression of great height by putting the internal pillars close together. There is a perfect triptych by Lucas Cranach the Elder, some striking thirteenth-century stone statues and a dozen or so departed Electors are buried under bronzes by Peter Fischer of Nuremberg, who worked from designs by Albrecht Dürer. Definitely worth the saving, even if Germany does have a unique collection of great churches. I partook of lunch in "Meissen's oldest restaurant", a pleasant little hostelry in one of the old houses alongside the cathedral. Here it was possible to sample not one but two varieties of Irish beer, a stout and an ale: somebody from the island of God and Guinness had clearly shown the kind of initiative which had brought Irish monks to these parts so many centuries ago . . .

It was high time to renew acquaintance with Dresden, last seen in glorious, high summer weather but now sharing the wintry gloom which had hung over Meissen for most of my stay thus far. The first time I had seen it in 1986, a young Dresden woman eking out her student income took my colleagues and me on a tour of Augustus the Strong's baroque capital. Among many other things, we were taken to the Salvador-Allende-Platz to see the courtyard of the Georg Schumann Building, now belonging to the Technical University but previously the state courthouse, where there is a memorial to more than 1,000 "anti-Fascists" executed on the spot by the Nazis. One thing led to another, so that we soon found ourselves discussing with her the event which makes Dresden irredeemably creepy for anyone of a certain age and with a modicum of imagination.

On 13 to 15 February 1945 the Royal Air Force by night and the US Army Air Force by day created a firestorm over Dresden, swamping it with incendiaries and high-explosive bombs. The lowest fatal casualty figure I can find in a large selection of reference books, German and English, is 30,000. The true total could well have exceeded 100,000, but nobody really knows because the city was crammed with retreating German troops, wounded and refugees. Radiation apart, the effect on the city, to judge from photographs, was indistinguishable from that of the first atomic bomb dropped by the Americans on Hiroshima. In terms of instant deaths the annihilation of Dresden could well have been the worst bombardment of the Second World War. The principal driving force behind it was the head of RAF Bomber Command, Air Chief Marshal Sir Arthur "Bomber" Harris, arch-advocate of the strategy of "area bombing" (carpet-bombing of cities), who was totally opposed to the Americans' stated preference for "precision bombing" (itself a contradiction in terms at the time and a serious euphemism from the viewpoint of those on the ground).

It was fortunate for Harris that there are by definition, might being right in these matters, no war criminals on the winning side, because the indiscriminate bombing of Dresden was strategically redundant and morally indefensible. By that time the European war was as good as won. It has to be added that in Britain there was little doubt during the war, whatever may have arisen after it, that the defeat of Nazism was such a high moral imperative that the end justified the means, including the "saturation bombing" of Germany, at the cost of the most concentrated casualty rate among British forces in the war. It also happened to be the only way the British could take the war to the Germans before the Anglo-American invasion of Normandy in 1944, given that the Royal Navy was embroiled until then in a vast defensive war against German submarines in the Atlantic. While no British leader ever criticised Harris in public, he was clearly an embarrassment after the war, subtly snubbed by being denied the most exalted of the honours which the Establishment heaped on the heads of so many other major commanders. He was made a Marshal of the RAF, yes, but well after the war, and was awarded a baronetcy (hereditary knighthood) rather than a peerage, and then only in

1953. In fact he was virtually sent to Coventry, an unhappy metaphor in this context: Coventry is linked with Dresden (and Rotterdam and Hiroshima and other heavily bombed places) in a conciliatory sisterhood of once broken, now restored cities on both sides.

It is a measure of the indigestibility, or at least the relativity, of the horrors of the biggest war in history that our young guide called the bombing of Dresden "the worst atrocity that happened in the war". The word Auschwitz was instantly on the tip of my tongue, but I left it there. I saw no point in getting involved in an auction of atrocities; and she was outnumbered seven to one by male journalists from Britain, most of whom knew no German, which put her at a linguistic disadvantage as well. Further, it was clear that she had acquired her view of the war from the GDR's "anti-Fascist" propaganda, according to which the Germans had been the victims of the brownshirted men from outer space as much as anyone else.

The centre of Dresden has been laboriously and lovingly restored since 1951; forty years later the job is still barely half done, there is no end in sight, and only now, in honour of Chancellor Kohl's sixtieth birthday in 1990, has a large sum of money been collected from private donations for the at least partial restoration of the saddest building of all, the Frauenkirche on the bare Neumarkt, which was once the most handsome and popular square in the city. What was left standing of the eighteenth-century church, which was very little, looked especially grim because the rubble was still in place, unlike the Kaiser Wilhelm Memorial Church in West Berlin, also kept as a commemorative ruin but very much tidied up. Even so, Augustus the Strong's palace, a mere scorched shell when I saw it in 1986, was coming along nicely this time and will soon transform the place. But one could still espy the little, burned-out, enclosed bridge linking it at first-floor level with the fully restored Court Church next door, now the Catholic Cathedral. This was somehow an especially sad sight, because it is a small and intimate detail amid the architectural megalomania all around, forlorn and apparently forgotten (as it has not been; its turn for restoration will come). One could imagine people scurrying away from the blazing palace to seek refuge among the sarcophagi of the Saxon princes in the crypt, overlooked, of course, by the urn containing the ashes of the heart of Augustus (the rest of him is buried in Polish Cracow).

Dresden grew round an important crossing of the Elbe and became a city of the Empire in 1226; the first bridge over the river was finished in

1275 and two centuries later the city became the official capital of the Dukes of Saxony, displacing Meissen. A fire led to the reconstruction as Dresden-Neustadt (new town, previously known as Altendresden or old Dresden) of the northern part of the city on the right bank of the Elbe, from the end of the seventeenth century. From here the redevelopment work rapidly spread across the river, encompassing what is still called the *Altstadt* (old town) today. The link between the two areas which together form the core of the city used to be the Georgi Dimitroff Bridge (one can hear the old despot's heart pounding in its urn). Dimitroff was a genuine anti-Fascist hero, a Communist from Bulgaria, of which he briefly became Prime Minister after the war. Accused of complicity in the Reichstag fire at the trial of the alleged conspirators at Leipzig in 1933, he ran rings round Hermann Göring, a prosecution witness, with his bravura cross-examination, which helped to get him acquitted. But I was not displeased to see a shining new, post-*Wende* name-plate on the bridge saying Augustusbrücke.

On the northern side of the bridge in a small square stands the Golden Rider, a wildly romantic, gold-leaf (mis)representation of Augustus the Strong as a Roman emperor; he is forever riding towards Poland on his rearing horse. Northward from there runs the Hauptstrasse, high street, known as Liberation Street under the previous dispensation, a pedestrian-zoned mixture of modern shops and a few restored baroque houses. On the northern bank of the river is the Japanese Palace, so called not from its architecture, which is baroque, but because it was originally used to exhibit the royal porcelain; now it houses prehistoric and an-thropological collections. At the north-western end of the bridge is another baroque building, the Blockhaus, where the guards used to stand watch. Between that and the Japanese Palace is a lavish modern hotel with a baroque core called the Bellevue, because from there one has a perfect view of the much richer, chocolate-box spread of grandiose buildings on the south bank.

From right to left, looking south, one first sees Semper's 1878 Opera House, built to replace one burned down. No expense was spared, within or without, in construction or reconstruction (completed 1985); whether the result is felicitous or indigestible is a matter of taste. Behind it stands the Zwinger Palace, a vast and breathtaking rococo extravaganza, built round a stately courtyard of grass, gravel paths and ornamental pools; the main entrance, the Kronentor, is dominated by a huge black and gold model of the Polish crown. Like so many other projects commissioned by

Augustus the Strong, it was designed by Matthäus Pöppelmann. It contains the porcelain collection and a zoology museum; the historical museum was closed and the Old Masters' Gallery, the finest collection in the ex-GDR, was temporarily housed nearby to allow further restoration work. As the eye moves leftward it next sights the Cathedral and former Court Church mentioned earlier, with the *Schloss* in its scaffolding cocoon looming behind. Running off from the left of the *Schloss* are the stables, whose north-facing wall is covered with a white and gold mosaic made of Meissen porcelain, the "Prince's Procession", 102 metres long and showing all the ancestors of Augustus. Behind it are the equally over-the-top former royal stables. If readers new to Dresden are beginning to gain the impression that the said Elector was not only strong (a soubriquet deriving from his sexual and philoprogenitive exploits as much as from his habit of straightening horseshoes with his bare hands) but also weak in the head when it came to self-glorification, they could well be on the right track.

Next in line is the Johanneum which, worthily but prosaically, houses a transport museum covering everything from trains and boats and planes to bicycles. The Schöne Pforte (pretty portal) next door is no such thing because it has yet to be restored; it antedates all the baroque, being a leftover from the pre-Augustan Renaissance Dresden. After the School of Visual Arts which stands in front of the Frauenkirche, and still moving from west to east, comes the Albertinum. This palace permanently houses a gallery of modern art and also has the Grünes Gewölbe, green vault, with Augustus the Strong's exuberant, enormous and vulgar collection of objets d'art, jewel-encrusted junk and countless contenders for bad-taste awards. The extravagant Augustus also collected mistresses, especially countesses, one of whom he put under *Schloss*-arrest for forty-nine years for getting above herself. He once gave a party at which the guests were prevented by the royal guards from leaving the banqueting hall until their protesting bladders and bowels "thundered in their trousers" – the German penchant for scatological humour at its right royal worst.

While I was in Dresden this time the Albertinum was showing a special exhibition of 360 paintings by 170 of the 665 artists known to have been *ausgebürgert* – decitizenised – by the GDR. It must have seemed like a good idea at the time and I am sure it was well-intentioned. I lingered for half an hour before getting down to the serious business, the old masters expected to be there until 1994, when they are due to return to the Zwinger. Going up the broad staircase to the first-floor landing I saw for the first time the magnificent row of five huge Canalettos of Dresden (no prizes for guessing who commissioned them). Inside the temporary gallery was the G D R's small but exquisite collection of masterpieces from the Italian Renaissance and paintings by many of the greatest German, Dutch, Flemish, Spanish and French artists. Works on view included portraits of a number of severely overweight Belgians by Rubens and seven Rembrandts, plus a fine selection of French impressionists and works by Caspar David Friedrich, Germany's great romantic painter. I have been fortunate enough to see many of the greatest art collections in the world from New York to Florence and Leningrad to Madrid, but the Zwinger collection struck me as rare for offering a really broad sample of all the main schools of European painting while remaining comfortably digestible by a lay person in a day. A triumph of quality over quantity, unmatched by any other gallery in the rest of Germany or even Berlin, east or west; worth a special trip. The Albertinum also houses an impressive permanent collection of modern paintings.

Just behind the baroque majesty of the southern river-bank, between the *Schloss* and the Frauenkirche, is a complex of yellow-stuccoed, modern but self-effacing buildings which to my untrained eye seemed to succeed in suggesting what was there before the war without presuming to imitate it. Even the new five-star Hotel Dresdner Hof does not obtrude. The east Germans are quite clearly at least as good at this kind of subtle infilling as their western confrères. Goodness knows they all had plenty of opportunity to practice. The *Ossi* architects seem to me as a layman to be a lap ahead of their *Wessi* counterparts in discreet urban regeneration – where they were given their head. Dresden is particularly impressive in this respect, as it is, of course, in its main effort to rebuild Augustus the Strong's monumental legacy.

I have to say that a heavy diet of German baroque with a Saxon accent is not necessarily an entirely uplifting experience, though fortunately there are other sights worth seeing in Dresden. To begin with, all those intrinsically grandiose buildings have been darkened again in the past three decades, after restoration, by air pollution. They would certainly look less overbearing if the fabric had its original sandstone colour. The *Schloss* will cheer the place up when it emerges because it is huge and will have its stucco coating again. But even when the winter sun came out brilliantly on my second and third visits, Dresden's baroque panorama still looked too much like an outsize mausoleum. Reborn after the fire of 1685, pounded by Prussian artillery in 1760, besieged and bombarded again during Napoleon's last victorious battle in Germany in 1813 and incinerated by the Anglo-Americans in 1945, Dresden has a rather stronger claim to the name of Phoenix than the capital of Arizona. On my mental map of the Saxon capital there will always be an empty space with the legend 'Here be Ghosts'.

Dresden and Meissen are at opposite ends of the same broad ribbon of conurbation along the Elbe. Halfway between the two on the B6, which runs along the south or left bank, is Radebeul. I almost caused an accident there when I saw a modest roadside signpost to the Karl May Museum. I am notorious, among the very few who have acted as navigator to me as driver, for reacting to a call to turn left by taking the very first opening, such as somebody's driveway. That perverse talent enabled me on this occasion to make straight for the museum, which I never knew existed, but which I correctly assumed to be devoted to the man who had been Adolf Hitler's favourite author. I had the place to myself.

Karl May, born in 1842, wrote, among many other books, derivative Indianocentric westerns – noble savage, decent white man – rip-offs of the works of R. M. Ballantyne and James Fenimore Cooper. Hitler adored not only the books, written for boys, but also the execrable German films based upon them, which he used to watch at private viewings in the small hours – when he was not boring people to death with his "table talk". Karl May's decent white-trapper figure was Old Shatterhand (pronounced Eault Shetterhent in German) and his noble Apache was called Winnetou. Another hero was named Old Shurehand (sic).

The museum was in the house where May had lived the last years of his life from 1896 to 1912. He renamed it (of course) Villa Shatterhand, and in the grounds was the Villa Bärenfett, bear-fat, a name lifted from the book *Unter Geiern* (among the vultures) published in English as *Son of the Bear-Hunter*. It is a huge, detached, suburban log-cabin containing an exhibition on the North American Indian. I was less than astonished to see the heads of wolves, bison and moose on the walls, even if the stuffed grizzly bear (not common in Apache country, I understand) gathering dust in a corner was a touch oversized for the average living-room. The centrally heated log-cabin had been specially built for the collection in 1926. Over 250,000 people had visited the place in 1988, said a notice. The house proper had served as a kindergarten until 1984, when the powers that were, doubtless sensing a nice little earner, dropped their official disapproval of Karl May and threw out the children.

The bulk of the exhibits had been sold by an American artist to May's second wife, Karla, and his publisher, E. A. Schmid (he must have seen them coming: one item, a long-handled, steel-bladed tomahawk is labelled, optimistically and unscientifically, "supposed to have been property of Sitting Bull"). There is an undated, Bayeux-style, narrative arras of the Battle of the Little Big Horn – the Sioux Tapestry? – which has no date and less artistic merit. There is also a superbly irrelevant record of the Indian protest movement in the 1970s and 1980s in the United States and Canada: it is no disparagement of the legitimate grievances of these people to dimiss this postscript in the context as Communist propaganda. It was clearly because the GDR regime held May to be an anti-colonialist writer that the old charlatan suddenly gained official approval. His works were apparently held to be *romans à clef* about the evils of imperialist exploitation of subject peoples rather than pot-boilers written at speed for profit.

Karl May's *oeuvre* includes not only *Heroes of the West* and such but also *Through Desert and Harem* (sic), *Through Wild Kurdistan* and the like. He travelled all over the Middle East and South-East Asia and, according to his many critics, never allowed the facts to get in the way of a good story. At home he liked to dress up like an eastern potentate. Indeed the controversy about the truth or otherwise of May's travel books generated a lively secondary industry which spilled over the German border into Holland, where formidable debunking campaigns were mounted. The embattled author fought a series of libel actions against one Rudolf Lebius, a German journalist, who defied popular sentiment by refusing to believe the outpourings of this literary mountebank.

May, who looks rather like Leon Trotsky in his photographs, caused a monumental scandal when he divorced Emma, his first wife, in March 1903 after twenty-three years of marriage and wed the divorced Klara in the same month. Revelations of a dissipated youth did him no good either in some circles. The son of a poor weaver, May briefly became a teacher but was sacked for theft. He eventually served seven years in various prisons before turning to pulp novels and then the "first person" westerns which made his name. So for most of his adult life May was able to laugh all the way to the bank; at the height of his enormous popularity he was publishing his books, like Dickens, in weekly parts at thirty pfennigs a time. The bookshelves of Germany and its neighbours were already groaning with his westerns when he condescended to visit North America for the first time in 1908. He confined his explorations to the north-eastern United States and part of Canada, and never went near the Apache country in the far south-west where his westerns were set. Rather remarkably for a resident of Imperial Germany in the years immediately before the First World War, let alone for a writer who had such trouble distinguishing between truth and invention, May declared himself a pacifist and wrote passionate diatribes against war. On the walls of the museum were testimonials from Bertolt Brecht, Albert Schweitzer, Heinrich Mann, Hermann Hesse and other celebrities who had all loved the "naive and innocent" books in their youth. But not a word from Hitler, undoubtedly the Saxon hack's most influential admirer.

My visit to Zwickau, birthplace of the composer Robert Schumann, the next day, was of long-planned intent. This grimy and crumbling town on Saxony's western border with Thuringia was the birthplace and deathbed of that most extraordinary means of human locomotion, the Trabant car, half-affectionately known as the Trabi, which became an inanimate television star in 1989, when east Germans were pouring westward via Hungary, Czechoslovakia and Austria. Most people will recall seeing on television car-parks full of abandoned Trabis in many parts of eastern Europe; others will have seen them on the road in the west (the west Germans relaxed their strict car-exhaust controls until the end of 1992 to enable their new fellow citizens to keep their "wheels"). A few have been sighted puttering further afield, most memorably at the side of the road, with bonnets wide open as if gasping for breath, on the long climb out of Dover. Since the *Wende* they have been photographed upside down in skips, stripped to the frame and abandoned in fields, propped up at crazy angles against the remnants of the Berlin Wall, burning on bonfires and queueing nose to tail at petrol stations. Travelling in one on a bad east German road (I speak from experience) is like a ride in a speedboat on choppy water – bouncing feet into the air off a cobblestone, landing yards further on and bouncing again. Or so it seemed; one's perceptions may be curdled by inhaling the exhaust-fumes from the filthy two-stroke mixture which powers them. In size and shape the nearest western equivalents were the early Riley and Wolseley variants of the immortal British Mini (the ugly ones with protruding boot). The design is of the same era, but without a trace of flair. I now venture to quote from the official 1988 (pre-*Wende*) history of the manufacturing plant, the VEB Sachsenring Automobilwerke, Zwickau:

High decorations such as "Factory of Socialist Labour" with the Karl Marx Order and the Banner of Labour are the expression of the high regard which Party and government extend to the Zwickau car-works. In 1986 our factory collective received, in honour of its outstanding performance in the preparation of the XI Party Congress of the SED, a banner of honour of the Central Committee, presented by the Minister for General Machine, Agricultural Machine and Vehicle Construction, Comrade Tautenhahn [picture of two men in dull suits shaking hands].

As producer of a highly valued and desirable consumer-durable we bear great responsibility for the fulfilment of the principal task decided upon at the VIII Party Congress of the SED . . . If in our republic today forty-six out of every hundred households have a car, then the Trabant workers have a not insignificant part in that. With the further intensification of production on the basis of a high development tempo of science and technique and the application of key technologies, productivity will be raised further and working and living conditions constantly improved . . .

Those were the days (and that was just from the introduction). How simple it must have been to live in a world of one's own, ignoring the fact that the Trabi was a menace to the environment, primitive, dangerous, noisy and noxious. It also cost about one year's average pay – and the average waiting time for a new one lay between ten and fifteen years. A second-hand Trabi was thus worth more on the "grey market" than a new one because it was available at once. The Trabi was at the bottom of the GDR automotive social scale. Next up was a Wartburg, then a Russian Lada, a Czechoslovakian Skoda (unusual among Socialist runabouts for being reliable), then a neutral Swedish Volvo or Saab – or a French Renault (made by a state-owned firm with a strongly Communist workforce!). The two-stroke Trabi, available as two-door "limousine" or three-door "estate car", was a people's car in the way the original Volkswagen "Beetle" never was. One of its main peculiarities was the unique material from which it was made – Duroplast, a sort of pressed, plasticised fibreboard. In spring 1991, German scientists announced the discovery of a chemical which could reduce a Trabi body to an easily disposable blob. History will probably confer on them the status of public benefactors.

I found the factory site easily enough; it was so vast one could hardly miss it. The trick was where to find the management. I was rather alarmed when I drove though the first gap I found in the long, grubby wall round the site, parked, got out – and found myself stepping into bloody water. A man with huge bloodstained hands and a similarly besmirched white coat appeared and demanded to know what I wanted. He explained that this was a meat-processing plant and gave me directions. At the correct gate a phone-call to upstairs established that the PR department was in a panic, with television crews from Belgium and the United States and west German newspaper reporters awaited; there was no time to handle an author from England as well, even if he modestly offered to trail round with the Germans with no need for interpretation. Would Friday week be any good? Not really.

I went to the works museum and "earwigged" on Herr Meese, who was explaining to a group of Dutch visitors that Zwickau had been a car-making centre since 1904. In the slump the four car firms there combined into one, the Auto-Union, whose four-ring symbol is used today by Audi (now part of the Volkswagen group). After the war, what production capacity was left following reparations to the Russians was applied to the manufacture of small trucks, then tractors for the new LPGs. From 1949 cars were produced again – two-stroke, wooden-bodied, 690-cc, twenty-horsepower bangers of a prewar design, but cars. The immortal Trabant was developed from 1955 for launch on a starving market in 1957. The name is German for satellite and was chosen to honour the first Soviet *sputnik* (one hopes the keen, thrusting operative who thought of it was suitably honoured with several of the countless decorations the GDR handed out to its workers in lieu of money). The first P50 model was a 500-cc, two-stroke, eighteen-horsepower box capable of ninety kilometres per hour. The P60 and P70 followed, the cubic capacity, speed, interior comfort and outer design slowly developing over the years until the three-millionth and last Trabi bounced off the production line in May 1990 – when the first locally assembled VW Polo was completed at Zwickau's branch factory at Mosel. Both historic cars are in the museum, side by side, ancient and modern, east and west. The D-mark killed the Trabi's thriving export markets in Bulgaria, Hungary, Poland and Yugoslavia. Trabis piled up in Zwickau and at the dockside in Rostock on the Baltic pending a decision from Bonn on whether to endorse a

DM2,000 export subsidy per car to get rid of them. At DM6,000 to 7,500, the two-stroke Trabi did seem expensive to the point of outrage.

In the museum there are prototypes of models which never went into production – stillborn post-Trabis which looked remarkably like the Renault 4, the Renault 5 and even a Jeep. I wondered whether the GDR, left to its own devices, would have produced a two-stroke, Duroplast, main battle-tank.

"If we'd had all the investment money the government promised us in the past," said the heavily pregnant young woman at the museum admission desk, "we'd have been able to make real cars. Nobody wants to pay D-marks for a Trabi; you'd have to be mad. They want DM9,000 for the new four-stroke model, you know." Most of the work-force of some 7,000 was on "short-time working" which meant they were doing nothing: the union treaty protected most workers from redundancy before the end of March or the end of June 1991. The girl on the desk said one shift instead of two was on duty each working day. The Treuhand was in charge in the meantime, doubtless scratching its head over what to do with this dirty white elephant of an antediluvian car factory. Very little activity was discernible at any of the three main plants, although there were thousands of (used) Trabis parked all round the site. I was relieved, if also mightily puzzled, to see a trailer full of live horses being driven away from the plant when I left.

The people's trams are deepest red in Chemnitz, thirty-five kilometres east of Zwickau on the way back to Meissen. My route into the city had an alarming sign on the boundary warning of rabies and imposing restrictions on cats and dogs, a real curfew. It was not long before I was gazing, in sheer disbelief at its crudity, upon the Karl-Marx Monument on Karl-Marx-Platz, just off Karl-Marx-Allee in what until recently was Karl-Marx-Stadt, third largest city in the German Marxist state, now restored to its old name after thirty-seven years. The monument is surely the world's biggest bust, a vast black model of the head of the founder of Communism, hacked out of some cliff by one Lev Kerbel, Soviet sculptor and holder of the Lenin Prize (why is not stated; surely not for this excrescence). It is so big that nobody quite knows how to get rid of it; explosives powerful enough to break up the head would considerably enlarge the square, which also has a Red Tower (no relation; it is a relic of the twelfth-century residence of the city governor). They will have to use power-tools and break it into fragments. In the vicinity I noted a Hotel Moskau, a Restaurant Irkutsk, a Street of the Nations and dear old Juri-Gagarin-Strasse. Anyone would think somebody had been trying to impress the Soviet Union. There are very few remnants of German history in the heart of this shattered and soulless city; they include the St Jakobi Church and the old *Rathaus* on the Market Square, both buried under scaffolding. At the nearby Theaterplatz, where all the buildings are from the present century, there is, on the Strasse der Nationen side, a relic of a 250-million-year-old petrified forest. It struck me as the perfect memorial for the now defunct SED municipal government. Unutterably depressed by what I had seen of Chemnitz, I decided that if I ever went there again it would be too soon, and departed, looking forward to Leipzig.

Kurt Masur, *Kapellmeister* of the Leipzig Gewandhaus Orchestra and the man who helped to prevent a bloodbath in the city in October 1989, was in America getting to grips with his new, "part-time" job as musical director of the New York Philharmonic. I spoke to Peter Gürtler, head of information, who is a music journalist by training, in the superb modern offices of the new Gewandhaus concert hall, completed in 1982. This was the last and by far the most impressive stage of the reconstruction of the Karl-Marx-Platz (formerly Theaterplatz) and Erich Honecker had taken a personal interest in the project. "People here, including Professor Masur, I would say, are not keen on the 'hero city' label," said Herr Gürtler, who had been on hand throughout the fraught events of the *Wende*. I had already seen Trabis proudly sporting a sticker saying *"Heldenstadt* [hero city] Leipzig". Masur, aged sixty-three and a work-aholic, had been one of six intermediaries between the demonstrators and the authorities, albeit by far the most famous. There were also Professor Peter Zimmermann, a theologian, and Bernd Lutz Lange, a cabaret artist (Leipzig too has a strong cabaret tradition) and three members of the SED secretariat for the Leipzig region.

When the Monday demonstrations after the peace prayers started to grow, the police and the Stasi took to surrounding the Nikolai Church, beating people up and trying to deter them from coming back. On 7 October 1989, the last officially celebrated anniversary of the founding of the GDR, they lashed out in all directions with truncheons, water-cannon and mass arrests.

A huge protest demonstration was planned for October 9; so were maximum turn-outs by police and army, with extra supplies of blood and hospital beds standing ready. But untold thousands of people converged on four churches in the city centre, filling them to bursting and massing in the streets round about. Things were clearly coming to a head. Herr Masur drafted a short appeal for peace and calm, which was signed by the other five and read in the churches, on local radio and on the public-address system in the centre of the city. He read it out himself and it worked. The security force commanders held their men back; the demonstration passed off peacefully. An emotionally charged concert took place that night in the Gewandhaus, with Richard Strauss, Siegfried Matthus and Brahms' Second Symphony on the programme, all relayed to the vast throng outside on the Karl-Marx-Platz. There was also a discussion with Kurt Masur inside the building and a debate on the square outside. This unique politico-musical evening is preserved on a double long-playing record put out by the Gewandhaus under the title, *Wir sind das Volk.*

The last and biggest demonstrations may have reached 200,000 and 400,000. The area outside the Gewandhaus (cloth house; the orchestra's first home was a converted warehouse and it is proud of its status as a city, rather than a state, institution since 1743) became a Speakers' Corner. After the opening of the Wall, Kurt Masur received visits from, *inter alios*, Chancellor Kohl and President Mitterrand of France; there was talk of making him President of the GDR, either alone or jointly with Christa Wolf, the East German writer and dissident. But in March 1990 the professor of music went back to the conductor's rostrum and the or-chestral director's office. He told a press conference that he would play no further part in politics. But he remains close to Professor Kurt Biedenkopf, the CDU politician (and for a while after the *Wende*, guest professor at Leipzig University) who became state premier of Saxony after the *Land* elections in the ex-GDR in October 1990.

Like so many other people I spoke to, Peter Gürtler thought it was sad that those whose opposition from within had begun the erosion of the SED regime were still in opposition after the *Wende*. "A lot of bad things have gone, but so have good things, like the solidarity among private individuals. That seemed to disappear in a matter of weeks. Here we used to sell cheap tickets and play to full houses every time; now tickets cost more, public bodies don't buy in bulk and there are empty seats for the first time – for the first time we are having to advertise! But not one musician has gone west for the much higher fees paid there. Some star players have been 'headhunted' but have stayed on. The Opera [on the other side of the square] reduced its tickets to DM1.50 – the same as a can of Coke – in a panic to fill the seats. That can't be right. We are just going to have to get used to the fact that what used to cost fifteen east-marks will have to be DM40 in future. Culture used to be heavily subsidised, part of a very substantial social wage. We are going to have to reach out and win over a new audience from among young people, who have so many new and competing calls on their time. Musical education in ordinary schools used to be bad here, but the specialised music schools are very good. They were free of charge, but their future is threatened by fees. All this kind of thing is the result of what was really an occupation by West Germany."

Leipzig was the GDR's second city with 560,000 inhabitants and may still have Germany's, if not the world's, biggest railway station (the first German railway ran from here to Dresden in 1839). Originally a seventh-century Slav settlement, it was German by the eleventh and a city in the twelfth, a university town in the fifteenth and the main centre of German book production in the sixteenth. Severely damaged in the Thirty Years' War, the Seven Years' War and the Napoleonic Wars, Leipzig and its famous fairs kept going. The academic, doctor, theologian and dramatist Gotthold Ephraim Lessing, as well as Goethe, Schiller and J. S. Bach, worked and studied in Leipzig. From 1871 to 1945 it was the seat of the Reich Supreme Court. The city was badly damaged in the same series of air-attacks which reduced Dresden to ashes, but the centre still possesses many worthwhile old streets and buildings, especially the well-restored *Rathaus*. The old Gewandhaus was destroyed in 1943; the renamed Karl Marx University has a fearsome 1971 tower-block, to make room for which the exceptionally fine, fifteenth-century Gothic university church was pulled down. There are several good churches still standing, however, including St Nikolai's and St Thomas's, outside which is the J. S. Bach memorial. These are some of the interesting buildings in and around the centre of a city which developed a cosmopolitan atmosphere unique in the former GDR, thanks to the large numbers of foreign visitors to the fairs (the latter were virtually ignored in 1990 but an urgent rethink was under way). I thought it was the liveliest place in east Germany, not excluding east Berlin. Its many good restaurants and cafés include Auerbach's Cellar dating from 1530, Goethe's old local tavern; its ceiling shows dramatic moments from *Faust*, which includes a scene set there.

The local newspaper is the *Leipziger Volkszeitung*, founded in 1894 and aimed at the then new working class. After the *Wende* it transformed itself politically from a Party organ to an independent, slightly left of centre paper, and modernised its layout. It enjoyed a thumping 480,000 circulation before the *Wende* and still had 400,000, despite an increase in price from a subsidised fifteen to a free-market forty pfennigs. Herr Manfred Arndt, the executive most in touch with local opinion – he edits the Letters Page – attributed most of the loss of circulation to the price rise and the new layout, but he thought sales, overwhelmingly by subscription, had already stabilised. The paper had been helped with its great leap into electronic technology by a partnership with the publishers of two Hanover newspapers; most ex- G D R papers had made such a connection as western publishers sought an eastern foothold.

After the events of 9 October 1989 the editorial staff declared themselves independent from the Party as from January 1, elected a new editor, Dr Wolfgang Tiedke, an occasional contributor and media lecturer at the University, and coverage changed dramatically, all to earn the trust of the readers. The paper is aiming to become "super-regional", to join the small band of quasi-national newspapers established in the west; the German press is essentially regional, but papers like the *Süddeutsche Zeitung* of Munich and the *Frankfurter Allgemeine* are available everywhere. For this reason it has taken to writing portentous leaders with a view to being quoted by news agencies and radio, and it runs new pages on national politics and international events. Herr Arndt was very proud of the fact that the *LVZ* journalists had taken just six weeks to adapt to an electronic system for which western colleagues needed two years. "We are also one of the very few local employers to be recruiting, on the publishing and distribution side." The *Volkszeitung* has a formidable base; with a readership of three per copy sold, it reaches 1.2 million out of 1.6 million living in the Leipzig region – even after the local editorial office in Thorgau left *en bloc* to open a local paper there.

One of the biggest local stories in the city during my east German explorations was the panic shooting by the police at a crowd of football hooligans after a match between Leipzig and Berlin clubs, killing one and wounding others. This was a dreadfully graphic illustration of the post-union deficiencies of the east German police forces: Saxony was reported to be no less than 4,000 officers short after national servicemen doing their conscription in the police had to be released and others resigned or were put on suspension pending investigation of their Party past. Football hooligans made their presence felt on several other occasions in east Germany during the rest of the unhappy first season after unification.

I went back to Dresden next because I wanted to learn something about how one set up a new, democratic state government from scratch. Professor Biedenkopf, who has taken up residence in a modest, heavily fortified former Stasi house half-concealed in the wooded outskirts of the city, was too busy to see me on any of the ten days I was able to propose. This was a pity because he is by far the best-known state premier in the ex-GDR, once regarded as Chancellor material in the west, former CDU leader in the most populous German *Land*, North Rhine-Westphalia, and one of the most gifted politicians in a country which offers worthwhile regional as well as federal roles to the ambitious in public life. He and Dr Kohl were not getting on, and it suited the Chancellor very well to see the much cleverer Biedenkopf take a job in Leipzig pending the state elections. His energy and impatience as well as his unique clout in Bonn made Biedenkopf, already known to Saxons as "our little king", the loudest and most influential spokesman for all five and a half eastern *Länder*. But his first, high-profile attempt to obtain tax concessions for the east was publicly slapped down in Bonn. He was not deterred, and if the "new" *Länder* are not to sink into a mire of debt, he will have to get his way in one form or another. In February 1991 the Ministry of Economics in Bonn conceded that the crisis had been underestimated and promised extra emergency measures costing more than DM10 billion. Nor was that the end of the story: tax increases were also announced in February, to take effect on July 1.

Dr Michael Kinze, an environmental administrator under the old system and now a senior official in the Saxon state chancellery, squeezed me into his schedule between two engagements at the vast, Wilhelmine riverside building which used to be the seat of the Dresden district government. In the transitional period a round table worked in Leipzig, as in many other cities, to reorganise local government. There was a co-ordinating committee of ten people covering the main departments of administration. It fell to Dr Kinze to consult the state chancellery of Bavaria about how a *Land* government worked, right down to sending its own representatives to Bonn and Brussels. All this was done from July

1990 with a view to enabling the new state ministers to get straight to work after the elections in October 1990. "We got as far as a structural plan for each ministry and the chancellery itself. There were also public consultation meetings every Thursday in the three big Saxon cities to inform – and to listen," Dr Kinze recalled.

State public servants came from Bavaria and Baden-Württemberg to help and advise – a good thing apparently, because Dr Kinze said that indigenous appointments were proceeding slowly owing to the hangover from the SED past. As he spoke, the state chancellery boasted a senior staff on duty that day of two, apart from himself, Dr Biedenkopf and the state secretary (the senior civil servant in a government department).

"The Allies instituted a process of de-Nazification after the war; who is to do the de-Communisation here? This is a very serious problem, because, among other things, a lot of people understandably want revenge. People will have to make a formal declaration that they never worked with the Stasi. But the problem should not be overstated. I should think that the old agents and informers won't be coming here and drawing attention to themselves by applying for government jobs at any important level. I don't think it matters much if a driver worked for the Stasi. I also think a lot of people are still paranoid; for example, there has been much talk of the Stasi still being at work and post disappearing. But everybody knows the post can't cope with all the extra work and the advertising matter they are suddenly having to deal with. The biggest problem is that nobody knows anything about how to run something as big as a state government. But I have every confidence that we shall learn," Dr Kinze said.

He naturally looked at the process of forming a government from an administrative and personnel viewpoint. But once the very vexed question of SED membership is resolved – no easy matter – the new states should be able to put together their public services from the staffs of the old *Bezirke*, of which there were usually three per *Land*. One positive result of the SED problem is that administrations have been obliged to reach down into the middle and even junior administrative ranks for new leadership talent. Some ambitious younger officials from western *Länder* have also been persuaded to take key posts in the east, seeing the chance to acquire experience of greater responsibility earlier than the normal career progression would offer. Recently retired civil servants were recruited in the west to help the east. But these early measures came nowhere near meeting the need and in spring 1991 Bonn began to consider using a measure of compulsion among public officials in the west – including judges – to fill the gaps.

The real threat to the future of the fledgling, reconstituted states was lack of funds. Bonn seriously overestimated the tax income of the new *Länder* because it underestimated the plunge in revenue-earning economic activity which was to follow the *Wende*. Dr Kohl had promised before the general election in December 1990 that there would be no tax increases to finance unification and integration. His ally, the FDP, went into the post-electoral coalition talks committed to making the ex-GDR a low tax zone and came out with nothing more than a higher income tax threshhold. But the FDP-run economics ministry admitted in February that the problem had been seriously underestimated and produced its DM10 billion-plus package. Professor Biedenkopf was surely entitled to say: "I told you so."

One did not need to be a cynic in east Germany in 1991 to know that in the end, whatever the political and economic difficulties, the public service would be reconstituted because government, like the taxes which finance it, like death and poverty, is always with us. For millions of private individuals in eastern Germany the uncertainty was rather worse. Because the old state had owned all but a few fragments of the "means of production, distribution and exchange" and the new one was bent on privatising, which is to say shedding, as much of that and the Communist social security system as possible, they had lost their job security forever, even when they had not actually or not yet lost their jobs.

This is not the place to go into whether the cradle-to-grave cocooning provided for conforming citizens in a Communist society is good or bad in principle, however much democrats disparage the constrictions and lack of choice associated with this level of nannying control. But it is pertinent to point out that the social wage in the ex-GDR was large enough to outweigh the value of the toytown wage packets of the bulk of the workforce. Everything from bread to circuses was heavily subsidised, much social welfare was totally free of charge, rent and energy costs and the prices of "essentials" (as defined by the state) were ridiculously low. Good, bad or indifferent as an economic system, this was a fact. All that is a powerful argument for immediate and enormous pay rises for all east Germans, who from 1991 were required to pay from their wages for so many items which had previously cost them little or nothing, when at the same time their employers were relieved of the social responsibilities thrust upon them by the previous dispensation.

The big reduction in the social wage had to be made up somehow if Dr Kohl's promise that nobody would suffer as a result of unification was to be made good. The general uncertainty arising from the fundamental upheaval in the labour market as the colossal economic shake-out got under way made it essential to have a look at unemployment – which quest took me to the Dresden Labour Office. There I met Frau Mayer, who had the same neat, competent and energetic air as her near-namesake, the school principal in Erfurt. Saxony has ten such offices; this one covered Dresden and environs. In January 1990 the area had about 2,000 unemployed; by the end of October, there were 15,468 (4.5%) and the trend was steeply upward (September: 12,070 or 3.5%; before the *Wende* – officially – nil). Nearly 60% were women. By contrast, there were 2,689 vacancies in October compared with 1,823 in September.

The closure of the Pentacon plant [the former camera subsidiary of Carl Zeiss-Jena) was the biggest setback for Dresden in the early days of united Germany: 5,000 jobs were lost at the end of 1990 as the Treuhand clearly saw no point in even trying to salvage such an outdated business, which could not hope to compete with Japan on the free market. Frau Mayer said that one of the most serious difficulties was to persuade people unaccustomed to using their initiative (which was usually unnecessary and discouraged in the GDR) to retrain. Workers on short time, even if they were actually doing nothing, were getting 90% of their pay. Unemployment benefit was set under the west German system at 68% of pay for the first six months, and after that 63% "unemployment support" for up to two years. "A lot of people seem unable to take the long-term view and they say, for example, 'why should I bother with retraining when I'm forty years old'; or else they sit around passively in a resigned mood waiting for something to turn up." The tragedy here is that this kind of Micawberism by east Germans makes it all the easier for well-organised, market-oriented western service companies to move in with their own staff and mop up all the work. "A year ago everybody was delighted with what was happening – freedom of movement, the promise of the D-mark and all the goods that went with it. I don't think anybody realised what was going to happen. This office used to function as an employment exchange because there was no unemployment before the *Wende*; now we are made to do a very difficult job for which we were not trained," she said.

The director of the Labour Office, Herr Günter Hollmann, said that the low point in unemployment was still a long way – many months – in the future. But he thought the rate of increase was slowing down. "I know a lot of people don't share my view, but I am actually optimistic for the longer term. I say that even as I recognise that it is really part of my job to spread optimism. Goodness knows there are enough pessimists and depressives around! For example – this city is getting a new state government. That is bound to generate all kinds of work, and not just for civil servants. Big companies want to come here; the city is being swamped by people who want to invest." Hence no doubt the intractable hotel problem; many firms were supplying their Dresden representatives with motor-homes to sleep in as a result. "We are hampered by the lack of unencumbered commercial property and land. Something drastic is going to have to be done about clearing that logjam."

Herr Hollmann believed that many qualified workers could be taken up by new companies after relatively short retraining. He thought sensible employers would see the value of hiring steadier, older workers for the sake of their reliability. "It is totally wrong therefore to say, as some older people do, that they are unemployable. We have to persuade them that retraining is worthwhile. What we need is some ex-easterners who went to the west before the *Wende* to come back and hammer home the import-ance – and the opportunity – of retraining. They all had to do it, and they obviously benefited from it. They can show that taking responsibility for your own fate as an individual is actually liberating. A *Leistungsgesellschaft*, a society based on performance, is not easy to adapt to, but it's what made them over there [west Germans] rich. That is the kind of positive thinking we need here. We have to persuade them that the old system degraded them in many ways." Regrettably, subsequent events in east Germany, in the economy and on the streets, made Günter Hollmann's optimism look even more desperate.

The GDR consciously modelled itself on the Soviet Union in many important respects, the economy and the Stasi being the two most obtrusive examples (more efficient than the original in each case). I was about to explore one other copycat aspect of the GDR, the local equiv-alent of the Soviet Union's special constitutional provision for its "nationalities", of which there are twenty-two numbering a million or more (and many smaller ethnic or linguistic minorities). East Germany had precisely one: the 60,000 Sorbs, all that remain of the Wendish Slavs who lived all over Germany east of the Elbe in the dark and early Middle Ages but were driven remorselessly eastward by the Saxons from the tenth century onwards. Today they live mostly in eastern Saxony and the south-east of neighbouring Brandenburg, a region known as Lausitz. In the GDR they were afforded protected status with their own educational and cultural institutions, and bilingual public signs in the areas where they are most concentrated. Since the latter include a high proportion of eastern Germany's enormous brown-coal deposits, the Sorbs got special treatment in another way too: they were all too often evicted from villages and even whole towns to make way for new opencast mines (but you did not need to be a Sorb to be bullied in this way). There was no special status for the 60,000 Vietnamese imported by way of "Socialist Solidarity" as extra labour in the early 1970s; they were treated as badly as any "guest worker" anywhere in the West, and after the *Wende* they were, if anything, finding conditions worse because of the epidemic of unemployment. They were being offered their air fare and a bounty of DM3,000 each to go home. The 30,000 Poles who lived and/or worked in the GDR were faring little better economically, but could hardly be treated so badly because their government, hypersensitive to the fact that Poland now had a looming united Germany on its doorstep, was well placed to make loud noises on their behalf.

More than half the 150-kilometre run to Zittau from Meissen was on the E40 autobahn from Eisenach, which peters out at Bautzen (Budysin to the Sorbs, whose "capital" it is). But the battered "motorway" goes into serious decline long before that, with stretches of undulating cobbles and of permanent single carriageway, crossing bridges one side of which had been closed for years (and in one case demolished). It looked as though tanks had been manoeuvring without restriction on the surface of one of the most important German routes to Poland. Appearances did not deceive, because Soviet and GDR military exercises frequently took place in this area. Here at least the nannyish speed limit signs restricting traffic not only to the overall maximum of 100, but often to eighty, sixty, forty and even twenty kilometres per hour were not unreasonable if one wanted to preserve one's suspension and one's vertebrae.

Zittau is where Germany comes to a full stop from west or from north. It lies in a *Dreiländereck* or three-country corner, of which there are many in Germany because it borders on nine other states, a world record. It is also part of the great "beer triangle" including Saxony and Czech Bohemia, where the oldest and purportedly finest lagers come from.

Czechoslovakia is due south, Poland is east across the River Neisse and Zittau is hemmed in, the terminus of three German roads – the B99 from Görlitz, the B96 from Bautzen via Ebersbach, and the B178 from Löbau, where the much diminished E40, all pretence to be an autobahn abandoned at Bautzen, actually ends. To get there one passes through fairly dreary, not to say dead, Saxon villages with tiled roofs, the tiles sometimes red, sometimes black, and frequently punctuated by "lazy eye" dormer windows: the graceful curve of the roof over the glass makes it look like a half-open eye, an effect which is redoubled when the roof is thatched, as in the north of the country, and has two such windows side by side. On the way down into Zittau, I saw a doe belting across a big open field as if her life depended on it; I could see no reason for her alarm. Once again Zittau offered a well-preserved centre and crumbling outskirts; the *Rathaus* could have been imported from Italy, but was designed by Schinkel, architect of so many mid-nineteenth-century public buildings in Berlin and elsewhere.

Concluding that life could be rather cramped in these parts, especially when the queues of trucks built up at the borders, I drove north along the Polish border to Görlitz, a town once Silesian-German, but now split in two by the Neisse, the eastern or Polish half spelling itself Zgorzelec (the Sorbs spell both halves Zhorjelc). On the way, in the pouring rain, after ten kilometres or so I passed through Hirschfelde (deer fields), an almighty concentration of chimneys and cooling towers, considerately placed on the Polish border so that the prevailing wind would export the filth. This appalling sight was duplicated twenty kilometres further north and just ten short of Görlitz, at a place called Hagenwerder; the capacity of both plants seemed out of all proportion to the surrounding population. And underneath the palls of smoke in each village were some encrusted wattle and daub houses which must have looked quite charming once upon a time.

Görlitz was gloomy and would probably have seemed so even without the rain, a hilly place with streets like canyons echoing to the wheels bouncing over the slimy cobbles, despite some fine new restoration work in the heart of the town. The place is highly unusual for having two market-places at different levels; the upper one, restyled the Leninplatz, is out of all proportion to the size of the town and looked like a good place for a rally: I noticed Willy Brandt was due to give one in a few days' time. Fortunately it was a Saturday, because during the working week the place tended to become constipated with fuming trucks and their fuming drivers, held up by the undermanned and unhurried Polish customs post on the other side of the Neisse bridge. There was a lot of smuggling going on, to judge by the hauls reported in the papers, but it was all in the other direction as Polish "entrepreneurs" took advantage of the weakness of the zloty and the strength of the D-mark which had just advanced to their border.

Bautzen lies about fifty kilometres westward of Görlitz on the River Spree, which eventually passes through Berlin, 150 kilometres north as the crow flies but not as the river winds. It is unlike any German town I have seen (which is saying a lot), having its inner centre in a crater-like depression, actually part of the Spree valley, with the tallest buildings poking their towers and roofs into the sky from below where you stand on the main road at the edge of the city: you survey the centre downwards and upwards at the same time, as it were. The outer centre is round the rim. The heart of the town with its elegant *Rathaus* and a market-place on which seven streets converge is mainly baroque; the Reichenstrasse (street of the rich) is perfectly preserved as a pedestrian shopping area with all the shop signs in both Sorbian and German. The Reichenturm, the tower at the end of this street, is nearly a metre and a half out of true at the top, and is one of the many substantial surviving parts of the old city defences. St Peter's Cathedral has an eighty-five-metre tower and is remarkable for having been used simultaneously, but separately, by both Catholics and Protestants since 1524: the former use the choir, the latter the nave, which is probably unique for having a kink in the middle. It must be the oldest example of pragmatic ecumenism on record, since the Reformation had barely started before this admirable arrangement came into force. The Sorbs are Catholic, the local Germans mostly Protestant, so it is an ethnic compromise as well. How heartening it would be if they could do this in Armagh . . . But behind the picture-postcard prettiness of the centre, one of the most intriguing in all Germany, the houses crumble in the back streets. Some had actually collapsed into heaps of rubble as if the bombers had been over last week. This degree of decay, remarkable even by GDR standards, was not infrequently cited as evidence of back-door discrimination against the Sorbs.

The Slav minority has been organising its own ethnic affairs in the Lausitz region since the middle of the last century, with flourishing scientific, cultural and publishing bodies; the Domovina, the main Sorbian cultural organisation founded in Hoyerswerda (Brandenburg) in 1912, sat in Bautzen (also regional capital of the Oberlausitz, upper

Lausitz) throughout the GDR's existence and will continue to do so in united Germany. The town also has a German-Sorbian People's Theatre and a State Ensemble for Sorbian National Culture, which its leaders sincerely hope will be subsidised by the two reconstituted *Länder* in which they now live. The day before I got there the Domovina had presented its literary prize for 1990 jointly to a local Sorbian author and a Russian writer.

Not having seen a decent *Burg* for quite a while, I resolved to spend the next day, a Sunday, renewing acquaintance with the Moritzburg, not far to the east of Meissen and due north of Dresden, and then driving down to see mighty Königstein and the stunning section of the Elbe Valley known as Saxon Switzerland. The Moritzburg was built as a Renaissance-style shooting-box by Duke Moritz of Saxony in the sixteenth century. Needless to say this was not good enough for Augustus the Strong, who told the indefatigable Pöppelmann to rebuild and expand it in the baroque mode. The result, however, is perfection: a square, yellow and white palace with four round towers and a red-tiled roof, standing in its own lake, surrounded at a distance by forest, yet visible from afar and approached by a causeway. Inside is a Museum of the Baroque with collections of porcelain, furniture, glass and paintings. Augustus could not resist lining the tall walls of one vast room from floor to ceiling with mounted antlers. How fortunate that the machine-gun had not been invented in his day. There is also a memorial in the basement to the artist and sculptor Käthe Kollwitz (born 1867) who was, like so many "decadent" (i.e. modern) artists banned from working by the Nazis. She died in the village in April 1945.

Just across the road is the Saxon State Stud (founded 1828), which breeds and trains horses for equestrian sport; it is not open to tourists, but puts on hugely popular parades and dressage performances in summer. In the grounds of the *Burg* to the east is the matching, eighteenth-century rococo Fasanenschlösschen (pheasant minicastle), built as a summer-house and now used as an ornithological museum. The surrounding area has been prudently and rightly declared a protected zone.

Königstein could hardly be more different. It is the stuff of the nightmares which lie just below the surface of the original Grimms' fairy-tales. Rapunzel's hair would have needed to be 240 metres long to reach a swain waiting on the Elbe Valley floor below this forbidding redoubt. In its day it was the mightiest fortress ever built in Germany and since the beginning of the thirteenth century the strongest Saxon outpost against the Slavs. The great sandstone crag had been a strongpoint since time immemorial and in its present form was built mainly in the sixteenth and seventeenth centuries. It was never captured, and it makes Colditz look like a glorified pillbox. Its fantastic walls encompass about twenty-three acres of rock on which stand a great fortified keep in one corner, entered by a steep covered way equipped with several means of seeing off the uninvited, a subsidiary fort on the north wall, a big barracks, a market-place, huge fortified casemates, an arsenal, a treasure-house and a church. There is a covered well-head over a shaft bored 153 metres through the solid rock; apparently the miners who dug it went on strike once, which made me wonder what their reward for such sturdy resistance would have been in the recently abolished workers' and peasants' state.

From the mid-seventeenth century Königstein also served as a prison – a detention centre for noblemen who offended the Elector of Saxony and a house of correction for rebellious peasants. Augustus the Strong sent J. F. Böttger (him of the porcelain) here to see if the rarefied atmosphere could help him turn base metal into gold (doubtless the conspicuously consuming Elector needed the money). The alchemist was told that he was being locked up for his own good (there was a war going on at the time). Earlier, the Chancellor of Duke Christian I from 1589–91, Dr Nicolaus Krell, was locked up for ten years, when the Duke died, by reactionaries who could not stomach his enlightened reforms. Then he was executed in 1601 – for being a Calvinist (We do not like thee, Dr Krell . . .). A former mayor of Leipzig holds the record for the longest stretch – forty years for embezzling enough money to build himself a palace; a young Saxon Army officer who killed his father in a drunken rage, however, got two years. Königstein was a prisoner-of-war camp in 1870–1, 1914–18 and 1939–45.

This part of Saxony has the most unusual rock formations. There are several other great, isolated crags like Königstein (king stone) in the Elbsandsteingebirge (Elbe sandstone mountains), as well as the extraordinarily tortuous rock formations of the Bastei (bastion), where labyrinths of square sandstone pillars rise like a petrified forest from the valley floor. Take away the water and the trees and one would probably be left with a miniature Arizona, complete with buttes and columns of rock. This is some of the best and most interesting walking country in Europe; you reach the Bastei from the pretty little *Kur*-centre of Rathen, or else from Bad Schandau, the most important local resort a little way upstream. There is a heart-stopping pathway (with safety railings) across the tops of the rock pillars, not recommended for those liable to vertigo, but quite all right for mountain goats in human form. Or you can take a river-boat of the *Weisse Flotte* (white fleet) which plies the Elbe for the warmer half of the year. I can attest that in summer the area is even more impressive, but also, inevitably, rather more crowded. This part of the Elbe valley matches anything the Rhine has to offer scenically and is one of the most spectacular sights of Europe – a useful reminder that by no means all of the ex-GDR is a polluted slagheap.

Passing through Dresden on my way back to Meissen, I noticed more than once that east German drivers were hooting at west German visitors waiting at traffic lights, even though they were on red. As a freshly qualified veteran of east German roads I knew the reason: the same treatment had been meted out to me on several occasions. Meanwhile I had become an admirer of the cause, the green arrow – a simple tag attached to many traffic lights and pointing to the right. It allowed a driver to ignore a red light and turn right onto the crossroad if there was a safe gap in the traffic. This pragmatic arrangement is also common in the United States, speeding up traffic flow no end. It also saves a lot of money spent elsewhere on elaborate filter lights. When the *Wessis* came they ignored the arrow, causing colossal jams all over east Germany; on unification they banned it. A protest led to a temporary reprieve for this useful idea until the end of 1991; after that east German municipalities are going to have to spend a fortune on filtering arrangements. This is a small but graphic example of how the *Wessis* were throwing out good *Ossi* ideas instead of copying them. Another eminently imitable custom was the large letter A (for *Anfänger*, beginner) sported by motorists on their cars for the first year after passing the driving test.

I was back on the road the next day, bound for broad Brandenburg, where the Prussians came from.

– IV –

BRANDENBURG

Länder – *history – forest – hidden horrors – brown coal – Cottbus – Potsdam – Sanssouci – Dutch and Russians – Honecker's Hollywood – Rheinsberg – Ravensbrück – Bundeswehr East – surrender – the other Frankfurt – Poland – city administration – Chorin – Wandlitz,* SED *nirvana*

– IV –

Brandenburg

Having seen Saxon Oberlausitz (upper Lausitz), I decided to begin my exploration of the wide-open spaces of Brandenburg from the south-east, in lower or Niederlausitz, and in general to work my way north. I would for the time being ignore Berlin, which is surrounded by Brandenburg, but is a *Land* unto itself.

The accession of east Germany to the Federal Republic served to revive the desultory debate which had gone on for years in west Germany about a reorganisation of the *Länder*, many being smaller than the biggest English counties. If this happens, the east German *Länder*, the average population of which is rather less than that of the "old" *Länder*, will also be affected. Indeed, such a rationalisation carried out at the moment of union could have been the salvation of the poor regions in the east, if a way could have been found of linking each eastern *Land* with one or more western ones. Three of the original western *Länder* – Baden, Württemberg-Baden and Württemberg-Hohenzollern – united into Baden-Württemberg in 1951 after a plebiscite and the resulting *Land* is now the most prosperous in the country.

If, say, Schleswig-Holstein and Hamburg in the west had combined with Mecklenburg-West Pomerania (MWP) in the east to form a single coastal state, MWP would have benefited in several ways. It would have been much easier to extend a viable regional administration eastward instead of forcing MWP to start a new one from scratch; MWP's financial problems would have been absorbed into the budget of a larger and overall more prosperous super-*Land*. Since western institutional models were to take over anyway, each organ in the west – *Land* parliament, police force, tax office and the rest – could have been enlarged by recruitment of east Germans *pro rata* and trained western officials would have been on hand in every department from the beginning, together with the necessary organisational structures. Towns in the western part could have helped towns in the eastern. Similarly, Lower Saxony and Bremen might have come together and absorbed Saxony-Anhalt; while Saxony and Thuringia, so long associated with the old Saxon ruling house, might have been more viable together than separate as the economically least weak region of the former GDR. Similarly, west Berlin might have acted as both catalyst and locomotive for the revival of east Berlin and also Brandenburg, the largest "new" *Land* surrounding the two parts of the new capital and Berlin's natural hinterland.

The east Germans, deprived of their *Länder* since 1952, were entitled to reassert the regional loyalties so important in Germany; but the emotional Volkskammer resolution to restore the previous states seems in retrospect premature, like so many other decisions connected with union. Doubtless the politicians in east and west would not have welcomed the added dimension of regional amalgamations coinciding with the fusion of the two Germanys; but after the event, especially in view of the unforeseen (or unacknowledged) problems arising from union, it does seem that the former measure might have contributed to the easing of the latter – if somebody had thought of it in time and tagged the necessary plebiscites onto the Federal election in December 1990. If the Bundeswehr can simultaneously absorb the National People's Army and drastically reduce its overall numbers in line with the European Treaty on Conventional Forces and the private deal between Kohl and Gorbachev, a real, trans-border integration of the two Germanys *Land* by *Land* does not seem beyond reach. It may yet have to come to *Land* mergers in the not too distant future. Each east German *Land* was already linked with at least one western state before unification, a connection which proved most helpful after it, when the western states sent officials, equipment, advice and often money to their eastern partners. Similar connections exist from before union between towns in east and west, "twinned" since the interGerman thaw of the early 1980s.

Today's *Land* was known historically as the *Mark* (march) Brandenburg – the main border zone where the Germans met the Slavs. The Germans were there first, but wandered south in the seventh century AD, whereupon the vacuum was filled by Sorbs and Wends, who were mostly driven out or overcome by the fourteenth. By then the area of Germany south of Schwerin and east of the Elbe was known as the Altmark, the disputed area east of the Neisse was the Neumark and the territory in between, essentially today's Brandenburg, was the Mittelmark – old, new and middlemarch. The latter was given over by Emperor Sigismund to the Count-castellan of Nuremberg, Friedrich VI of Hohenzollern, in 1411; four years later he was made an elector (one of the handful of leading German princes with a vote at the formal election of the Holy Roman Emperor) and hereditary imperial arch-chamberlain. It was only 503 years thereafter that the Hohenzollerns released their grip on Brandenburg, the springboard for the conquest of Prussia.

Brandenburg, then with its capital in Berlin (the city has been administratively autonomous only since 1881), became the unifying force in Germany from the days of the Great Elector after the Thirty Years' War. The possession of Prussia, in Poland (but independent of it by 1660) and outside the Empire, made it possible for the Hohenzollerns to become kings in Prussia (1701), which was therefore adopted as the official name for their entire collection of fiefdoms all over Germany in 1807. The dominant power in Germany and a major one by any standards before Napoleon briefly conquered it, Prussia became a world power after the internal reforms, begun in 1807, helped it to make a decisive contribution to his final defeat in 1815.

Brandenburg's population trebled to more than three million in the nineteenth century, in the latter part of which the writer Theodor Fontane published five books about his native region, a unique guide to a land rich in history. The great municipal reform of 1920 established Greater Berlin in the city's present boundaries, which almost made a ghost-province of Brandenburg, stripped by a stroke of the pen of two million people and two thirds of its revenue. In October 1990 it was the only state in the ex-GDR in which the SPD was able to form a government (the CDU dominated in the rest, and after December 1990 in the whole of Berlin as well).

The widely respected Prime Minister, Dr Manfred Stolpe, comes from the Evangelical church and has behind him the only SPD-led *Land* coalition in east Germany (all the others including Berlin have CDU-led governments). He soon became unofficial joint chief spokesman for the ex-GDR alongside Professor Biedenkopf (CDU) of Saxony in the Bundesrat (the Federal upper house representing the *Länder*), conferences of *Land* Premiers and elsewhere.

Among Brandenburg's most obvious deficiencies is fertile soil, a short-coming in which it closely resembles the lost province of Prussia. Known as the sandbox of Germany, it was once seabed, as its generally flat surface suggests. There was thus little or no stone from which to make monuments, so that Brandenburg's historic public buildings, sacred and profane, are made of brick, sometimes with, more often without, stucco dressing, which does not detract from the beauty of the best of them: brick Gothic can be just as majestic as stone, but looks warmer. Berlin, as capital, and Potsdam, as alternative royal seat from the mid-eighteenth century, have public buildings of imported stone; otherwise Brandenburg is a land of brick – and of the beech, the birch and the silver birch, which flourish in the sandy soil of its glorious forests.

Stick to the main roads and you could be forgiven for thinking, the odd open space and distant chimney apart, that the whole of rural Brandenburg is covered in trees, nicely spaced and stretching in all directions. But not far off the highways and byways of the former administrative district which bears the name of the city of Cottbus there are gigantic black holes in the ground, vast manmade valleys which it is an insult to Earth's only satellite to call moonscapes. These are the frightful scars of the lignite or brown coal industry, the outlandish opencast mines, with their huge digging-machines resembling fearsome insects from afar and beached oil rigs close to. Three quarters of the GDR's lignite supplies came from southern Brandenburg. Scars in this context are more literal than metaphorical because the GDR's passion for brown coal after the world oil crisis of 1973–4 strongly resembled a physical and mental disease – physical for the damage it did to the people and the environment, mental for the associated stress and the obsessive-compulsive quality inherent in the regime's policy of maximum extraction regardless of social cost. The excavators often scoured so deep that the water-table was ruined and the surrounding area went dry. Germany's leading novelist, Günter Grass, saw these pits as perfect symbols of the GDR state and was moved to make a series of stark charcoal drawings as well as writing about them in summer 1990. Whole villages, even small towns, were razed as the SED ordered all possible industries to switch from oil to brown coal to save imports (and to reduce dependence on the Soviet Union for oil – which did not come cheap and was often so badly refined that it had to be re-refined, with equipment imported from Sweden, in the great petrochemical complex at Schwedt in north-eastern Brandenburg, neatly positioned between the prevailing wind and Poland).

Lignite is harder than peat but softer than any other solid fossil fuel and tends to contain inordinate quantities of sulphur and other noxious impurities. It is an inefficient, bulky and filthy, but also dirt-cheap, means of obtaining energy, either by direct burning or by conversion in mountainous quantities at antediluvian power stations or distant-heating plants. It is delivered in heaps of flat oval briquettes dumped without sacks on pavements; as noted above, the initially nostalgic smell of burning brown coal is ubiquitous in the ex-GDR except in summer. You can taste it at the back of your throat. One obvious benefit of union is the abandonment of further exploitation of the east's huge deposits as the word goes out: switch back to oil. This meant that a lot of communities, notably Sorbian ones, threatened by new pits which would have been opened without so much as a by-your-planning-permission, could relax. The SED regime did not have to worry about public inquiries, but simply bullied people into leaving their homes. Sometimes communities were made to move twice, even three times in a few cases, when the area to which they had been relocated was needed in its turn. The Sorbian village of Lakoma on the B97 just north of Cottbus held out from 1983, even when a new Lakoma was built on the other side of the trunk road and people started to move to it, until the *Wende* saved the village well after the thirteenth hour. For environmental reasons work has stopped at the monster pit at the edge of the village. The defiant banners were still up when I passed through.

Cottbus (Chosebuz in Sorbian; it has a large Sorbian/Wendish-vernacular church) stands on the River Spree at the south-eastern edge of the Spreewald forest – which is menaced by the retreat of the water-table resulting from opencast mining. Where Britons lisp, "the Leith Police dismisseth us", Germans may be heard to splutter: "*Der Cottbuser Postkutscher putzt den Cottbuser Postkutschkasten*" (the Cottbus mail-coachman cleans the Cottbus mail-coach chest). An early example of a grid-patterned city, Cottbus was wrecked in the Thirty Years' War and regenerated by the migrant Huguenots who played such a prominent part in Prussian social history (they built themselves a church also). It was Saxon and Prussian by turns, like so many other places in this part of the world. The town still has bits of its wall, the main gate and the Spremberg Tower, all built of brick, to remind it of its fortified past. Also near the town centre is the baroque *Schloss* Branitz, adapted in 1850 by Semper of Dresden Opera-house fame and now used as the local museum and art gallery. It has a splendid ornamental garden dominated by two unique earthen pyramids; one of them is the burial mound of Prince Hermann von Pückler-Muskau, who built the place.

The capital of Brandenburg, Berlin being otherwise engaged, is Potsdam, which is not an unworthy choice. On a map of Greater Berlin, as we may now call it again, Potsdam looks like a south-western suburb on the point of absorption. But if there was anything at all that was good about the Berlin Wall it must be the fact that it sustained the separate identity of Potsdam, which now seems assured by the city's new and important regional role just as the Wall is demolished. Previously the only connection between Potsdam and what the SED called the "special political entity" of West Berlin was the famous Glienicke Bridge over the River Havel, scene of so many real-life and rather more film and television exchanges of spies and dissidents between East and West. The Communists had to use the Berlin Ring autobahn to bring their human parcels round to Potsdam from East Berlin, while the Americans (it was their sector) just drove across West Berlin. The bridge itself is a modest affair of green steel girders and nineteenth-century provenance. Its special role as the crossing-point of the King of Prussia between his two neighbouring "residence cities" is marked on each side by a few classical stone pillars. They look out of place not only because the bridge is made of steel but also because they serve no obvious purpose, architectural or otherwise. The road on the western side is magnificently straight and broad; on the eastern side the street was a narrow, cobbled shambles as reconstruction work got under way. I made a point of driving across, because whenever I had seen it previously it was out of bounds.

But on my first visit to Potsdam for this book (I had been before to see the sights, which are superb) I took the s-bahn from the centre of Berlin to Wannsee station, the end of the line, and then transferred, because it happened to be standing there, to an east German s-bahn train bound for Potsdam – a new connection. The eastern train was made up of double-decker carriages, one of those brilliantly simple ideas which to me seemed as sensible and obvious as the double-decker bus (an old Berlin tradition). The Deutsche Reichsbahn deserves credit and imitators for this, if not for the devastated stations on the line. What a pity that the service ran only about once an hour in each direction and that it was much easier to leave the station and get on the new 99 West Berlin bus-route, which runs fast and often to Potsdam – a small but prime example of western superior resources and initiative stealing a march on the *Ossis*.

To see the most spectacular building in Potsdam, if not in all Germany, you get out of the s-bahn at Potsdam-West (not Potsdam-Stadt, which is for the town centre) and walk a few hundred metres north-west across the Park Sanssouci to the palace of the same name. This is Frederick the Great's impeccably restored and maintained rococo residence, over the top in at least two senses. It stands on a little plateau, looking south over an elaborate terraced garden of six levels, each equipped with rows of glass doors for the greenhouse effect. Frederick the Great wanted to be buried with his hunting-dogs and without pomp at dead of night on this terrace, but his successor and nephew, Friedrich Wilhelm II, had him laid to rest in the Potsdam Garrison Church (when that was destroyed, he and his father were moved to Burg Hohenzollern in Swabia, whence the family originated). Prince Louis Ferdinand, modern head of the House of Hohenzollern, made arrangements for the fulfilment of his great ancestor's wish on the 205th anniversary of his birth, 17 August 1991, which must make Frederick the oldest and deadest beneficiary of the *Wende* by a large margin.

Frederick himself roughed out the basic design of his fun palace, which was then executed by Georg Wenzeslaus von Knobelsdorff. Egged on by his obsessive master and a bottomless purse, he cast aside the restraint shown in his earlier work on *Schloss* Charlottenburg in Berlin and built the last word in overripe baroque extravagance in 1745–7. The saving grace of this fantastic building is its size, which is small as palaces go: twelve rooms in line abreast on one level across the eighty-metre front (not counting the two little "service" wings slightly set back). The entrance is at the back on the north side, where there is a semicircular colonnade of Corinthian pillars with a gap in the middle to admit carriages. At each end of the building proper is a circular room and at the centre-front an oval one (the marble room). The others are the king's study-cum-bedroom, a couple of reception rooms and five guest-rooms. One of these is where Voltaire came to stay for long periods (there is a famous picture of the French *savant* seated in the presence of the standing King) – a room with pale green walls festooned with fake vegetation, all painted with loving attention to detail. Another room has gold-leaf spiders' webs on the ceiling.

This is only the beginning of what there is to be seen in the park. No sooner was Sanssouci finished than Knobelsdorff started work on some extra rooms (Neue Kammern) in a detached annex to the south-west, originally intended as an orangery. Further west is the actual Orangerie, built in the Italian Renaissance style in the middle of the nineteenth century and now a state archive, twice as big as Sanssouci. As spectacular as the latter in its different, slightly less self-indulgent way, is Frederick's New Palace, built in the 1760s as proof that Prussia was not broke after the Seven Years' War with Austria. This three-storey, "conventional" late baroque palace, with stone statues round the edge of the roofs and a copper-clad dome in the middle, has an east-facing frontage of 240 metres and became the summer residence of the Prussian royal family. Behind it, to the west, are the "Communs" where the army of servants lived, now a teacher-training college.

Also in this amazing architectural orgy of a park are a picture gallery with a small but priceless collection of old masters, a Neptune grotto, a Sicilian garden, several "roundels" including an elaborate Chinese teahouse and a "Greek" temple, a church, two theatres, "Roman" baths, a hippodrome, artificial lakes and waterways, a poets' grove, a pheasantry, the little *Schloss* Charlottenhof with another collection of paintings, and the waterworks which supplied and powered all the fountains, now a technical museum. As if this were not enough there is also the New Garden to the north-east of the town, which contains the Cecilienhof. This palace was built for his daughter by the last Kaiser, Wilhelm II, at the beginning of the century, as a copy of an English Tudor country house. It would be convincing but for the straightness of the roof and other lines, and the geometrically exact angles of the half-timbers. This was where the Potsdam Conference was held by the victorious Allies in July 1945. A right-wing arsonist set it on fire after the *Wende*, in protest against the preservation intact of the conference scene with its furniture and fittings – including the bizarre library of the British delegation, complete with romantic prewar novels. Various other fakes and follies bespatter this end of town, including the Marble Palace, which contains a branch of the German Army Museum (I had seen the main one in Dresden so I spared myself this – by now I was suffering from monumental indigestion).

Then there is the town itself, the Prussian Aldershot (though without the Home Counties functional-brutalist architecture), an insignificant place in a beautiful setting until the Hohenzollerns took an interest in it as an alternative residence in 1617. The ultra-Catholic Louis XIV's revocation, in 1685, of the Edict of Nantes, which had established religious tolerance in France, prompted the Great Elector of Brandenburg to issue his Edict of Potsdam in the same year, inviting the gifted and energetic Protestant Huguenots to settle in Brandenburg. But it was the "soldier King" Friedrich Wilhelm I who began to build up Potsdam for military purposes in the early eighteenth century. There are still whole streets of houses with dormer windows in their roofs, showing that the original owners had been obliged to lodge a couple of soldiers from the garrison in the attic. Since the gout-ridden King required his Life Guards to be 1.90 metres tall, they had no need to visit a tavern to get sore heads.

He had much of the town rebuilt, bringing in Dutch workers to drain the ground (Potsdam stands by the lakes and waterways linked with the Havel river) and carry out the construction work. He allowed them to build themselves houses in the typical Dutch urban style of unclad, rust-red brick with tall, stepped gables. The Dutch Quarter in the heart of modern Potsdam is the striking result – though it badly needs the preservation work recently begun. Other buildings and streets have been restored with the customary close attention to detail, but the town as a whole is sadly down at heel, and areas near the centre have been disfigured by infelicitous modern buildings. No doubt its proximity to Berlin will boost both tourism and the accelerated refurbishment of the town's fabric, which will encourage more visitors.

The soldier-king treated his son Frederick the Great rather less kindly than his workers, but the younger man added much of beauty and style to his father's garrison town and military headquarters, finally electing to live there. Textiles (for uniforms) and brewing (for thirsty soldiers) boomed. The town was partly rebuilt and considerably expanded to the designs of Knobelsdorff and other leading architects of the day. A good road linking Potsdam with Berlin to the north-east and Brandenburg city to the west (today's B1) was built at this time. Frederick and his harsh drill sergeant of a father probably spun in their graves in the Garrison Church when Napoleon's troops occupied Potsdam from 1806–8, after the Battle of Jena. From 1809 the civil servants of the reformed Prussian adminis-tration joined the soldiers in Potsdam and in 1838 it was linked by Prussia's first railway to Berlin. Only after 1918 did Potsdam lose its royal-military character as garrison and imperial summer residence.

One elite, ceremonial regiment, the 9th Infantry, was kept on there by the Weimar Republic: several of its aristocratic officers abandoned the Potsdam military tradition of unquestioning obedience to join the July

Plot against Hitler in 1944. Its last adjutant, in 1945, was First Lieutenant Richard Baron von Weizsäcker, subsequent first President of united Germany and so often the conscience of his nation. One of the last major air-raids of the European war caused much damage to Potsdam in April 1945, destroying the castle, the town-hall and many other historic buildings, and damaging the splendid Garrison Church (its remains were blown up for ideological reasons in 1968; its tower may now be rebuilt). In 1952 Potsdam became the administrative centre of the GDR's geographically biggest *Bezirk* and thus had no rival for its new function as capital of reconstituted Brandenburg.

The partly restored, partly rebuilt town centre offers a baroque *Rathaus* (1753) and a German classical Nikolaikirche designed by Schinkel, the architect of Unter den Linden in Berlin, as well as a French Huguenot one designed by the hyperactive Knobelsdorff. There are three impressive ornamental city gates, all in different styles: the Brandenburg (vaguely Roman triumphal), the Jägertor (hunter's gate with matching statuary) and the Nauen. The latter is described as English late Gothic, but must have been copied from an England I have never visited; even so it is the best of the three.

Carry on due north for a few hundred metres and one comes to another unique feature of this remarkable town: the Alexandrowka Russian Colony, a scattered collection of a dozen large, dark, log houses with fancy, painted wooden trim laid out on grassland along streets which form a St Andrew's Cross (an Imperial Russian motif). These impressive dwellings were built on the order of King Friedrich Wilhelm III. Sixty-two members of a Russian Army choir which had defected to Napoleon's colours were captured by the Prussians in the campaigning which followed the Corsican's retreat from Moscow. Under the later Prussian-Russian military alliance against the French, these men were allowed to transfer to the Prussian Army. The twelve who elected to stay on for good were each given a house for life which could be passed to direct descendants; the last such heir was still in possession in 1990. To the north of the very authentic-looking settlement is a Russian Orthodox church.

As one approaches the centre from the Potsdam-Stadt station to its south, one sees on the left a long, single-storey baroque building of sandstone and red stucco, all the more striking for being the only old building in this section of town, to the left of the broad Friedrich-Ebert-Strasse. Rebuilt by Knobelsdorff in 1746, it is the former Royal Stables

Brandenburg

and now houses the (ex-)GDR Film Museum. I wanted to see this by way of homework before investigating Potsdam's modern role as the German Hollywood. I duly learned that even this unmartial activity derived its inspiration from the Army: a letter from General Erich Ludendorff, Hindenburg's right-hand man at the head of the German Army in the First World War, complained to the War Ministry in July 1917 that the Allies had built up a commanding lead in the use of motion-picture technology for propaganda. This was the formative impulse behind the foundation in December that year of the Universal Film AG (UFA, from 1945 Deutsche Film-AG or DEFA) at Babelsberg, across the Havel from the centre of Potsdam.

After the First World War the huge waterside facility blossomed as the heartland of the thriving German film industry. Early successes included *The Cabinet of Dr Caligari* and *Nosferatu*; Fritz Lang made the weird and wonderful *Metropolis* in 1926 (he emigrated to Hollywood like so many others in 1933). Marlene Dietrich and Greta Garbo became famous here, and Bertolt Brecht's *Threepenny Opera* was filmed at Babelsberg, even though he distanced himself from the picture later. Under Goebbels the Nazis made exhaustive use of the studios for propaganda purposes, producing such vibrant dramas as *Hitler Youth Quex*, *SA-Man Brand* and the infamously vicious *Jew Süss*. Lang and Brecht meanwhile combined their formidable talents in Hollywood to make the celebratory *Hangmen Also Die* in 1942, about the assassination of Reinhard Heydrich, the SS security chief and "Protector" of occupied Bohemia. The Soviet occupiers licensed DEFA in 1945 and the studios were diverted seamlessly from Nazi to Communist propaganda. The first production was *The Murderers are Among Us*, starring Hildegard Knef (1946). Helmut Käutner notably filmed *The Captain from Köpenick* in 1956 – by no means all GDR films could be dismissed as mere propaganda. The museum was imaginatively reorganised and "decommunistified" after the *Wende* and any film enthusiast would find it well worth a visit. Yet its annual budget was DM200,000, whereas its west German rival at Frankfurt-on-Main had DM5 million!

The Film Museum was yet another reason why I regretted not having had the chance to base myself in Potsdam for several days: the lodgings lottery had assigned me to exceedingly modest quarters in Berlin this time. It was from there that I drove with extraordinary care through the aftermath of a blizzard for my appointment to view a desirable riverside site, incorporating 100,000 square metres of open land and 24,000 square metres of warehouses containing theatrical props, within easy reach of Berlin: DEFA, Babelsberg.

Herr Scheinert, public relations chief at DEFA, could have been an American – tall, bespectacled, extrovert, fast-talking, crew-cut, wise-cracking, wheeling and dealing round his big, ground-floor office. Like the citizens of Leipzig, the DEFA people had had rather more to do with foreigners and westerners than most GDR citizens, even east Berliners. The east Germans who for the time being worked on at DEFA are widely recognised as fine craftsmen, who might need technological updating but otherwise probably had more to teach than to learn. Scheinert's first move was to show me a half-hour video tape telling the story of the studios and their importance – a professional salesman's pitch for the survival of the facility, which is classically east German in that it is equipped to do almost everything it needs in order to function (and was therefore heavily overstaffed in western terms). I learned that Billy (*né* Wilhelm) Wilder started work here, that Fritz Lang needed 36,000 actors for *Metropolis*, that the site spread over half a million square metres and had 127 buildings on it, was the biggest film studio in Europe and had made the Continent's first talking picture in 1929.

Although in recent years many foreign film and television companies (including French, Japanese and west German film-makers), had come to DEFA to exploit its assets, its low overhead and its proximity to Berlin, DEFA had been largely cut off by the Cold War from the international links it had enjoyed before Goebbels took over in 1935. But it had been used to make 700 feature films since the war. It could offer 2,000 wigs, 150,000 costumes and a million props stored in hangar-like warehouses. With the abolition of the inter-German border DEFA was now able to make free use of the cultural facilities of the whole of Berlin, including artistic and musical talent (not to mention five-star hotels and rented mansions for the stars).

After the video show I was told that the plan mentioned in it, to set up a holding company and ten limited companies (GmbH) on the site handling its main functions, still existed on paper but was subject to change at any time; no firm decisions had been taken by the Treuhand, which now owned DEFA. "The need for self-sufficiency among big organisations in the GDR in fact makes us better equipped in many ways than any other film studio," said Herr Scheinert. "We have facilities here which would be classed as industrial and would be separate anywhere else – even including a timber-seasoning yard."

Until the turn of the year DEFA employed about 2,300 people, but up to 800 were to go at the end of December 1990. No new projects were being taken on, so all the work being done was on the eight films already in hand and still unfinished before monetary union. All such work was due to come to an end by March 31, whereupon the workforce would be reduced again, to below 1,000. Some of those who had gone or were going were people past retirement age, as usual in the GDR – but, as Herr Scheinert said, in this business a lot of people did their best work when old. "I wonder if anybody ever tried to get Olivier to retire when he was sixty-five – and if so, how such a person reacted on his eightieth birthday," he mused.

DEFA had a turnover of 37 million marks a year (including state subsidies) making feature films, and another 44 million or more making television films. But the GDR broadcasting corporation, DFF, had already cancelled most of its unactivated projects at the end of 1989; DFF survived the *Wende* pending a shake-up of broadcasting in the GDR, but had no money to splash around. The GDR had spent 500 million marks a year on television, a fair part of which had flowed to DEFA; Scheinert hoped that the five new *Länder* would do better by way of financing television. Talks were going on with the Brandenburg government with a view to establishing a European media centre at Babelsberg; Berlin might support such an idea, as might Brandenburg's western partner *Land*, North-Rhine Westphalia. There were rumours of French interest, of a visit from MGM, the European Commission and the umbrella organisation of European film producers. "Our problem is a short-term one; I'm sure the future will be all right. What we need now to keep going is a lot of new TV work."

DEFA acquired a reputation, among other things, for making good, non-political children's films which exported well. Two new directors used to make their film debuts at DEFA each year, a record nowhere in Europe could match. Herr Scheinert said that DEFA film-makers had been the first among GDR media people to confront controversial social topics in a country where such experiments were dangerous. Homosexuality had been tackled as a theme well before the *Wende* and almost everything made at Babelsberg in recent years had been bought and shown in west Germany. "Whatever the jests about 'Honecker's Hollywood', DEFA films won prizes almost every year round the world. We probably need to spend DM100 to 150 million modernising, but there is so much space here that this need not get in the way of new production."

For most of its existence Babelsberg was controlled by censors, whether the Kaiser's for a year, Hitler's for a decade or the Communists' for over forty years, but was admired for its technical prowess. It would be a bitter irony indeed, I thought, as I plodded through the snow back to my car, if DEFA were to be destroyed just when it could once again exploit the freedom of expression which made it one of the cultural glories of the Weimar Republic. Were it to die now, it might go down in history as little more than a lavish propaganda factory where make-believe Nazi super-men had seen off seedy Jews and Communist peasant heroes had driven their tractors over the horizon of the collective farm to garner a crop of Socialist realism. A nation yawned in its subsidised cinema seats until the restrictions were eased in the early 1980s and DEFA began to re-emerge as a name to conjure with.

Apart from Berlin, which has thirty times the population, Potsdam offers visitors the widest variety of architectural, cultural and historical sightseeing in eastern Germany, although they cannot expect to wander around DEFA at will. Even the mechanised rubbernecks who prepare the green Michelin guides would need a special trip of not less than three days to do the place justice. Small wonder that 4,000 *Wessis* have reportedly laid claim to houses in the "Prussian Versailles", whose only garrison now (until 1994) is the Red Army, which finally put paid to the Prussian militarism that was born here. They include Prince Louis Ferdinand, who has graciously passed up Sanssouci, the New and Cecilienhof palaces in favour of the relatively modest Villa Ingenheim, a Hohenzollern property now housing a military history institute – and Marika Rökk, dancing star of many old Babelsberg films, would also, please, like her villa in the old film-stars' quarter returned.

One place I would not wish to live in for the next million years or so is Rheinsberg, a delightful spot ninety kilometres to the north with 5,300 inhabitants. It lies in the Ruppiner Schweiz (Ruppin Switzerland; east Germany is full of little Switzerlands, for which title the qualifications seem to be no more than a couple of hills and lakes). As Crown Prince, Frederick the Great commanded his own regiment here in the rank of colonel at the age of twenty. It is, therefore, perhaps not surprising that the frenetic Knobelsdorff managed to pass through and dash off the plan for the local rococo *Schloss* (1739), now a sanatorium for diabetics. It was at this northern Brandenburg end of the Mecklenburg Lake Plateau, famous for its sanatoria, that the GDR chose to site its first nuclear reactor, a Soviet export which came on stream in 1966. It seemed right to pause briefly and reflect on the vandalism involved in choosing such a place just because it had so much surface water available for cooling purposes, an advantage which hardly made it unique in a country of so many lakes. Like the ex-GDR's two other nuclear power-plants, this piece of Chernobyl technology was being wound down.

Rejoining the main road through these parts, the B96, I soon came to Fürstenberg, less than twenty kilometres to the north-east, an unremarkable town of 6,000 souls which I had not come to see. I was about to make my second foray into the historical remains of Heinrich Himmler's "empire of screams" – Fürstenberg-Ravensbrück, the only concentration camp built for women, by men from other camps in the area, who completed the place in six months. It opened in May 1939 and 867 female detainees were moved in at once. Eventually more than 130,000 women (and hundreds of young children) of twenty nations passed through the camp, of whom about 47,000 died in or near it from gassing, shooting or else being tortured or worked or marched to death. The camp held 70,000 prisoners at its busiest. In the last two years of the war the births of more than 800 babies were recorded at Ravensbrück, a start in life so awful as to defy imagination. But in nearly all cases the life in question came to a very early end. The women were forced to labour at the camp and its "branches" in the area producing leather, shoes and textiles as well as munitions; they also did assembly work for Siemens AG, the huge electrical concern which flourishes to this day. The fact that so many died at the workbench was immaterial because the SS and Gestapo were always overfilling the camp in any case. The camp was equipped with a gas chamber, a crematorium and a little alley where people were shot in the back of the neck. The German medical profession fell over itself to exploit the unique opportunity to conduct experiments in the sterilisation of women.

The wooden huts have gone, but the two-storey, stone cell-block with its seventy-eight solitary-confinement cells still stands. One can see the whipping block with straps where women were lashed on the buttocks up to twenty-five strokes at a time at the twice-weekly flagellation parade – by fellow prisoners set on by the guards. Other punishments available in this block were forty-two days' bread and water with one hot meal every fourth day, or three days' bread and water, the prisoner to sleep on the bare concrete. On the upper floor many of the cells stand open with a memorial to one or other of the nationalities incarcerated in this lakeside hell on earth. At the end the psychopaths in charge took it into their heads to march all the prisoners westward, except for the 3,000 too sick or broken to move, away from the advancing Red Army in April 1945. Thousands more died on the various segments of this macabre and pointless last death march. The SS destroyed the records before leaving, so nobody knows precisely who went there or the true number of dead. The barracks once used by Himmler's guards and adjacent to the site, now a tastefully maintained memorial, still house a Red Army garrison complete with married quarters.

In the old administration block, now a museum, is a display of mainly photographic and cartographic material on the concentration camps in general and Ravensbrück in particular. The entrances to the first set of rooms were blocked by stools bearing notices saying they had been closed as a protest action by the museum staff against the Communist propaganda in the commentary and the selection of illustrations. Walking without difficulty round these symbolic obstructions one immediately saw the point and admired this heartening stand. The concentration camps, like the Hitler regime which built them, were described as the product of unbroken German imperialist tradition, serving the profiteers of monopoly capitalism. The chief targets and victims were allegedly the Communists, and the Soviet Union comes across as the chief agent of their demolition. In fact the Russians used some of these places, notably Sachsenhausen near Oranienburg in Brandenburg, as soon as they took them over (mass graves of Soviet origin have been found at Oranienburg). No mention either, in the Ravensbrück rewrite of German history, of the Nazi-Soviet Pact, of the KPD's cooperation with the brownshirts in fighting the SPD as the "evil greater than the Nazis", or of the Soviet role in training the Panzers and the Luftwaffe. The SED regime obliged teachers to bring children to see these lies of omission, which ensured that a couple of generations of east Germans learned a very strange version indeed of the purely German phenomenon of Nazism and its consequences.

The sudden blizzard which brought real winter to the central region of eastern Germany in mid-December (the higher lying southern area had already experienced snow and chaos late in November) added another hazard to my lodgings lottery: route roulette or the find-a-passable-road game, the object of which was to see how little ground one can cover in a day. Having listened carefully to the radio, I rashly resolved to stick to my programme for the day in question, visiting "the other Frankfurt" (due east of Berlin on the Oder and the Polish border) for the first time. Unfortunately the GDR's snow-clearance vehicles were themselves snowed up, unable to cope with the continuing blizzard on the Berlin Ring autobahn (E30) south of the capital. Having advanced twenty kilometres in the first two hours of daylight and hearing of one massive jam after another ahead (Poland was closed) I turned north towards Berlin and then worked my way eastward to Strausberg; only undiluted stubbornness got me there on the treacherous roads. The Bundeswehr eastern command headquarters for which I was bound would probably have stayed in business for another day or two, but I was determined not to waste the day.

Arriving at government offices, whether municipal, state or federal, without an appointment was one thing. Turning up in a mobile snowdrift at the former supreme headquarters of the National People's Army (NVA), now Bundeswehr Kommando-Ost, very nearly threw the system. I had already been misdirected to an airbase at the other end of slippery, slidy Strausberg, a straggling town with unhelpful signposts, and it was lunchtime. As the military hierarchy – sentry, corporal of the guard, duty officer and finally the civilian receptionist on the desk, who was the only one who knew how to find anyone on the internal telephone – adjusted itself to my egregious presence, I attacked my emergency cold-weather chocolate supply. Eventually I was handed, with exemplary pfennig-wise economy, an overstamped NVA admission form, and directed to the office of Major Hubertus Kunze, on the staff of Lieutenant-General Jörg Schönbohm. The General has the not inconsiderable task of winding up the NVA, cutting its numbers drastically while absorbing it into the Bundeswehr. At the same time the Defence Ministry in Bonn is arranging to reduce the Bundeswehr as a whole from its pre-union level of 495,000 in the old Federal Republic to 370,000 in the new one by 1994.

The latter total was agreed between Chancellor Kohl and President Gorbachev at their breakthrough meeting in the Caucasus, which paved the way for Soviet consent to unification, and was confirmed by the November 1990 European treaty on the reduction of conventional forces. One could hardly avoid the impression that a military attack on Germany during this period of unprecedented turmoil would find its defence forces in a state of total chaos. The absorption of the NVA was already proceeding at high speed, one immediate benefit being the release to the civil authorities of hundreds of surplus bases and buildings and no less than 12,000 kilometres of road previously reserved for the military.

The defence apparatus of the GDR was much weightier than the size of the country would warrant in the West. Leaving aside the menacing presence at 2,000 facilities of a million tonnes of ammunition and 422,000 Soviet troops plus their dependent civilians (reduced by unification to 380,000, all of whom are to leave by 1994, if not sooner), the GDR was an armed camp. The NVA had an army of two corps or six divisions (two armoured, four motorised infantry), a total of 120,000 men, of whom 71,500 were conscripts; the reserve amounted to 330,000. The naval arm of the NVA, the Volksmarine, had 16,000 men (including the coastal border brigade with forty patrol-boats) and three frigates, twenty-one corvettes, eleven missile boats, twenty-seven torpedo boats, forty-six minesweepers and more than 100 auxiliary craft (quite a lot for a short coastline in the enclosed Baltic). The Air Force had 40,000 men and 375 combat aircraft. Also run by the National Defence Council (chaired by Erich Honecker) and the Ministry of Defence and Disarmament (*sic*) were the Volkspolizei with 25,000 police and 46,500 border guards; and 450,000 militia based in factories and other large plants. (As a comparison, the Netherlands, which has a slightly smaller population than the GDR, has an army of two divisions and 68,000 troops, a navy of 16,900 including marines and air personnel with eighteen frigates, six submarines and about ninety auxiliary vessels, and an air force of 18,300 with about 150 combat aircraft.) What really startled the Bundeswehr was the fact that the GDR's forces had been up to eighty-five per cent combat-ready, even at weekends (when western forces are about twenty per cent available). On the other hand most main equipment was not up to the best Soviet standards. But Nato regarded the NVA as the Warsaw Pact's all-round best troops. They came under direct Soviet command just as the Bundeswehr has always been under direct Nato command.

The GDR was also a gigantic munitions dump, with an estimated 90 billion marks' worth of equipment and ammunition which would be surplus to Bundeswehr requirements when it swallowed up the NVA. Between the Volkskammer election in March 1990 and union in October, huge quantities of this matériel were disposed of, either to other members of the Warsaw Pact, notably Poland, or onto the international arms market. Chancellor Kohl's first offer of $3 billion in aid to the

United States in the Gulf crisis, which blew up on Iraq's invasion of Kuwait in August 1990, was originally meant to be handed over in the forms of ex-NVA equipment! Immediately upon unification, investigators from several Federal agencies in Bonn moved in to probe a series of deals which disposed of huge quantities of GDR munitions before the treaty of union took effect: Iraq may have benefited from this unique closing-down sale. India was offered enough cut-price, modern Soviet tanks for a division as late as August 1990. Stasi involvement in the last-minute disposal of military equipment was strongly and not unreasonably suspected. At the same time the Bundeswehr had to allocate 6,000 extra men to guard NVA gear, including a third of a million tonnes of ammunition, because the high-voltage electric fences which used to do the job are banned by FRG law – a rare example of reverse automation where the west substituted manpower for eastern technology. In the end 11,000 troops had to guard the stores, which included 1,200,000 small arms left by NVA, border police, militia and Stasi, 10,000 heavy vehicles, 2,140 cannon and 450 planes (including two dozen modern MiG 29 fighters, though they lacked the latest Soviet accessories).

As union approached, all East German generals resigned or retired in the knowledge that none of them could be politically acceptable to the new masters. Full colonels similarly had no future, lieutenant-colonels were borderline cases, majors, captains and lieutenants wanting to stay on faced investigation, probation and then retraining at the Bundeswehr's internal leadership centre in Koblenz. All NVA men over fifty had to retire at once on pension (at East German rates). A lot of officers took early retirement; many others faced a one-step drop in rank in the over-officered, over-promoted NVA (SED membership was all but universal in the NVA officer corps, due to be slashed from 24,000 to 4,000). The border guard and militia were wound up, and the police removed from defence ministry control for subordination to the new *Land* governments. Conscription, from eighteen months to two years and for some up to three years in the GDR, was immediately cut to the west German twelve months. All these measures reduced the ex-NVA component of the Bundeswehr to 83,000 men (the only women in the Bundeswehr are in the Medical Corps) by the end of 1990. The east German component of the integrated and reduced Bundeswehr will amount by the end of 1992 to 50,000, of whom half will be conscripts.

Many Germans, east and west, thought it remarkable that the NVA "surrendered" to the new dispensation as it did, given the pro-Soviet, anti-western indoctrination and orientation of the GDR's armed forces. Were they all merely continuing to obey orders, regardless of their origin? Or had they never believed, in which case why had they not rebelled against the SED? Or if they did believe, why was there no protest against being plucked out of the Warsaw Pact and tossed into Nato overnight? The military being the military, the *Wende* was marked ceremonially at midnight on October 2–3 at the larger NVA bases by a final rendition of the GDR anthem "Risen from the Ruins" and the hauling down of the hammer-and-compasses version of the German tricolour for the last time. At that moment and in such a context the whole business of unification must have seemed like a surrender. It certainly did to some of the Bundeswehr people who witnessed it. Dismay and reluctance were reported as Bundeswehr uniforms began to be issued from 0000 hours, Central European Time, on unification day, 3 October 1990. Interestingly the strongest resistance to the new military arrangements came from the east German Evangelicals, who said they would not supply chaplains because this western custom compromised the separation of church and state. There were no scuttlings of ships or immolations of tanks in protest (as half-feared), but General Schönbohm did receive many anonymous threats to his life and was given a heavy bodyguard.

The almighty, instant about-turn from east to west, even more remarkable politically and psychologically than the recruitment of ex-Wehrmacht officers and NCOs to found the democratic "citizens-in-uniform" Bundeswehr itself in the 1950s, was under the supervision of fewer than 2,000 western officers and NCOs under General Schönbohm's command. One of them is Major Kunze, who gave me a crisp briefing amid a series of interruptions, their effect magnified by the boom of boots on wooden floorboards. "We are still in stage one of a three-stage operation to reduce, overhaul and integrate the new eastern command," he said. "It has not yet been decided who will be allowed to stay on, nor how many of those not kept on will be allowed to work as civilians." No women would be retained, but some of them might get civilian jobs. "The whole of the ex-NVA is in a state of social insecurity about its future until the process of deciding who will leave, who will stay on for a while and who will be allowed to become career soldiers can be completed." But the manpower position of the Bundeswehr had been transformed by the uniquely difficult twin tasks of absorption and reduction, from struggling to keep up numbers (because of a steep decline in the west German birthrate in the early 1970s and the 1989 reduction from fifteen months to twelve of the conscription period) to being able to pick and choose.

Those non-conscripts leaving at the end of the year (1990) would receive a gratuity of up to DM7,000 to tide them over. Those left had to remain "in waiting" until a decision about their future was made case by case. It would not be easy, because it was not only the suitability of the candidate but also his specialism which would decide his future. Many ex-NVA people wanted to stay on and applications would be processed as quickly as possible. The first NCOs had received their confirmations a week earlier. Those who had decided of their own accord to leave by the end of 1990 had to hand their notices in by December 14. Those who waited and were not kept on were promised a minimum of two months' notice and gratuities, part-pensions or other support, depending on age and length of service. The task was "unique in history", the Major said: two defence forces from opposed alliances were being fused in two years and reduced from a combined total of 630,000 at the outset to 370,000 in four years (a level at which it might be not only possible but also necessary to convert the Bundeswehr into a wholly professional force, I learned elsewhere, because each conscript-year would be far too big for requirements in a country of 80,000,000 people). "What's more the Bundeswehr is constitutionally made up of citizens in uniform, whereas the NVA may have been called a 'people's army' but was really a Party army," the Major pointed out.

There were and are bound to be problems of morale. Uniformed *Wessis*, regular or conscript, receive about twice as much pay as their *Ossi* comrades, who faced up to two years' probation even if admitted to the Bundeswehr in 1991. There was not much opportunity and apparently not much appetite for socialising between western and eastern soldiers; both elements in the new eastern command seemed to be keeping themselves to themselves, an unremarkable fact encouraged by the initial trend towards absorbing, reducing or demobilising the NVA by units rather than by individuals. At least a reduction in rank did not entail a cut in pay, and any *Ossi* lucky enough to be posted to the west got the western rate. The Bundeswehr seemed to me to be unlikely to function as a wholly integrated force again until the overwhelming majority of ex-NVA people had left, which might take a decade. And it would be against human nature if someone with "ex-NVA" on his otherwise impeccable service record did not find this fact an embarrassment, if not a positive disadvantage, at some stage in his future career. One can hardly fail to sympathise with the German Bundeswehr Association, the soldiers' union, and its demand that there should be no discrimination in the service. "We have not come as victors to the defeated but as Germans to Germans," said General Schönbohm when he arrived at Strausberg. No German general has had a harder task in peacetime: living up to these well-meant words is likely to be the hardest part of it.

By the time I made my second attempt to get to Frankfurt-an-der-Oder the blizzards had stopped and an iron-hard frost had set in; the autobahn was clear of snow if not of idiots who were prepared to ignore black-ice warnings and speed limits alike. But the radio was warning of twenty-kilometre, eight-hour queues to enter Poland at the end of the E30. Since Frankfurt could hardly be closer to Poland without being in it, that meant I would reach the tail of this queue before I could get to the Frankfurt exit. They had thought of that on "Radio Aktuell", advising departure from the autobahn at the Müllrose (literally rubbish rose) exit. This was easy. Unfortunately nobody had thought it necessary to signpost Frankfurt from there. When I enquired the way of a gnome-like man pushing a bicycle he laughed and said, "This is not the way to Frankfurt," overlooking the patent fact that I had hailed him precisely because this had already dawned on me. He made off, shaking his head but imparting no further information. Finally a vanload of *Wessi* television sets and I agreed that (a) we had taken the wrong road and (b) we should get out of the snow-covered field into which the wrong road had dumped us. Soon a convoy of the lost was slithering about the landscape until a more helpful bucolic personage issued reliable guidance. We eventually got back to the autobahn, to find that the eastbound carriageway had been abandoned to the trucks now blocking both lanes for miles on end and the westbound was now split into two, with a lane each for local traffic leaving and approaching Frankfurt. Coming into the city I met what could well have been half the Red Army coming out, as I drove past endless Soviet barracks before crossing the Leninallee into the city centre.

It was worth the effort to reach the other Frankfurt, a city of something over 80,000 people, one tenth the population of its western namesake on the Main, the financial capital of Germany. Brandenburg's Frankfurt with its big bridge provides the most important crossing to Poland. The historic summit meeting in November 1990 between Chancellor Kohl and Prime Minister Mazowiecki of Poland, which did not, as intended by the Germans, help the premier to beat Lech Walesa in the December election for the presidency, was highly symbolic for both countries and for Frankfurt itself. The two leaders also went to what used to be Frankfurt's suburb on the eastern bank of the Oder, Dammvorstadt, just fifty metres away – now the Polish town of Slubice. There are other places which were divided by the postwar truncation of eastern Germany, such as German Guben/Polish Gubin, but none compares in importance with Frankfurt, which bestrides the main road from Berlin to Warsaw. The Polish connection can only grow in importance as Frankfurt struggles to cope with the threatened collapse of the local economy. It was the GDR's centre for the manufacture of electronic semiconductors, but the factory was some distance back from the frontier of knowledge in this western-dominated field and the jobs of 8,000 workers were on the brink of disappearing when I got there.

German-Polish relations are highly sensitive and have become more so since the *Wende*, a fact which is reflected in intensified form at this chief border crossing – so much so that concerned Frankfurt citizens have formed a metaphorical "Frankfurt Bridge" to work for a better atmosphere. In the days when the GDR and Poland were both members of the Warsaw Pact, the citizens of each could cross freely into the other's territory – until the SED grew scared of "infection by the Solidarity virus" and effectively closed the border. With this kind of discouragement it is hardly surprising that vague Polish plans to modernise their customs posts were shelved, leaving them totally unprepared for the boom in traffic which ensued upon democratisation and the extension of the all-conquering free market to Poland. Before the SED restrictions the Poles used to come over, change their zlotys into east-marks at a reasonable rate and buy scarce, heavily subsidised goods from under the noses of east Germans in the GDR shops, better stocked than their Polish counter-parts; they would then either resell on the black market at home or for hard currency in the west. After German currency union and before political unification the East Germans could return the compliment by taking their new D-marks to Poland to change them at a huge advantage and buy Polish food at ridiculously low prices. For their part the Poles during this phase poured into West Berlin, pawned the family heirlooms for D-marks and bought western consumer goods, especially audio equipment, for resale at a high zloty-profit at home. Once these goods spread all over the ex-GDR, Poles with visas and hard currency (say from relatives in the United States or Britain) could go to the nearest German town – especially Frankfurt – and buy there.

On unification both governments imposed visa restrictions to stop this economic tourism, but the Poles regained the moral advantage by unilaterally reopening their frontier in October 1990 to Germans with GDR-issue identity cards (which also brought in some much-needed hard currency). Both governments promised further easements in the New Year; Poland lifted visa requirements for all Germans on January 1. Poles with jobs in the ex-GDR met hostile demonstrators who saw them as threats to German jobs. At the semi-conductor factory there were demands that the 500 Poles working there should be sacked first. Poland feared that the Oder would become the frontier not just between itself and the new, historically frightening united Germany but also between rich West and poor East in Europe. This fear was reflected in Germany, where politicians tried not to talk about the possibility of a huge westward migration from the hungering Soviet Union via Poland. Frankfurt and Slubice, the former about twice as big as the latter, are still bound together by more than a bridge. Frankfurt continues to supply its former eastern suburb with gas and there are many family connections through intermarriage, even though the Poles of Slubice, who moved into the houses vacated by displaced Germans, are mostly easterners from Polish territory taken by the Russians and given to the Ukraine after the war.

Herr Isken runs the office of Dr Wolfgang Denda, *Oberbürgermeister* (mayor) of Frankfurt. He told me the city was effectively bankrupt. The biggest problem (as ever) was property claims, which were preventing the city from providing land and buildings for would-be investors. This was particularly frustrating because there was nearly as much land inside the city boundary as in Leipzig. "At the same time we have to face the closure of the semiconductor works, and we don't have an independent middle class from which new businesses might be expected to come; there are just a few artisans. We would like to attract new firms here, but, apart from the lack of unencumbered space, we have to recognise that being on the Polish border is a problem – unless it is a fully open, free border. That is why we attach so much importance to Brandenburg's plan to set up a European University here, to which we hope young people from all over Europe, east and west, will come." Frankfurt had a university until 1811, when it was moved to Silesian Breslau (now Wroclaw in Poland). The *Land* government was also considering basing some of its functions in Frankfurt to help the city.

Meanwhile Herr Isken produced a most impressive "organigram", as the French call it, of the new city government. This developed from a local round table in the tense pre-revolutionary days of 1989. In the local elections in 1990 no party got near a majority of the seventy-one council seats, so the SPD with nineteen, the CDU, controlling sixteen, and New Forum with seven, formed a coalition which elected Dr Denda, a previously apolitical electronics engineer. The structure of the city government was based on one of several west German municipal models, with eight departments (mini-ministries). Officials and staff were being (re-)recruited, avoiding as far as possible the 10,000 citizens who had been in the SED and known Stasi agents (though it was proving impossible not to rehire secretaries, drivers and others who had been informers).

While I was in town a crisis was brewing over Dr Denda's allegedly high-handed style of government and delay in confronting local unemployment (which he strongly denied). I was in no position to judge, but from what I heard of Frankfurt's problems Dr Denda would need to be a magician to deal with difficulties which affect the entire ex-GDR and could not be dealt with by any municipal or *Land* government without massive aid. The Federal Government in Bonn seemed to be faring no better, but it alone had the means to tackle the looming economic disasters. That local initiative was not dead in Frankfurt was shown by a bang-up-to-date buy-out from the Treuhand of a local road-building business (ex-VEB). Ten managers had just bought eighty per cent of the fledgling GmbH and the workforce of 260 took up the balance of the stock. Management buyouts are rare enough in old west Germany, conservative as it is in business practices; this confident display of enterprise was certainly the first of its kind in Brandenburg and may even have been the first in the ex-GDR.

At least Frankfurt, heavily bombed during the war and generously overlaid with concrete after it, boasted a very fine *Rathaus* indeed, of Brandenburg brick inlaid with stucco and with a superbly intricate Gothic gable. The most impressive local church, again of brick with ornate, half-timbered white gable-ends, a former Franciscan monastery chapel, is now used as a concert hall. Apparently its acoustics are near perfect. Even the late nineteenth-century brick and stucco main post office verges on the majestic, and the modern reconstruction in the centre and the medium-rise inner suburbs is no more soulless than the surroundings of its much richer western namesake – which might well envy its poor eastern relation the space in and around Frankfurt-an-der-Oder (if only it could be put to positive use unencumbered by the accursed accumulation of claims upon it).

Brandenburg has one other important town apart from Potsdam, Cottbus and Frankfurt: the ancient capital of Mark Brandenburg, which gave the *Land* its name. Brandenburg city, just a few miles west of Potsdam, has nearly 100,000 inhabitants and was once a fortified Slav settlement called Brennabor. The Margrave Albert the Bear reconquered the place in 1157, the Germans having lost it in 983, and it became the capital of the *Mark* until displaced by Berlin at the beginning of the seventeenth century. At its end the Huguenots arrived to revive its economy as an important leather-working centre and trading town on either side of the River Havel. A garrison town until Potsdam took over, Brandenburg gently declined, despite a gradual accretion of surrounding communities and land, and some modern industrialisation. The brick cathedral of SS Peter and Paul was nearly seven centuries in the building (from 1165 to 1836, restored in 1966). The modest exterior conceals a wealth of interior features, fixtures and fittings dating from Brandenburg's long-gone heyday as a regional capital.

When I passed through, there was a cheerful *Weihnachtsmarkt* (Christmas fair) in the bitter cold and snow, which did not discourage the many passers-by from lunching off sausages from a street stall. One stallholder was repeatedly calling out for someone to sell her a Trabant for cash. Understandably nobody seemed to take her seriously, but it seemed that her runabout had finally given up the ghost and she wanted a replacement at once. She may have been the only person in the whole of Germany after the arrival of the D-mark who publicly confessed, with no trace of embarrassment, to wanting a Trabi.

The day I went to Eberswalde-Finow, some forty kilometres north-east of the centre of Berlin on the B2 and at the heart of one of the most popular areas for day-trips in the former GDR, I may have been the only tourist of the week. The snow was thick on the ground (though fortunately not on the roads) and it was bitterly cold. As its name indicates it is a municipality of two towns dating from the thirteenth century but joined only in 1970. Water, wood and local iron-ore made the area an early ironworking centre; now it has a steel-rolling mill, a pipe works and makes cranes. It is also packed to the brim with Soviet troops.

My destination was Chorin, ten kilometres further up the road, where there is a most magnificent brick ruin of a monastery in a superb lakeside and forest setting. Built in 1273 by the Cistercians, the monastery was dissolved in 1542, when the Reformation triumphed locally; it then passed into the ownership of the Elector. Chorin itself was pillaged several times and set on fire in the Thirty Years' War, then reduced to serving as a quarry for new buildings. Even so there was more than enough left at the beginning of the last century to move the architect Karl Schinkel to arrange for the first conservation measures. In 1861 the place was incongruously handed over to the Prussian forestry department for preservation. None the less a good job was done, including considerable restoration and even rebuilding. The GDR forestry administration kept up the good work, reasonably profiting from the 100,000 visitors who came each year to admire the splendid ruin. Top-class concerts are put on in summer, featuring orchestras and bands from Germany and abroad. It struck me as a highly imaginative use of the place as I warmed myself over an excellent lunch at an inn nearby.

About ten kilometres on back roads to the south-east of Chorin is a spectacle of an entirely different order, at Niederfinow. The lower Havel and upper Oder rivers pass through this area only one or two kilometres apart and it seemed obvious they should be joined by a little canal. But the Havel flows thirty-six metres lower than the Oder, so that the first attempt at a link in 1748 required no less than seventeen locks. The second, in 1914, still needed four locks. So, in 1927, it was decided to build a ship-elevator. The barge or boat would sail into a steel basin full of water, which would then be raised from the Havel, hauled along a steel transporter bridge built into the side of the bank sloping up to the Oder and unloaded there; or vice versa. Although it came into use only in 1934, this stupendous and still functioning device belongs in the same category as the great engineering achievements of the Victorian/Wilhelmine era.

On the way back I made a detour across the E28 Berlin-Szczecin autobahn onto the B273 to Oranienburg. The area is deeply afforested with no immediately obvious sign of human habitation.

The unremarkable turn-off brings the visitor onto one of the broadest and finest non-motorway roads in Germany, if not the world, even though it runs for only five kilometres through dense forest to the point where the B273 crosses the B109 Berlin-Prenzlau road. It is only a few kilometres due south from the crossing to a big junction with the northern segment of the Berlin Ring, from which a special spur of autobahn runs south to Pankow, the section of east Berlin where foreign ambassadors and senior GDR diplomats used to reside. But, if one looks carefully to the left on passing along the B273 towards the crossroads, a long, low, green-painted concrete wall can be seen running parallel to the road inside the trees. By taking an unmarked leftward turn into the forest one reaches a corner of the wall, where there is a watchtower and a guardhouse. This is Wandlitz, a spot which appears in no known guide book to the GDR.

Here the SED leadership lived in seclusion in luxury houses (though of extremely boring external design). They had heated indoor swimming-pools, all the latest domestic appliances and fittings from west Germany, servants and their own independent heating and electricity plants. Food and drink of a variety and quality unknown to the ordinary citizenry were brought by special delivery at the merest whisper of an order down the bug-proof telephones linked to the secret Stasi network. It was here that Honecker, Stoph, Krenz, Mielke and all the top people from the *Politburo* were lodged.

Having worked together during the week, they took in each other's metaphorical washing in the evenings and at weekends, which must have been extremely tedious and the opposite of relaxing. Puritans and conservatives believe that Socialists should not be well off, which is a matter of opinon rather than logic. It is not unreasonable to be ruled by people whose material circumstances are comfortable enough to help them do their important jobs properly (and to reduce the temptations that inevitably come with high office, the corruption of power).

What was obscene about Wandlitz was the fact that no ordinary GDR citizen, no matter what he or she did, how hard he worked or saved, or how loyal to the regime or the system she was, could ever aspire to a fraction of this level of personal consumption. A poor individual in England, if sufficiently obsessed with a material luxury, at least has the right to scrape the necessary money together and go to Fortnum & Mason for a kilogram of caviar or to Savile Row for a hand-made suit. In the GDR there were far too many quite ordinary physical comforts that money, even hard currency, simply could not buy – and too many privileges which even the most ravening ambition could not aspire to unless the Party, which answered to nobody west of Moscow, gave its blessing. No wonder many east Germans exploded with rage when they overran the settlement after the *Wende* and saw how their departed *Bonzen* had lived. The Wandlitz settlement is now closed to visitors again, but is being used to look after sick children, which sounds right; a 200-bed sanatorium is also being built for them.

– V –

MECKLENBURG-WEST POMERANIA

Lots in a name – backwoods – best scenery – worst economy – Neubrandenburg – Rügen Island – Stubbenkammer – end of the line – Greifswald – nuclear shutdown – university – rotten road – Wismar – resorts – Rostock – cars – recycling punctured – Schwerin – silent shipyard – why the rush?

– V –

Mecklenburg-West Pomerania

This is the *Land* which I was most keen to see during my exploration of the ex-GDR for two reasons: it includes the entire east German coastline and I had never seen any part of it before. The user-unfriendly Communist state had simply closed much of the coast to foreign visitors because of its naval and radar defences. People who come to know Germany well tend to divide into northern and southern camps: there is the school which favours the Alpine, *Lederhosen* and beer-festival atmosphere of the Catholic south and the tendency which likes the big skies and complicated coastline of the Hanseatic, Protestant north. I confess that I was a committed "northerner" (doubtless because of my Dutch origin) before I got this chance to explore the German east in detail: Munich is much the more beautiful city, but I prefer Hamburg any day. I was interested to see whether my northerly bias would be strengthened or weakened by Mecklenburg-West Pomerania, MWP for short.

The name is partly untranslatable, the German being Mecklenburg-Vorpommern. The prefix *vor-* usually translates into English as "fore-" or "pre-" and indicates physical or temporal priority; in the former mode the converse is *hinter*, meaning "behind", and in the latter it is *nach*, meaning "after". The Germans use the expression Hinterpommern for the part of Pomerania you get to on leaving Vorpommern; but Hinterpommern is now in Poland, which makes the use of the name Vorpommern a touch tactless. English does not allow the translations Forepomerania and Afterpomerania, while Upper and Lower do not work because the whole of Pomerania is flat; all this obliges us to make do with West Pomerania. At any rate it was the part you reached first heading east from Mecklenburg, if you were a Teutonic knight on your way round the Baltic in the white soutane with the black cross, bible in one hand, sword in the other. Mecklenburg straightforwardly takes its name from what is now shown on the map in tiny print as Dorf Mecklenburg, a village of no significance today. There, in the tenth century, the Germans built a fort on a hill in their efforts to reconquer from Wendish-Slav rule the region which they had abandoned in the seventh, when they were pushed south and west by the great Eurasian mass migrations.

The area or various parts of it at various times passed in and out of the hands of Germans, Slavs, Germans again, the Hanseatic League, Danes, Swedes, the French and more Germans. It was carved up, reunited and carved up again, only differently, as Saxony was over the years. There were counts and dukes and finally grand-dukes of Mecklenburg-Schwerin and Mecklenburg-Strelitz, and the whole of Mecklenburg was unique in Germany in having no regional constitution before 1918: until then it was corporatist, with four estates (in the political sense) – nobles, landowners, mayors and peasants. Backward is not the word for this arrangement, which makes pre-revolutionary France seem radical. Only in 1934 were Schwerin and Strelitz reunited as one Mecklenburg. Modest Mecklenburg Village bestrides the line from Wismar due south to Schwerin and Ludwigslust along the B106 road, where the British and Soviet armies joined hands in 1945. All Mecklenburg went into the Soviet Zone on 1 July 1945; in 1952 Mecklenburg was divided into three *Bezirke*, Rostock on the coast and Schwerin and Neubrandenburg inland. West Pomerania is the area between today's coastal town of Ribnitz-Damgarten and the River Oder and was fought over by Poles and Germans in the Middle Ages; it has also been ruled in its time, in whole or in part, by the Hanseatic League, Danes, Swedes and Brandenburg-Prussians.

Bismarck used to say of Mecklenburg that, if the world came to an end, its inhabitants would hear the news a century later. He thought rather more highly of Pomerania, remarking that Schleswig-Holstein, over which he went to war with Denmark in 1864, was "not worth the healthy bones of a single Pomeranian grenadier"; but he would, wouldn't he? His family owned lands in what is now Polish Pomerania. The Pomeranian capital used to be Stettin, but the Oder-Neisse line was bent west of the mouth of the Oder, where Vorpommern ends, so that the Baltic port was incorporated into Poland as Szczecin in 1945.

With only 2,100,000 inhabitants washing around in almost 23,000 square kilometres, MWP has the lightest density of population of any *Land* in the old GDR and all united Germany. The "land of a thousand lakes and castles" in fact boasts 650 of the former and rather fewer of the latter, but the poetic licence is entirely permissible. In Lake Müritz it has the largest in the European Community and there is (of course) a "Mecklenburgish Switzerland" to the north-west of Neubrandenburg. The main economic activities are, as one would expect: fishing and shipbuilding on the coast, agriculture including horse-breeding inland, tourism everywhere – and one big nuclear power-station outside Greifswald, a gently crumbling former Hanseatic city which otherwise seems to have done no harm to anybody. All in all the many "good bits" of MWP struck me as the most beautiful in the former GDR, even allowing for my admitted bias. The coast surpasses most things on offer in northern Holland and west Germany, but where the North Sea has tidal *Watten* (sand flats) the Baltic has non-tidal *Bodden* – great swathes of shallow water just off the coast with their own delicate (and seriously threatened) ecology.

MWP is also the most vulnerable *Land* economically because, for example, its shipyards have effectively lost their semi-captive Comecon markets round the Baltic and stand no chance in a free market which long since all but destroyed shipbuilding throughout the West. Its agriculture is not geared to European Community requirements; its fisheries were so heavily subsidised by the GDR that the free market was all set to drown them within weeks of union; and its nuclear-power industry is shutting down because it does not conform to west German safety standards. Its seemingly endless chain of holiday resorts on the Baltic, though intrinsically offering as much as anywhere on the narrowest German coastline (indeed more in some ways because there are no "concrete cliffs" in MWP to compare with Schleswig-Holstein's), will need massive investment to attract tourists from outside the ex-GDR. Meanwhile they have lost their standby trade of workers' subsidised holidays and most of their "cure" and convalescent business. And if communications in the ex-GDR can fairly be described as poor, those in MWP are generally shocking. The main coast road (B105/E22) from Lübeck on the old West German border via Rostock to Stralsund, opposite the wonderful island of Rügen, is a nightmare – the best argument outside London I have seen in a long time for the abolition of the internal-combustion engine and a reversion to MWP's superb horses. I was fortunate in being able to pick and choose when to travel, but there were times when I miscalculated and regretted.

I first strayed over the MWP border from Brandenburg on the B96 trunk road (alias the E251, from Berlin to Greifswald). My first stop was

Neustrelitz, a little town of 27,000 people which had nevertheless once been a grand-ducal capital (old Strelitz was relegated to a suburb of the new one when its castle burned down in 1712, whereupon the Grand Duke moved to his hunting *Schloss* of Glienicke to the north (destroyed in its turn in 1945), ordering the construction of Neustrelitz in 1733. The late-baroque town centre has a market-place around which the buildings stand in star-shaped layout. The park of the lost palace is still there, neatly landscaped in various styles from baroque to modern.

Thirty kilometres further north stands Neubrandenburg, three times the size, its name misleading because the Margraves of Brandenburg, having founded it in 1248, gave it as a dowry to their peers of Mecklenburg in 1292, of which it has been a part ever since. That it survives, complete with some impressive old buildings, is little short of a miracle. The Thirty Years' War, two massive fires in 1676 and 1737 and a fierce land battle between the Wehrmacht and the Red Army in April 1945 (which destroyed eighty-five per cent of the buildings) happily failed to remove the place from the map. Ironically, the best-preserved ancient monument is the virtually complete stone city wall (late thirteenth century) which so signally failed to fend off disaster – 2,300 metres in circumference and seven high with towers, four city gates, moats, half-timbered watch-houses and other defensive features. The fifteenth-century, Gothic brick gates have been splendidly restored and the surrounding area includes Lake Tollense and much forest. In the heart of the town stands one of those bad Communist jokes, all fifty-five metres of it, raised in 1965. Q: What is the best place in Neubrandenburg? A: The House of Culture and Education. Q: Why? A: Because it's the only place in Neubrandenburg from which you can't see the House of Culture and Education . . .

On my return to MWP I took the only autobahn which passes through it, the E55 from Berlin to Rostock, by far the biggest city in the *Land* with its modest population of 250,000, where I had arranged to stay for a week. By and large this is the best main road in the ex-GDR and I covered the 228 kilometres in two and a half hours door to door. But it was a Saturday and I was very lucky with the weather.

Thus encouraged, I resolved to make my longest exploratory run the next day, the Sunday, right the way along the most promising-sounding section of coast from Rostock eastward to the great island of Rügen. This entailed following the B105 to Stralsund and driving over the 1936 causeway with its folding bridge and onward, via the B96 across the island, to Sassnitz. The coast road was deceptively attractive and empty on a winter Sunday; the weather had turned threatening and doubtless kept most would-be day-trippers indoors like sensible people. Stralsund, a former Hanseatic city with an obviously Scandinavian name, stands on the Strela Sound between the mainland and Rügen. Wandering Franks (who also gave their tribal name to Frankfurt-on-Oder) and Saxons threw out the local Slavs in the thirteenth century and developed among the coastal swamps a major port and trading centre which joined the Hanseatic League. When the League, originally formed to combat late-Viking piracy in the Middle Ages and then transformed into a littoral common market, went into decline, so did Stralsund.

Helped by the Swedes to beat off Imperial troops in the Thirty Years' War, Stralsund remained Swedish until 1815. After that the Prussians took over and turned it into a modern fortress, which did not save it from serious damage by bombing in the Second World War. The RAF battered the German Baltic coast, which was used for shipbuilding and repair, the training of all German submarine crews, for experimental rocketry (at Peenemunde) and the care and maintenance of major surface warships.

Stralsund has a most attractive centre round the Alter Markt, with a Gothic brick *Rathaus* going back 700 years and the Nikolai Church next door, which is full of the treasures only a Hansa city could afford in the late Middle Ages. With water so close to the centre of town, the place only needs a little attention – work was already in hand on the market-place – and should then become a good draw for western tourists because it is in the middle of the best coastal stretch of east Germany.

Rügen is Germany's largest island (926 square kilometres) and was the constant inspiration of its greatest Romantic painter, Caspar David Friedrich, born in nearby Greifswald (1774–1840). He made the most of the dramatic local land- and seascapes, which is to say a great deal. The most spectacular spot is the strangely named Stubbenkammer on the Jasmund Peninsula at the north-eastern end of the island. Here are spectacularly steep, white chalk cliffs up to 161 metres high, laced with streaks of flintstone and topped with a forest of beeches. A few metres back from the edge the SED had unfeelingly placed a defence complex with radar and watchtowers in a compound walled with rough concrete, now apparently abandoned. Otherwise it was a breathtaking spot with spectacular views; in the distance, on inaccessible cliffs, rare birds of prey of the hawk family have their nests, which you can inspect through public telescopes. One can only commend the fortitude of the owners of the waffle-stall for selling their irresistibly aromatic wares on a bitter and eventually rainy Sunday morning. There were not many around to succumb to the temptation, but those of us who were present did our best to make a thorough job of it.

A few kilometres south, still on the Jasmund Peninsula, stands Sassnitz, northernmost town of the ex-GDR. It is a surprisingly modern one, its main claim to fame being the ferries to Trelleborg in Sweden and Klaipeda in (reluctantly) Soviet Lithuania. Founded in 1824, it used to be a seaside resort which enjoyed fashionable status when the railway arrived around the turn of the century and encouraged the development of the ferry services. Lenin is commemorated at the station (how fitting, in view of his remark about the German revolutionary's need for a platform ticket) by a commemorative carriage recalling his 1917 journey in a sealed train from Switzerland via Germany and the Baltic to what we now know as Leningrad, carrying the bacillus of revolution with the blessing of the Kaiser. A plaque on the wall of the seamen's hostel says he stopped over in Sassnitz.

Carrying on southward from there along a minor road with water on either side you reach the Mönchgut (monks' estate) Peninsula, once owned by the Cistercians. It is surely the remotest place in eastern Germany and the people who lived there had their own dialect, costume, unique folklore and way of life well into the present century. The weather was pretty rough by now and the area looked wild in the extreme, with glowering thatched cottages (one or two with those "bedroom eyes" in the roof) at the very edge of the tideless water, black fishing boats bottom-up alongside.

I had a Nuremberg number-plate this time, and a gnarled man in oilskins and Prince Heinrich (or Helmut Schmidt) cap paused to stare at me as if I was mad when I emerged from the car into the rain to snatch a picture of Thiessow, the last hamlet on the peninsula. He may have had a point. The coast is lined with a series of small, bracing, east-facing seaside resorts separated by forest or marshy land. On a clear day, which this wasn't, you can see across the Greifswalder Bodden all the way to the town from which its name derives. It is a pale and shallow sheet of water which depends on wind, rain and current rather than non-existent tides for its survival as a marine biosphere; but already half the Baltic has been killed by pollution. I planned to visit the town itself the next day.

I had felt obliged to return after my first month in the former GDR to honour a long-standing engagement, to contribute a lecture to a course on the British press being run by Reuters news agency in London for east European journalists. The worthiness of the cause seemed to outweigh the expense and inconvenience of the interruption. But my virtue was rewarded. Among those attending the course was Jan-Peter Schröder, the youthful Chief Reporter of the *Ostsee-Zeitung*, Rostock's daily newspaper. When I told him what I was doing, he insisted I look him up when I got to MWP. By the time I reached Rostock it was 1991 and he had left the city without notice to take charge of his paper's new district office in Greifswald. A news emergency prevented him from keeping our appointment in Rostock and all attempts to reach him by phone failed, so I followed my usual practice of trusting to luck and setting off without an appointment. In Greifswald exhaustive research yielded the whereabouts of the public telephone, a vertical coffin in a post office next to the railway station where, even to make a local call, you had to queue to tell the counter clerk and pay the thirty pfennigs in advance.

We met and repaired for a very early lunch to the *Rathauskeller*, a fine example of the cellar-restaurant under the town hall which is a marvellous German urban institution valued rather more in east than west Germany these days. Herr Schröder volunteered the information that he had been a member of the SED, albeit a critical one. "I was one of those who thought the system might still be capable of reform from within," he said. The *Ostsee-Zeitung*, with its mouthwatering local circulation of 250,000 (the same as the population of its home town – one subscriber for every eight people living in MWP) had been the official paper of the administration of the Rostock *Bezirk*, the Party organ. When the *Wende* came at the end of 1989 the journalists got together and elected a new editor, Gerd Spilker. They knew they would have to fight to hang on to their huge circulation, the result of an effective monopoly now vanished. The Springer Press group, west Germany's and Europe's biggest, had already begun to invest in the paper before the Treuhand considered how to dispose of it. The four largest west German press groups had descended on the newly liberated but uncertain east German newspapers. "This has helped a lot of papers to make the transition to the latest technology, but I don't think it's a healthy trend from the point of view of having a genuinely free press, which must mean variety of ownership as well as titles. It could just become an extension of the cosy, unofficial cartel which operates in the west," Schröder said. I was to learn more about the paper's position when I went to visit its head office.

Of all the problems of the West Pomeranian area the most pressing, economically and environmentally, was the nuclear power station at Lubmin outside Greifswald, the only full-scale and functioning one built by the GDR. Rheinsberg, the first, completed by 1965, was small, essentially experimental, and the third, at Stendal in Saxony-Anhalt, had not reached the production stage. All three faced shutdown, partial if not total, temporary if not permanent. As happened when the British government decided to privatise the electricity industry, the nuclear sector had to be left out of the arrangements for denationalising the east German power supply because it was not economically viable on its own. The fact that it did not meet west German safety standards either may have doomed it altogether, although there was talk of keeping the newest facilities going if they could be made to meet west German regulations (reputedly the world's strictest) or adapted in some way, if only for research. Meanwhile the three east German nuclear plants were handed over to a new joint-stock company, Energiewerke Nord A G, controlled by the Treuhand and entirely separate from the Berlin-based Vereinigte Energiewerke A G, which manages the conventional plants due to be converted from lignite to oil as soon as possible.

The first reactor of the four built in phase one of the development of Greifswald went on stream on 18 December 1973 and the fourth in 1979. For the next eleven years Greifswald and Rheinsberg supplied up to 12% of the GDR's electricity (oil accounted for less than 4%, hydroelectricity 1.5% and lignite the rest). From 1983 the town relied on its nuclear power station for all its distant heating and in 1989 the first of four new reactors planned for phase two went critical for the first time; the other three, which would have enabled it to supply a quarter of east Germany's electricity, were still under construction until the *Wende*, as were the first two at Stendal. All work on these has stopped, and on 18 December 1990 Greifswald was taken out of the national grid, its usable reactors completely shut down. An oil-fired power station was put up in four months outside the gates of the Greifswald plant to take over its work; otherwise there would have been no winter heating in the area.

The imminent loss of 4,700 jobs at the nuclear plant could only be a crushing blow to a town of less then 64,000 people in a part of the country where alternative sources of employment are even less obvious than elsewhere. The local port and associated economic activity, food production, clothing, construction and outdated information-electronics industries are not up to such a task. The loss of the massive investment in Lubmin only compounds what amounts to a social and economic tragedy, in which Greifswald was damned if it carried on with nuclear power and no less damned if it did not.

Somewhat removed from these problems, but with not a few of its own, is Greifswald University, founded in 1456 and as such the oldest on former Prussian territory (as the town once was). It is also the smallest in the ex-GDR and in all Germany with just 4,000 students (German universities tend to be colossal: Bonn, for example, is ten times the size of Greifswald). Even so, it was the only university in the GDR which offered the entire spectrum of mathematical and physical science. Its main building is a very handsome, purpose-built, lilac baroque affair; this and its various annexes suggested that this "Uni" could be a very pleasant place at which to study. Amazingly, until the end of 1990, it employed a total of more than 5,000 people, including 1,400 academics, and ran a "clinic" (i.e. a full-blown hospital) with 1,500 beds. This was an extreme case of the kind of feather-bedding which was universal in the GDR, where economic activity and social provision were inextricably linked; large institutions became almost self-contained socio-economic entities whose budgets were determined by the regime without reference to market forces.

I was given these figures by Dr Siegfried Lotz, mathematician and the spokesman for the new Rector, Professor Dr Hans-Jürgen Zobel (a theologian elected to public office, like so many other east Germans with church connections, for his politically clean hands). Dr Lotz, who has a cosy study bulging with books and papers under the roof of the main building, was just recovering from the trauma of *Abwicklung*, the "deconstruction" of ideologically suspect or superfluous departments. The university had formally been taken over by the new MWP *Land*-government, which decided to close two departments: Marxist-Leninist studies, including the associated Economic Sciences Institute, and Socialist Factory Management with its section of the same Institute. The Disaster-Medicine department would also go as part of a rationalisation of MWP's medical schools. Further, the Institutes for Educational Psychology and Counselling, for Teacher Training, for Philosophy and a sports institute were to be reconstructed, or else dissolved and their functions reassigned. This did not mean, I learned, that students would be cut off in mid-course and thrown out; they would instead be reallocated to reorganised or different departments. Staff would be pensioned off if old enough, or else reassigned or given long notice. "Passengers" on the old pay-roll would, as elsewhere all over the former GDR, have to get off the gravy-train and make their own way. "It was obvious that this kind of thing could not possibly continue," said Dr Lotz. "But there are people here now who would accept the return of the Berlin Wall if it meant they got their old social security back."

Protests by students and academics against *Abwicklung* took place in Leipzig, Berlin and other places while I was in east Germany. Their object was not to preserve Marxist-Leninist studies and the like, but to oppose state interference in the running of the universities. Dr Lotz acknowledged that there was no euphoria at Greifswald about this interventionism – on the contrary – but the university had been obliged by law to meet a turn-of-the-year deadline for completing its arrangements for *Abwicklung*, which in itself was only the beginning. The new state government was planning a law governing the entire future organisation of tertiary education in MWP and was collecting opinions before tabling it in the Schwerin parliament because there was a great deal of controversy on the subject. Dr Lotz thought the eagerly awaited new budget for the university would have a bigger effect on it than the *Abwicklung* process. Three expert committees, including west German advisers as well as east German academics, would reorganise the education, psychology and philosophy departments and the university as a whole. "There are going to be some very difficult personnel decisions about the future of people associated with the SED. Quite a few of its members were actually decent people, you know. Lots of people have their little secrets, but we must hope that the necessary task of restructuring doesn't become a witch-hunt. The political and spiritual readjustment we have to make is a lot harder than our day-to-day work, which is tough enough at present. We are having to learn or relearn to be professional academics; we too have to adjust to the new conditions, the only way we'll ever have prosperity here."

The university is geographically the remotest in Germany and during the GDR period it was also largely isolated from the intellectual mainstream of the free world, its academics (including a few of world repute in their fields) unable to travel at will, if at all, and hemmed in by a closed society. Some progress had already been made with the acquisition of previously unobtainable books and equipment, and a little extra money was coming in from western foundations even before the new budget was known. "If we have to sell ourselves," said Dr Lotz, "I think we can make something out of the smallness and unique intimacy of the place." If that means more attention to the personal academic and social needs of students it would be no bad thing: British universities score most heavily over their German counterparts in this area. One reason why German students spend so long at university is that they have to use so much time orienting themselves and coping with the often highly impersonal academic bureaucracy.

So far I had explored coastal MWP east of Rostock. My plan to drive the 120 kilometres or so from there to Lübeck on the former west German border had to be given up about halfway, when I had reached Wismar after two and a half hours. Even though the sun was out and the road was bone-dry, sheer weight of traffic on the B105/E22 slowed us all to a crawl on a single-track, two-lane highway in serious need of modernisation.

Wismar was the GDR's second port (after Rostock) and long ago a Hansa city, a shipbuilding centre where huge blue cranes towered over the northern part of town. The very large and graceful market-place was obscured by acrid clouds of brown coal smoke issuing from the chimney of the municipal offices. Wismar joined Lübeck and Rostock in 1259 as a founder-member of the Hanseatic League. The town belonged to the Swedes from 1653 to 1803, when they leased it back to Mecklenburg; it was legally restored to Germany only in 1903. It was another one of those places which it was virtually impossible to enter legally in a car. It was also the only place in east Germany where I was issued with a parking ticket (DM30 for parking on a tatty piece of grass like everybody else). I await the extradition proceedings with interest. There was no other reason to remember Wismar.

I struggled back eastward along the coast road as far as Neubukow, a nondescript village with one claim to fame: it was the birthplace of Henrich Schliemann, the man who found Troy and to whose exploits we shall return: his memorial seemed an awfully long way from the Museum Island in Berlin (and rather further from Troy). Here I thankfully turned down a minor road which promised to take me to the main Baltic sea-side resorts along the Mecklenburg Bight. The biggest of these is Kühlungsborn, which looked very much like an early nineteenth-century coastal spa in terminal need of a coat of paint. Most resorts, from the Venice Lido to Llandudno, look pretty grim when deserted in midwinter, but Kühlungsborn was the most decayed example I have ever seen, with one dreary, shuttered hotel after another. Even the public lavatory was padlocked, driving me to antisocial emergency measures (there was absolutely no danger of being seen in this windblown ghost town). Now that east Germans were belatedly discovering the delights of Mallorca and Tenerife, I did not fancy the chances of a place like this when the west German seaside resorts had so much more to offer (at a price, admittedly). A mighty vote of confidence as well as a massive investment would be needed to regenerate the place, even if it does have four kilometres of clean, sandy beach behind a sandbar.

Heiligendamm is the oldest German seaside resort, which opened for business in 1793, an outlying suburb of Bad Doberan, the summer residence of the dukes of Mecklenburg-Schwerin. Heiligendamm was launched by Duke Friedrich Franz I, who was advised by his doctor to take to the water. Once past the tastefully positioned heating-plant to one side of the road, the village looked well kept. You reach the splendid, curved and sheltered beach through trees 500 metres off the through-road. There are – or were – several pleasant-looking sanatoria and convalescent homes "for workers"; one hopes a way will be found to enable east Germans of modest means to continue to come to such charming spots.

The forest gives the impression that this is lakeside rather than seaside and the atmosphere is only slightly dampened by a loud noticeboard with a list of rules and restrictions. The Wall-orientated Germans have a habit which fills the average foreigner with amazement or rage, depending on when he gets to the beach. They build themselves a *Strandburg* (beach fort), a carefully made wall of sand firmed up with water and even decorated with seashells, which is their inviolable territory for the day. The Dutch in particular take a very dim view of this practice on their beaches and tend to kick the walls over, which can be deleterious to international relations. Rule number four said: "Beach forts must – insofar as their construction is territorially permitted – be at least two metres away from the dunes! Undergrowth and flotsam and jetsam must not be utilised for the construction of forts!" Have a nice day, I thought. The call for "environmentally conscious conduct" should have been returned to sender long ago. I was slightly startled when a nun popped out of the wood with a man, but I later discovered there was a cemetery nearby. There could hardly be a nicer setting for it (the cemetery, that is).

Bad Doberan (a *Bad* because of its purportedly health-giving, natural mud baths) is unusual for having a delightful, narrow-gauge steam railway to Kühlungsborn running along the streets in the heart of town, the first English-style race course ever built on the Continent (1807, the Duke again) and a huge, fourteenth-century brick minster built by the Cistercians and unique in the entire Baltic region. The village's central open space is called the Kamp (Low German for a field) and is unusual for being grassed and triangular. It is described in the guide books as "a park in the English style" but once again struck me as coming from that England I had unaccountably missed. This may refer to two graceful "Chinese" pavilions on the Kamp; they and Heiligendamm once made Doberan the modish German equivalent of Regency Brighton. The handsome buildings round the Kamp date from the beginning of the last century and were used by the Duke and his family and guests in summer. Altogether it was an exceptionally pleasant town.

Having been a journalist for more than a quarter of a century and still practising on an irregular, part-time basis, I am inclined, on going to a part of the world of which I know little or nothing, to barge into the local newspaper office and pick the brains of its occupants. In my experience they are collectively omniscient and in touch with the people as nobody else, including local politicians and municipal employees – and even the ubiquitously quoted taxi-driver. That is their job, and especially in unfree societies they usually know far more than they can print. Only their readership knows more, but, unlike a newspaper, is not organised for the dissemination of information. On the other hand, if a journalist relies too much on other journalists for his information, there is an incestuous element to his work. He risks paying too little attention to the real world with its less articulate but real people. I wandered into the *Leipziger Volkszeitung* because I wanted to include at least one newspaper among my collection of institutions; I called on Herr Laasch, one of two deputy editors of the *Ostsee Zeitung* in Rostock, because I had an introduction from Herr Schröder, who worked under him. But this courtesy call turned into a two-hour *tour d'horizon* not only of the problems of the east German press but also of east Germany as a whole.

We talked of newspapers first. Herr Laasch, in his mid-thirties, is married to a radio journalist who was about to go back to work from full-time mothering of their small child. She comes from Berlin and that is where they lived and he worked until July 1990, when he answered the call to return home to his old paper, to take charge of its all-important regional coverage. As a Party organ it had enjoyed a monopoly circulation of just over 300,000, even though newsprint had been rationed (and the contents, if like that of the other SED papers I used to see in the bad old days, was doubtless extremely tedious).

"As journalists we used to go in for tightrope-walking. Some exploited the admittedly rare possibilities to the limit, but the Party kept a very close watch on everything that went in. Some subjects were just never touched. Younger colleagues tried to push back the frontiers; older ones found it harder and harder to resist the pressure. It was a kind of schizophrenia. For example, we knew, when the government ordered all factories to devote five per cent of production to consumer goods, that one of the results was a huge and useless glut of lawn-mowers, but we were prevented from reporting it," said Laasch. "People at the deep-sea fishery would tell me they were ten days ahead of their catching norm, but in fact they were ten days behind. People lied to you to protect themselves, and you knew they were lying, and you lied as well, to the readers, because you didn't have the choice if you wanted a quiet life. The Party used to interfere in the tiniest details of news coverage."

Herr Laasch felt the region was faced with imminent economic disaster. Agriculture, fishing and shipbuilding were all terribly vulnerable. Nuclear energy was as good as dead. Food and fish would go under because of the European Community regulations which were introduced overnight. MWP had been swamped by western fish, though those which could be caught on the doorstep were just as good and rather fresher. The farms had the same problem. There was also serious local pollution in the Baltic and on land, as well as a lack of investment and the closely related problem of countless claims for the return of property, which came up so often in my travels. Most of the shipbuilding had been for the Soviet Union, notably deep-sea fishery vessels, but the arrival of the D-mark and the departure of the transfer-rouble had probably killed that market. The related unemployment problem was exacerbated by the fact that all plants kept huge stocks as a cushion against shortages – and also retained extra staff and storage space to service them. MWP had obvious prospects of tourism, but the infrastructure was a disaster crying out for improvement, and standards would have to be raised in most hotels, restaurants and other services.

Local telephone lines were so bad that fax-machines and modems for computer transmissions would not work properly; fortunately old-technology teleprinters do work. When there was a big fire in Wismar the local brigade tried to telephone for help from Lübeck and Stralsund but could not get through to either. There is an estate of 40,000 people on the edge of Rostock – nearly one sixth of the population – and they had just four public telephones, of which one worked. "Private phones? Don't make me laugh! We need a decade to catch up with the demand for phones . . . And we must have an east-west autobahn to replace that awful coast road. At present all transit traffic has to come through Rostock . . . And so long as nobody knows what is going to happen to their homes, their factories, their jobs, nobody is going to take any chances and nothing much is going to get started. There are so many past injustices to correct as well," said Herr Laasch, producing a cutting revealing a police racket in the 1950s – Operation "Rose" – which had hotel-owners expelled from the GDR on spurious allegations of speculation or black-marketeering so that the regime could take over the premises.

In the local economy not everything was black. Rostock had won over a shipping line from west German Travemünde because the port was better placed to serve eastern Scandinavia and the Soviet Union. These were the links on which Rostock needed to concentrate. The arrival of the D-mark had caused the cancellation of a lot of contracts with the Comecon countries, which could not afford the hard-currency prices – "and the Soviet Union, which has terrible problems of its own, no longer has the political motivation to keep us going, as it did in the GDR days. It used to take everything we could make here, even if it wasn't up to western standards. Mind you, our ships were very good, but they were also heavily subsidised. We had to pay a lot for Soviet oil, but we didn't have to pay in dollars as one does on the world market, but in transfer-roubles. We also had to take a lot of lousy Soviet goods in barter deals or part-payment for our exports, such as buses which never worked properly. We had to send builders to the Soviet Union to build shops there, though we desperately needed new shops ourselves. On top of that, money that should have been spent on development here and all over the country was swallowed up by the insatiable needs of Berlin. One result is that we have a quarter of a million people here and 40,000 of them are in the queue for new homes because what they have now is grossly inadequate."

Herr Laasch was warming to his multiple theme, speaking at machine-gun speed. What, I managed to ask, about the future? "What indeed!" he fired back. "This year [1991] is going to be the worst. We have to survive this year and then, with luck, it can only get better. But it is going to be bad. We ourselves, as a paper, will probably be all right. We are being paid about sixty per cent of western rates, which is better than most people get here and is fair for the moment. We have developed a partnership with the *Lübecker Nachrichten*, a newspaper in which the Springer group has a minority holding, and we hope the connection will enable us to re-establish our position." The *Ostsee Zeitung* had new technology and the advantage of habit among readers, with 245,000 subscribers (who could not, however, be taken for granted). "We must expect some new rivals, which is fair enough, but we are at home here – even if we have to charge fifty rather than fifteen pfennigs a copy nowadays."

The main psychological requirement was that people had to change their habits of thought after forty years of SED Socialism. "We have to realise, like any business, that we have to supply a service to customers with a choice, and we aren't used to that in these parts. We still have too many of the old bosses in new jobs. People get very angry indeed when they are sacked by these characters, who have done very nicely, thank you, out of the *Wende*. Some of them behave like old Manchester capitalists. And people are coming over from the west and buying up land and everything else they can, cheap, unless the local authorities manage to prevent it."

Herr Laasch thought people would soon get the message that their future depended on hard work – if they find or keep a job – which had not been the case before. Meanwhile the *Ostsee Zeitung* was one of the few enterprises recruiting: sales and advertising staff as well as journalists. "We can't find many qualified people locally, and if we get them from outside the city we can't find them anywhere to live. And if we do finally manage that, public transport fares have more than doubled, so everybody is switching to cars – which means Rostock is blocked solid half the day with no bypass to ease the jams . . ."

Fortunately both of us had to move on to other appointments, because by this stage my wrist was seizing up and my internal translation-computer was overheating. "We have an enormous amount of frustration to contend with but if we get the investment in the infrastructure, we'll survive. I'm not moving: I like it here," said Herr Laasch as he showed me to the stairs.

Northerly Rostock, its character informed by water, unsurprisingly emerged as the most attractive city of the ex-GDR in my entirely subjective opinion (Berlin being in a category of its own as far as I am concerned). It has terrible traffic jams and its fair share of other east German urban problems arising from chronic under-investment, neglect, poor housing, pollution and rustbelt industry. But the architects let loose on rebuilding the centre were or are several cuts above those who drearified other GDR cities. As a key Baltic port Rostock was severely bombed in 1942 and a major reconstruction began ten years later. The Lange Strasse (long street) which runs west from the looming and forbidding Marienkirche to the impressive Kröpelin Gate (under restoration) is lined by tall brick buildings, mostly modern, with understated Gothic references.

To the south and running parallel is the pedestrianised Kröpelinerstrasse, rather more than a kilometre long, most attractively restored and, where necessary, rebuilt. The new buildings inserted in the gaps left by the bombing are obviously modern, yet do not obtrude from the narrow, gabled, older houses. Halfway along this principal shopping street is the University, founded as the first in northern Europe in 1419 and soon known as "the light of the North". It consists now of a converted baroque palace (1714) and several imposing nineteenth-century buildings originally put up for various other purposes, including a guardhouse and a court, plus a library with 1.6 million books. In the little square round which these are grouped is a statue of Rostock's most famous son, Field-Marshal Prince Blücher, who set the seal on Wellington's final defeat of Napoleon at Waterloo in 1815 (thus avenging the French occupation of Rostock in 1806).

The strategic importance of the harbour, on the River Warnow some twelve kilometres from the open Baltic, is shown by the list of powers which occupied and/or ruled it over the centuries, including the Slavs, the Hanseatic League, Imperial troops and then the Swedes in the Thirty Years' War, Danes, Swedes again, Russians, Prussians and Mecklenburgers. The Swedes occupied Rostock's outlying port, originally a fishing village, at Warnemünde and exacted a toll on passing ships, which ruined the local economy in the eighteenth century, though not for the first time – and clearly, as the magnitude of the post-union crisis in the ex-GDR became clear in 1991, not the last.

The city centre, which still has much of its medieval wall, also boasts two former monastery churches and two others; all are rather more inviting than the Marienkirche, which looks neglected (but houses an astronomical clock dating back to 1472 with a built-in calendar valid until the year 2017). Among several other interesting and well-restored old buildings, pride of place must go to the originally thirteenth-century *Rathaus* with the seven towers of its Gothic façade looking over the pillared baroque extension covering the main entrance. Rostock has a sevenfold obsession with the number seven: according to an ancient rhyme the Marienkirche had seven doors, the market-place linked seven streets, the city had seven gates and seven quays, seven towers and seven bells on its *Rathaus*, and seven lime trees in its park.

None of this brought it much luck in 1990 and 1991, when it lost its role as the GDR's principal port and link with the outside world: for forty-five years it was protected from having to compete against the west German Baltic and North Sea ports. Now it will be limited to exploiting its proximity to Denmark, Sweden and the Soviet Union, always assuming the latter's trade with Germany can be revived. When I was in Rostock, the last seventy-eight Trabis were shipped from the huge quayside car-park to Poland. Another 999 plus 732 Wartburgs had been sold to Bulgaria and, when they were shifted, the park would be empty.

Norsk Hydro, Norway's multinational chemical company, moved in to buy the Rostock fertiliser plant, founded in 1905 as the world's first producer of nitrate fertilisers and now the biggest of its kind in the world, for DM75 million. The region's truck-drivers, however, brought Rostock and several other towns in MWP to a standstill in protest against alleged official slowness in delivering promised alternative work for what they used to do for the local VEBs. The one-hour warning strike was organised by the western public service and transport union, the ÖTV; its effects were staggering and many people feared that this was just a foretaste of what might happen later in 1991, when unemployment was due to reach levels unheard of even in the Slump, which did so much for Hitler's career.

Despite all this, Rostockers found the time to engage in a particularly lively debate on the renaming of their streets, a subject which aroused interest all over the east. Lots of letters reached the *Ostsee Zeitung* and the city council, not only seeking the removal of the repetitive and limited Communist repertoire but also objecting to the imposition of its west German equivalent. The Ernst-Thälmann-Platz should not be restyled Bismarck, but rather Lloydplatz in honour of the independent north German maritime company, they said. A lot of people took exception to the idea of an Adenauerplatz because the first West German Chancellor had no connection whatsoever with Rostock. What was more, one indignant citizen wrote, "he was one of those who brought on the division of Germany under which we in particular suffered here". There was a widespread feeling that the money would be better spent on cleaning up the city, and many people reasonably objected to the bureaucratic consequences: they would have to get all their official documents – identity card, driving licence, car registration – changed yet again, as if they did not already have enough to do.

The first car registration in Rostock under the west German system introduced on January 1 (with two years' grace for conversion of number-plates) conferred the proud number HRO-AI upon Frau Heidi Stein's Volkswagen Golf. The 'H' stands for Hansestadt, Hanseatic city, as in HB for Bremen, HL for Lübeck and HH for Hamburg. Her son Thomas, a twenty-three-year-old medical student on vacation from Cologne University, was taken aback to be confronted by a big bunch of flowers and a "photo opportunity" for the local media when he received the certificate after queueing all night. When the doors opened, some 400 people had lined up, but the officials could cope with less than twenty applicants an hour. Sadly a man of fifty-nine dropped dead in the queue, from a heart-attack. All this was more evidence that the east Germans were as much in love with the motor-car as their western fellow citizens had ever been. After the *Wende* many east Germans scrapped their smaller number-plates in favour of the west German type, even though they had to rest content with their GDR numbers until 1991 arrived – whereupon they had to buy another new pair of plates.

Something else about to be thrown away during my time in Rostock was one of the city's and the GDR's few positive contributions to environmental protection, the Rostocker Rohstoff-Recycling GmbH, privatised successor to the Rostocker Sekundär-Rohstoff VEB (SERO for short, secondary raw material). The SED regime was, as has been seen, not user-friendly and indeed showed acute symptoms of the arrogance of office when it came to the needs and desires of the people, which it ignored whenever possible. But it was also desperate for foreign exchange, which led it a long way down the road of import substitution (an environmental disaster, admittedly, when it came to preferring local brown coal to imported oil). But one unquestionably beneficial, not to say exemplary, result was the creation of SERO VEBs all over the country.

Their job was to gather systematically all reusable materials for process-ing and recycling to industry; those who took the trouble to collect it and hand it over were paid by the kilogram for their trouble. This "secondary raw material" saved the state hundreds of millions of marks and involved far more than do-gooders collecting piles of bottles and wandering down to the bottle-bank in the Volvo in order to feel virtuous for the rest of the weekend. Glass, paper, metal, wood, rubber, plastic and reusable scrap of all kinds, even rags and bones, were gathered and recycled on a scale matched by few if any countries. Contributing to this admirable good housekeeping became effectively a social duty for which Party organisations awarded the Communist equivalent of Brownie points.

East Germany acquired a massive rubbish disposal crisis within months of the *Wende* as people bought the new western goods with their fancy wrapping. They also scrapped Trabis in favour of western cars, threw out old furniture so they could spend their converted savings on mail-order substitutes and threw away the piles of new junk mail, doubtless drinking from throwaway cans or non-returnable bottles the while. The Treuhand seemed wedded to its philosophy of privatise or bust and would not give its blessing to a loan to tide the firm over and enable it to buy extra equipment. So when I was there it was about to go to the wall, even though it had lined up contracts from several municipalities to do what the defunct SERO VEB had done. Local organisations accused the Treuhand of refusing even to let a western waste-disposal firm take it over and of having set its face against the survival of the recycling industry. However, as the embattled GmbH was now receiving world-market prices for its scrap rather than the higher prices paid perforce by GDR plants, it could not afford to give even the tiniest token sum to local collectors. The privately run collection points therefore stopped taking any more rubbish, which had to be temporarily dumped in hundreds of containers along the coast instead. Private citizens were still collecting twice as much reusable refuse per head as the *Wessis* (who created several times more rubbish) but returning home frustrated after being sent away full-handed. Doubtless their zeal will fade very quickly. Of the 630 local SERO workers, nearly two thirds had lost their jobs by the end of 1990.

All in all the failure to safeguard, and indeed to imitate and expand, the GDR recycling network in the enlarged Federal Republic seems sin-gularly short-sighted. Free-market dogmatism is no less stupid than the totalitarian dogmatism of a command economy: the strengths and weaknesses of each system are secondary to the blind, doctrinaire application of either. Recycling should be seen as an essential public service in a place as polluted as east Germany and not treated like a "business" which must make a profit or be shut down.

Until I saw Schwerin I have to confess that I did wonder why Rostock, with twice the population, had not been made capital of MWP. The answer is that Schwerin looks like what it was and now is again – a capital city, albeit on a small scale, and it has the grand public buildings to go with the job. The oldest and stateliest town in the region, its present aspect derives from the decision of Grand-Duke Paul Friedrich in 1837 to take up residence here rather than in Ludwigslust to the south, where his forebears had spent most of the previous century. The magnificent palace, an irregular pentagon to fit its tiny island in Lake Schwerin, was done over in the middle of the last century as a faithful imitation of a French chateau of the late Renaissance (Semper of the Dresden Opera had a hand in this); it has a strong claim to be the poshest parliament in Germany now that the MWP state assembly sits there. On the "mainland" opposite are buildings which were put up for the grand-ducal court and now serve the state government as headquarters, with the Mecklenburg State Theatre and Museum buildings adjoining, and the thirteenth-century Gothic brick cathedral in the near background: altogether a very imposing place to walk around in the winter sun.

With the *Landtag* (state parliament) in session in the palace, I took in some of the debate on the financial disaster this *Land* (and the rest, together with the vast majority of municipal governments in the east) was facing in 1991. Little MWP's *Land* budget alone (i.e. excluding those of local councils) was likely to have a deficit of DM3 billion in 1991, the legislature was told. It was the ruling CDU, Chancellor Kohl's party, which introduced the emergency motion demanding more Federal aid, and all other parties supported it. Deputies had been looking at the small print of the West German constitution freshly extended to the east and focused on Article 107. This provides for a financial levelling of *per capita* resources among the *Länder* by a special law. MWP was not alone in wanting such a law passed as soon as possible, instead of having to rely on the German Unity Fund (a kitty to which Bonn and the western *Länder* contribute in aid of the east and which does not appear in the Federal budget, thus helping to fudge the true cost of unification), on unpredictable individual hand-outs from other *Länder* and panicky, one-off emergency payments from Bonn. When the new Federal Government finally presented its 1991 budget in February, it conceded that the election promise not to raise taxes to fund unity was dead and that heavy new imposts would have to take effect on the first anniversary of monetary union – 1 July 1991.

The political instinct which had so successfully inspired Dr Kohl to exploit both east German yearnings for freedom and the window of opportunity for union in Moscow did not extend to making a plan for the consequences. Those who admire the great German virtues of thoroughness and organisation will probably join me in finding this an omission staggering in its magnitude, yet not altogether surprising. Staggering because the disaster which so many economic experts in east and west (and abroad) saw coming was simply ignored in Bonn, except by the unfortunate SPD, which was promptly and unjustly condemned as killjoy, and even unpatriotic, for daring to mention the problems associated with instant union; unsurprising because Dr Kohl's traditional approach to a crisis always was to sit it out. This usually worked, if not like a charm, then like a wet blanket in such contexts as the Bonn cabinet, the CDU executive and the European Community, where in the end it defeated even the implacable Mrs Thatcher when she was premier.

However, in east Germany this immobilism, presented as unconditional trust in the free market and distrust of the economic planning which had brought the GDR so low, entailed millions of individual personal catastrophes for the new citizens of the Federal Republic. The captive east European markets to which the GDR had sold its exports were thrown away without a second thought. The cash, profits and indirect taxes which flowed west in huge amounts as the east Germans went on their spending spree stayed mostly in the west. The colossal subventions which Bonn paid to West Berlin, to areas along the old inter-German border, and even to industries which needed a hand after the war but surely not in the 1990s, continued for the time being instead of being switched wholesale to where they are most needed – the new *Länder*. Their GDP looked set to fall to half its 1989 level in 1991. To judge by the instant recovery of the SPD and the slump of the CDU in the Hesse and Rhineland-Palatinate state polls within months of the "unification election" triumph of 2 December 1990, the CDU's fortunes in 1991 were also set to revert to 1989 levels, when nobody would have given a pfennig for Dr Kohl's chances of re-election until the east German revolution saved him. His government's failure to anticipate the collapse in the ex-GDR – and I believe it is that rather than suppression for electoral gain (even if the latter was hardly absent!) which was the main problem – seems a poor reward indeed for the almighty boost which the east Germans gave him as the lucky incumbent at the moment they jumped to freedom and landed in the Federal Republic.

Nowhere was likely to be worse affected than Rostock, which is why I arranged (for once) to visit the Deutsche Maschinen und Schiffbau AG (German engine and shipbuilding, formerly VEB-Kombinat Schiffbau), the town's and the state's biggest employer with 46,000 then still on the payroll (many on "short time") and facilities all along the coast. However the company spokesman, Herr Dietrich Strobel, personally charming, was quintessentially east European in his approach to information. He would have made an exemplary spokesman for the British Home Office: the Prisons Department has a remarkably similar outlook. I cannot blame him for declining to speculate about the combine's future, which was completely incalculable but decidedly unpromising at the time; yet he had precious little to say about the present either. So we had a polite conversation about the past, including naval history, trade in the Baltic and reparations to the Soviet Union after the war, and I came away with one more bundle of paper.

There is not much industry in MWP, and DMS-AG accounted for one industrial job in four in the state. Small wonder that the Chief Minister, Dr Alfred Gomolka, was elected to the supervisory board of the holding company. Its principal works were at the old Neptun yard in Rostock and three other yards in Rostock, Wismar and Stralsund; in all DMS had twenty-four plants, newly reorganised as subsidiary companies. The GDR built up this industry effectively from scratch to pay off part of its Soviet reparations with ships, to acquire a merchant fleet of its own and to earn hard currency in the West with cut-price ships. West Germany meanwhile, from 1975, slashed its shipbuilding capacity by more than half to 700,000 tons, production-time by three quarters and the workforce by more than three fifths to about 30,000. This makes the DMS payroll at the turn of the year 1990–91 look grossly inflated, but it included the staffs of polyclinics, holiday homes, even horticultural and children's nurseries, as well as the usual extra staff needed to cope with shortages of materials and services and to make the required contribution to consumer needs. (All

GDR plants in latter years were compelled to divert a minimum of five per cent of output to consumer goods; DMS thus got into various forms of metal-bashing, including making caravans, furniture, refrigerators and even truck-trailers for distributing goods.) But its main trade was ship-building, and up to eighty per cent of that was for the Soviet Union. Of the 1.6 million tons of shipping on the stocks, seventy-five per cent was still for the Russians. The contracts were drawn up on the basis of 4.67 east-marks to the transfer-rouble, amended to DM2.34 in the second half of 1990, after German monetary union – i.e. hard currency, which is in very short supply in the Soviet Union. The rate was due to fall by an unspecified amount thereafter.

Even though one Soviet fishing vessel in three, including those in the largest classes, comes from Stralsund in MWP, there was no guarantee that the Russians would be able or wish to pay in hard currency for ships even if tailor-made for them. There is no alternative buyer. DMS was therefore burdened with a potential total debt in lost or loss-making contracts, losses on deliveries of materials and money owed to the banks, of DM6 billion – in a murderously competitive industry where many governments notoriously pay their shipyards huge subsidies and their workers low wages. The rump of a shipbuilding industry survives in west Germany because the three remaining builders went up-market with high technology; DMS did not need to, being geared to its own market, the Soviet Union, just as the exports of so many other east German under-takings used also to be tied to eastern Europe.

Surely it was not beyond the wit of Bonn to have found a way to hang on to these markets, at least transitionally, to give the GDR economy, so obviously wide open to annihilation by western competition, the chance of a soft landing? This could have been done by formalising political unification – say in a confederation – well before, rather than almost immediately after, monetary and social union. Such minimal political union would still have secured the release of the GDR from the Soviet bloc to the FRG, which undoubtedly had to be done as quickly as possible while the chance existed. Economic union could then have been organised in phases, during which the east Germans would have had their freedom of speech and travel, and could have been supplied with judicious quantities of hard currency to satisfy all reasonable material desires. That would have been much cheaper than the ocean of money, ultimately calculable in trillions of marks, now needed to keep the ex-GDR afloat in a chaotic sea of troubles. Such thoughts are not hindsight: plenty of experts advised such a course in advance, including those in New Forum and others who led the revolt against totalitarian rule in the GDR.

One may reasonably hark back to the breathtaking, but all too familiar, complacency of Bonn under Dr Kohl; one should also remember the spinelessness of the last, CDU-dominated, government of the GDR, which could surely have done more to protect its citizens from the economic and social hurricane which was to follow union. Its Prime Minister, Dr Lothar de Maizière (CDU), resigned as post-union minister without portfolio in the Kohl cabinet over allegations that he had been a Stasi informer. His east-CDU, having previously gone along with the SED regime, lay down in front of the Bonn steamroller. This is surely the most far-reaching example of how ruling elements of the old dispensation seamlessly transferred to the new – leaving ordinary citizens to suffer the pain of union. Much has been made of the fact that not one senior state post in united Germany – President, Speaker, Chancellor, Vice-Chancellor or one of the most senior ministries – went to an *Ossi* in what would surely have been an appropriate gesture. But one could also take the view that there was no deserving candidate after such a desertion of ordinary easterners by their homegrown leaders. The reward of Dr Günther Krause (CDU), the GDR's chief negotiator of the surrender which the Unification Treaty can now be seen to represent, was the Federal Ministry of Transport – a political bed of nails if ever there was one.

It was time, however, to move on, in response to the siren call of Saxony-Anhalt (the siren being of the species found on the factory roof rather than the Lorelei Rock). The logistical wheel of fortune had decreed that my headquarters for this last part of my anti-clockwise circuit round the former GDR would be Dessau, which was at least well situated for most of the places I needed or wanted to visit. I therefore took to the autobahn once again for the longest single run of the whole undertaking – 300 kilometres of mostly corrugated road, mercifully and unusually free of heavy traffic. I thus progressed more rapidly than I expected, which was comforting because the travelling was certainly more hopeful in this instance than the arrival.

– VI –

SAXONY-ANHALT

More history than most – Dessau – Bauhaus – Wittenberg – Luther again – the Harz – Magdeburg – how to start a government II – structures – old guard resists – PR man confesses – minister's poisoned chalice – filth trail – Halle – Altmark – Stend(h)al – Bitterfeld

– VI –

Saxony-Anhalt

As a political unit, unlike the other "new" *Länder* which are the reasonably faithful legacies of past provinces, fiefs or kingdoms, the reconstituted Saxony-Anhalt has a history of just seven years; its name has only five. Created in 1945, it was wound up with the rest in 1952, when the infant GDR took the view that the *Länder* might develop into alternative centres of power or loyalty and broke them up.

The historical paradox is that Saxony–Anhalt as a region actually has more "history" than the others. The western part was in Charlemagne's empire; Magdeburg and Halle, its biggest cities, date from the ninth century; and it was part of the first kingdom in the Empire, Heinrich I's Saxony, in the tenth. Divided among various bishops and princes, most of it fell to Prussia from the late seventeenth to the early nineteenth centuries (old German political boundaries kept changing because of the dynastic habit of dividing inheritances among all sons; there was no English law of primogeniture to keep estates together). Napoleon gave part of today's Saxony-Anhalt to his brother Jérome's Kingdom of Westphalia, but it went back to Prussia again after Waterloo. The small but influential principality of Anhalt with its capital at Dessau, seat of the powerful Ascanian margraves and princes who fought the Slavs and ruled Brandenburg before the Hohenzollerns, managed to retain a separate identity for seven centuries from the Middle Ages until 1945, when it was lumped together with Prussia's Province of Saxony.

In the south-eastern corner of the old-new *Land*, at Torgau on the Elbe, the American and Russian armies linked up amid jubilant scenes marking the death of the Third Reich. The north is the rural and sparsely populated Altmark, the old border region west of the Elbe which was the launch-pad for the German (re)conquest of Brandenburg and points east and more recently the home of a spanking new nuclear power-station (at Stendal, only partly built). When the Russians dismantled Prussia in 1947, the region's name was changed to Saxony-Anhalt. In 1952 it was divided into the two *Bezirke* of Halle and Magdeburg. Its principal modern claim to fame is singularly unhappy: the area round Halle, home town of the famous émigrés Georg Friedrich Händel (or George Frederick Handel, according to taste) and Hans-Dietrich Genscher, Bonn's Foreign Minister of unification, is the base of the GDR's notorious chemical industry and may be the most thoroughly polluted spot on the face of the earth. I was not keen to leave the ex-GDR on a depressingly low note; happily I didn't, even though my last call was at well-named Bitterfeld, probably the most devastated town of them all.

Dessau, eighty-five per cent destroyed by the RAF in March 1945, is a long, thin town on the busy B184 road from Magdeburg to Bitterfeld and stands close to the junction of the rivers Elbe and Mulde. In terms of ancient monuments it is of minimal interest. The rebuilt Bauhaus and associated modern buildings are of special interest, however, to those keen on twentieth-century architecture. After its foundation at Weimar and its eviction from there by local Philistines, Walter Gropius's Bauhaus school of architecture and the fine arts moved to a purpose-built structure at Dessau in 1925. This has been carefully restored and maintained as a prime example of its own unmistakable style and still functions as a fine-arts school. Before the Bauhaus architects were driven out again, to Berlin in 1932 (where they were soon shut down altogether in the Nazi drive against the artistic *avant-garde*) they designed a housing estate and several public buildings in the area, which can still be seen.

Dessau has no real centre, and its main hotel (where the Prussian roulette reservation system had allocated me a room on my last blind date with accommodational destiny), though clean and well run, is built internally like a student hostel, with vinyl floor-covering and chipboard furniture. The room heating was demented in its enthusiasm, running up amazing temperatures as a boiler somewhere below rattled itself to pieces round the clock. Fortunately it was so bitterly cold out of doors while I was in Saxony-Anhalt that I needed to open only two windows to be able to bear sleeping under the duvet, which had all the lightness and elegance of a sack of potatoes. The staff, who were unfailingly friendly and efficient, never forgot to remind me to let my tea draw in the morning. Dessau was undoubtedly the most boring of the six places I stayed in during my explorations, so I spent as little time there as possible.

Lutherstadt Wittenberg, as the GDR officially styled it, in the same way as the English do not refer to Augustine-city Canterbury or Shakespeare-town Stratford, requires an act of faith if you approach it from Dessau, about thirty kilometres to the west along the B187. The road is lined with one heavy industrial plant after another, a huge rubber works, a big nitrate plant, a filthy confectionery factory and so on. Was there any point in pressing on to the centre? Given the historical significance of the place, and how readily it could have been preserved as a jewel of a town with all its monuments, it is hard to understand the minds of those who allowed these stinking factories to spring up on its downwind outskirts (although it has been noted above that the GDR only came late, albeit all the more enthusiastically, to the idea of making the most of Luther).

As the capital of the Wettin dynasty which held the Saxon electorate in the late Middle Ages, Wittenberg flourished in the reign of the Elector-Prince Friedrich the Wise from 1486. The name is however Flemish, because Flemings settled the place in the Middle Ages. In 1508, six years after Friedrich opened the university, Brother Martin Luther of the Augustinians came to study theology. Four years later he was teaching it as a professor. In 1517 he turned the world upside down when, according to legend, he nailed his famous "ninety-five theses", against the corrupt ecclesiastical confidence trick of selling "indulgences" absolving the buyer from punishment for past sin, to the door of the *Schloss* church. The famous door was lost in a fire but a bronze commemorative one stands in its place. The church of which it is a part is rather more impressive than the outwardly threadbare khaki remnant of the adjacent castle. Rebuilt a century ago, the church has a round tower, tall and stout with a spire on top of its dome and a "collar" with a Lutheran motto written round it in gold leaf. Inside are the graves of Luther and his friend and supporter Philipp Melanchthon (*né* Schwarzerd, black earth, which he translated into Greek) and a life-size statue of Friedrich the Wise who hid Luther in the Wartburg.

From the castle, the Schlossstrasse (or the parallel Dr-Richard-Sorge-Strasse, named after the anti-Nazi spy) leads you eastward to the nicely proportioned, square Marktplatz which has a fine, restored *Rathaus* and, looming behind it, the *Stadtkirche* (town church), the oldest building in

Wittenberg, where its famous adoptive son rattled the rafters with his sermons. Inside are works by Lucas Cranach the Elder and the Younger; the father was mayor of the town for seven years as well as portrayer of Luther, and the son was born here. Their neglected house was the subject of a local preservation campaign in 1991. Also born here was Wilhelm Eduard Weber, the inventor of the electric telegraph (who might have come in handy in the post-*Wende* communications crisis). The town was occupied by Napoleon's troops, and when the Prussians won it back they closed its university, amalgamating it with Halle's. Its position on the Elbe and good road and rail connections explain why Wittenberg became an industrial centre after Bismarck's unification.

Luther has a worthy principal memorial in the Lutherhaus Museum, the most important monument to the Reformation. This magnificent but not overlarge building, originally an Augustinian monastery and later the centre of the former university, stands round a courtyard which one crosses to get to the Museum and Luther's private apartments. Original manuscripts and first editions of all Luther's books are on show as well as his rooms and furniture, and many important contemporary paintings. A few steps westward along the Collegienstrasse is Melanchthon's more modest but no less well-tended house, the only sixteenth-century private house still standing in the battered town. It was a lovely, if bitterly cold, Saturday afternoon in Wittenberg and the place was completely dead, apart from a handful of western tourists and me. The town is deeply grimy, many of its tiled roofs showing powdery chemical deposits; even the carefully restored, seventeenth-century merchants' houses round the *Rathaus* were looking grubby as the *Wessis* and the Dutch dismantled the last market stalls and headed for home. Wittenberg badly needs a dose of the Weimar treatment because what happened here is no less important in German history. The diminution of local industrial activity at least offers the inhabitants' lungs a silver lining in the form of less polluted air.

On the Sunday I drove into the Harz Mountains, a region which was unevenly divided between the west and east Germans after the war, with the latter holding the lion's share of this popular holiday region. The border ran by the eastern village of Stapelburg on the B6, a strip of black ice that day; the village has disintegrating roads and indifferent houses, whereas the neighbouring western resort of Bad Harzburg has streets like carpets and houses glowing with fresh stucco.

I drove up a treacherous by-road to Elend because of its name: it means "misery", but does not live up to it, a pleasant village above the snowline. Schierke to the north-west came next, a true mountain resort with hotels and lots of people with sledges and skis.

A few miles further on in the same direction is the Brocken, at 1,142 metres the biggest mountain in these parts, slap bang on the old inter-German frontier. Before the *Wende* the Brocken was said to be the highest mountain in the world because it was unclimbable from east or west; each side used the mountain to spy on the other from sealed off installations. The air was so clear that my eyes hurt from the glaring snow, yet even up here on a cold and still winter's day there was the inescapable whiff of burning lignite.

On the way back down the winding B6 I passed through Wernigerode (one of many local places with names ending in *-rode*, which I believe means "clearing"; nearby is the quaintly titled Benzingerode which, as far as I could see, did not even boast a petrol pump). This town has a spectacularly beautiful little market-place lined with fairy-tale wattle and daub buildings including a lovely pink, yellow and black *Rathaus*. The partly medieval castle still stands guard above the town and houses a unique museum dedicated to the history of feudalism, seen by all good Communists as the direct ancestor of capitalism. The town is also the northern terminus of the narrow-gauge Harz Railway, which twists and turns for sixty kilometres (and four hours) through stunning scenery and forests to Thuringian Nordhausen in the south of the Harz Mountains.

Not far away to the north-east is Halberstadt, a name which seems to mean "half a town"; it was nearly no town at all because the GDR authorities began demolishing many old houses in its medieval heart just before the *Wende*, an act of official vandalism which was halted by a west German television exposé. Now the town looks as if it was recently bombed and only partly rebuilt, though the disproportionately large and handsome, unpaved central square (Domplatz) with a Gothic cathedral (*Dom*) at one end, a Romanesque basilica at the other and some delightful old houses in between, is fortunately intact. One of the latter contains an ornithological museum with 16,000 stuffed birds and a big library on the subject. The town was a religious centre from the ninth century and was badly bombed in 1945. The main buildings were restored, but in recent years the authorities apparently gave up the effort; medieval houses therefore crumbled and seemed to the official mind to cry out for demolition. In fact what was being built in their place in some parts of the demolished area was commendably harmonious in design. The gaps in the town map ought to be refilled and the entire place preserved.

One problem of this economically backward but beautiful area is the embarrassment of monumental and cultural riches it offers. Back on the B6 south-east of Halberstadt is the better-preserved Quedlinburg, which boasts a Renaissance castle plus several fine churches and religious foundations. The aforementioned Heinrich I, first King of Saxony, is buried here. Some of the town's lost treasure mysteriously turned up somewhere in Texas shortly after the *Wende*. German and American lawyers met on neutral ground in London and delicately negotiated its return. Other "lost" German artefacts have, since the revolution, been reappearing mysteriously in the United States, doubtless smuggled there by soldiers returning from the Second World War. Perhaps the collapse of Communism stirred a few old consciences.

In general the eastern Harz Mountains are bound to benefit from increased tourism from the west, which should justify the expense of the much-needed restoration work for these wonderful old towns and villages in one of the most attractive parts of Germany. Heartened by this lovely scenery, I was ready to confront the city of Magdeburg, capital of Saxony-Anhalt, first thing on Monday morning – even though 7,500 police had demonstrated there for better pay and conditions at the weekend, claiming that the state force had lost 3,000 officers and was fifty per cent under strength.

Dessau and Magdeburg are linked by about sixty-five kilometres of the B184, a journey which was to take me ninety minutes in each direction outside the rush-hour. This slow-motion experience is commonplace in Britain, but hardly on a road which is not especially overloaded with traffic. The unusual features of this stretch included the large number of busy level-crossings and the even larger number of Soviet Army convoys. I was mildly astonished not to witness an accident or its aftermath.

When I reached Magdeburg, it lived up to the impression I had fleetingly gained of it from railway journeys to and from Berlin over the years – a bleak and battered place, even in the sun which kindly shone throughout my days in Saxony-Anhalt. The *Rathaus* is not bad, there are a couple of impressive churches, including the cathedral, and one more kept as a ruin in memory of the war which devastated the centre. Most of it has been rebuilt in modern, windblown concrete with no trees; the Maxim

Gorki Theatre (sic) was presenting *Was ihr wollt* by W. Shakespeare, alias *As You Like It*. The British Army raced as far as here from Hamburg at the end of the war but withdrew in favour of the Russians. One of the few other decent buildings is the state chancellery, a former princely palace now serving the Chief Minister of the *Land*. It was there that I called upon Herr Michael Gentsch, the government spokesman.

A Bavarian of Thuringian ancestry with recent experience as spokes-man for the president of the West Berlin city parliament, Herr Gentsch said he had come to Magdeburg for the challenge; if all went well he would be happy to work there for ten years. The work had been so hard that it actually made him ill for a while – he is in his early thirties – but it was so obviously worthwhile. His large, parquet-floored office contained one desk, two chairs, a ladder, a map and stacks of newspapers round the walls. How, I asked once again, did one set about creating a state government from scratch?

"It works like a pyramid," Herr Gentsch said, "except that you start building it from the top." The parliament had been elected on 14 October 1990 and the CDU won the right to form a government. Dr Gerd Gies presented his CDU-FDP coalition cabinet on November 3. Fourteen state secretaries – heads of government departments – were appointed next. A personnel commission including coalition and opposition members and representatives from Lower Saxony, the western "partner *Land*", was working its way through the civil servants of the two GDR *Bezirke* now reunited in the *Land*, determining whose records were politically clean enough for their subjects to be re-employed. Magdeburg beat Halle to the status of capital because it said that it had the office space, but property claims turned this into a serious exaggeration. The fledgling government and the city council were desperately seeking more administrative space, which is why Dr Gies had to put off his first representative function – receiving the British Ambassador from Bonn – for more than a month, until his office was ready.

The former German-Soviet Friendship society, now renamed Inter-klub, was sitting on some much-needed offices; the state government hoped to winkle it out before 1991 was much older. "We got the Environment Ministry settled in first because its task is the most urgent." The least enviable ministry in all Germany snatched its offices from under the nose of the university. "We are having to improvise from day to day and fit in offices wherever we can. Meanwhile people from all over the place are asking us for statistics and information as if we had been functioning for decades," said Herr Gentsch. "Quite often they simply don't exist."

Saxony-Anhalt is unusually badly off in having only one western partner-state whereas most other new *Länder* have two or even three. And the partner, Lower Saxony, has an SPD-led government which is not madly keen to help a CDU-FDP one. Gentsch said it had unstintingly loaned plenty of valuable officials and advice, but was not exactly throwing its money about. But without the 500 borrowed civil servants very little would have been achieved. "Public finance as practised in the west is of course completely new here. The revenue and expenditure systems are extremely complex, and there is not much scope for the kind of buck-passing and figure-bending which used to go on under the old regime. The government exists to serve the people now, not the other way round, which for many takes some getting used to. Ordinary people here are still very submissive to authority."

Following the example of a number of western states, Saxony-Anhalt has been divided into three new administrative districts centred on Magdeburg, Halle and Dessau; below them are thirty-seven *Kreise* (small counties) and three city governments (the three just named). All these too were starting or restarting from the top of their respective pyramids and working downwards. Britons accustomed to an ever-centralising (but not overwhelmingly democratic) national government and ever more circumscribed local authorities will find this elaborate administrative structure in just one *Land* (population only three million) quite startling. However, the economic success and political stability of West Germany before union does rather suggest that the huge investment in local government pays off, not least because the Federal Government which sits on top of the heap tends to delegate decision-making as far down the scale as possible. This excellent principle has been given the singularly ugly name of "subsidiarity" in Brussels. One simply knows that Saxony-Anhalt will work well as soon as it gets the revenue and structural investment it needs, because the models it is copying work better than just about anyone else's. The Germans are obsessed with order, which is not always an unmixed blessing, but their proficiency at local government is among the most positive manifestations of this foible. And it is local government, down to the smallest municipality, which has always been the principle conduit of social and structural investment in west Germany.

Gentsch detected some resistance from the remnants of the old system. "It isn't necessarily deliberate, but . . ." Adaptation was much quicker at the political than the economic level, where it was noticeably slow, he thought. "Workers don't know their rights yet" – this from a declared political conservative; note the enviable consensual attitude, proof of the reality of the social market economy – "and some employers have gone over the top since the *Wende*, behaving like the worst nineteenth-century capitalists. Some old bosses went off and did a six-week management course and started issuing orders without regard to workers' rights." The staff were often too scared to assert themselves and lots of people had been sacked, even though the unification treaties specifically forbade this for six to twelve months after monetary union. Some parts of industry had "sunk into anarchy", though others continued to function more or less normally.

Herr Gentsch thought the Treuhand was overloaded at the second and third levels of management with bosses from the old regime, doubtless recruited for their knowledge of the ex-GDR but hardly likely to inspire confidence in a bewildered and insecure workforce. He saw this as a sign of how the old order was able to put up some resistance to the new; so was the slow and clumsy way the old "HO" – *Handelsorganisation* or trade organisation which ran shops, restaurants and hotels – was being broken up. Too many such places, having been privatised but still run by the same people, were gaining competitive advantages over new businesses. "The boards of some enterprises have stayed exactly the same after the change from VEB to GmbH – you can't expect the workers to like that, especially when it comes to mass dismissal notices. And western trade union officials who have come over here are quite depressed about the reluctance of people to stand up for themselves, even to speak out. But they are beginning to learn, and once it starts I'm sure it will be very fast, if only out of self-preservation. At the same time, when you meet people privately, one to one, you often find they can't stop talking. It is as if they need a catharsis for all their past sufferings – and for having done nothing to help themselves." Herr Gentsch has political ambitions; I shall not be surprised if he achieves them.

My next port of call could not fail to be the Environment Ministry: I wanted a briefing before I descended into the sump of Europe. My contact was Herr Johannes Altincioglu. If this name seems rather un-German, appearances do not deceive, even though its owner was born in Swabian Heilbronn, Baden-Württemberg. His parents were immigrants from a Christian minority in Turkey; their son had been "headhunted" for his unenviable but unquestionably challenging job as press officer. He was well suited in two senses: he came from the PR department of Mercedes-Benz and he had his clothes and shoes hand-made in London, he told me.

"It is a terrible list," he said. The north-south Halle-Merseburg axis with all the chemical works, Stendal with its nuclear plant, the nuclear waste dump near Helmstedt on the former border, the Eisleben-Halle-Bitterfeld east-west axis, the Mansfeld area at the eastern end of the Harz . . . "The situation is so desperate that about the first thing the new government here did was to take emergency measures. There are more in the pipeline. Laws are being drafted to tackle the problems more fundamentally. We are pressing not only Bonn but also Brussels for massive help because we can't possibly be expected to tackle something on this scale by ourselves. But don't forget we've got the Harz and a large number of animal and bird sanctuaries as well, even if we are the most polluted of all the states, new or old."

The emergency measures had already reduced water pollution by thirty and air pollution by eighty per cent, he claimed. Some of the offending plants had simply had to be shut down, but there had also been improvements in working practices and some reduction in the use of lignite, which was going to be phased out altogether as soon as possible. "We shall be going back to oil-burning for power, and we shall then have the latest anti-pollution technology." Meanwhile public education, recycling of industrial waste, free advice to factories and general dissemination of information designed to raise awareness of the environment at all levels was being organised throughout the state. The campaign had even been extended to Soviet officers as they prepared to take their troops home, so that their bases could be left in a decent condition and better run from an environmental point of view in the meantime. The Bundeswehr could do its bit in clearing former NVA sites before handing them to the civil authorities. Some areas left deserted because they were near the border offered chances to create more nature reserves.

"But no area in Europe, or at least western Europe, can be as bad as this," said Altincioglu. "We are lucky that Martin Bangemann [a German EC commissioner] comes from this region: he has a personal as well as a professional interest in our problems, so we are fairly optimistic about getting help from Brussels." Essentially, nothing whatsoever had been done for, and everything against, the environment of the Elbe-Saale river region for more than half a century, whether by the Nazis during the war or the Communists after it. "There are no water meters here, so everybody wastes it. Water used to cost nothing, not a pfennig. Some people are still in the same management or other executive jobs as before – how on earth are we going to get them to think completely differently about the environment?" Meanwhile the *Land* government was installing measuring devices all over the affected areas in order to quantify the horror as precisely as possible and establish where it is worst. Awareness was being raised in the schools, where it mattered most for the future. And all five east German environment ministers were meeting regularly to coordinate joint measures and exert combined pressure on Bonn and Brussels. "After all, the Elbe is already polluted [by Czechoslovakia and Saxony] before it gets here. Our problems are very different from those of the environment in the west."

It was hard to believe that Herr Altincioglu, an FDP member like his minister, Wolfgang Rauls, had only been in his strenuous job for five weeks. "Herr Rauls has the hardest ministerial post in the whole of Germany," said his chief spokesman almost proudly. "He is working twelve hours a day or more every day, and the staff are just as keen – not many of them take the whole of their thirty-minute lunch-break." The ministry had the best and newest building in the gift of the government and was furthest advanced in staffing, with seventy-seven out of 150 already recruited. "But we have the toughest and most urgent job." Thanks to the usual chronic housing shortage, the top personnel were living on three floors of a down-at-heel hotel previously favoured by itinerant building-workers. "But morale is very high," Altincioglu insisted. "East Germans are very good at improvisation, which I would not say is a typical German quality; but then they had to be in order to survive under the old regime." A good symbol of what his department and the new administrators of the ex-GDR are really up against was the gleaming new fax-machine in a corner of Altincioglu's ultra-modern office. "It's a cul-de-sac because most of the media organisations I deal with haven't got one, or else we find the telephone line is so bad that it doesn't work. So we are using it as a photocopier," he said. Doubtless Herr Genscher (also FDP) will not be backward in coming forward to speak out for his native *Land* in the Bonn cabinet.

I approached Halle from the north via the E51 autobahn, turning onto the B100, which comes from Bitterfeld and runs west-south-west into Halle. From there you take the B91 which runs due south through industrial southern Halle, then Schkopau, home of the notorious Buna works, then Leuna with its two vast chemical plants, then Merseburg and onward to Weissenfels, which proudly sells itself as "shoe metropolis of the GDR". After that, if one is really serious about having a good look at the quintessence of industrial rot, one can turn round and do the whole stretch in reverse order, as I did, so as not to have the morning sun in my eyes. It is only about forty kilometres each way. The sun was out, but there had been no wind for several days so a bright smog was brewing up over the entire area. It was actually possible, in a closed car, to taste the different flavours of the air from plant to plant because they stuck in one's throat and sinuses before being displaced by the next sample; and the air also varied in colour from place to place, doubtless depending on what was being pumped into it. Over Halle it was yellow-brown, over Schkopau at a distance it looked dark grey, with lighter grey plumes of steam set off against it. Outside the fug-belt the sky was its proper colour, a cloudless bright winter blue. I noticed that several standard yellow roadsigns with black letters, as used all over Germany, were turning white in the abrasive air. I wondered what this implied for the lungs of local residents and workers. I also wondered what this area had been like before Herr Altincioglu's emergency measures.

Many of the filth-producing plants in the Halle-Merseburg-Bitterfeld triangle used to belong to what has already gone down in history as the world's most infamous industrial company: IG Farben AG. IG stands for *Interessengemeinschaft* or "cartel", *Farben* means "dyes". This monopoly was created in 1925, in Weimar Republic days, out of Agfa, Bayer, BASF, Hoechst and others, a rationalisation to meet foreign competition. It made the Zyklon-B gas used to massacre the victims of Auschwitz; and it set up a branch of the Buna works of Schkopau next to the death camp in 1941–2 so that a total of 300,000 inmates could make synthetic rubber before they died; the factory itself actually worked 25,000 of them to death. IG Farben was the biggest single contributor to Nazi coffers and its synthetic oil and rubber technology, though uneconomic in free-market terms, helped the Wehrmacht to overcome Germany's lack of these commodities, so essential for waging modern war.

The western Allies broke IG Farben into its constituent parts in their zones of occupied Germany, thus enabling them to re-establish themselves among Germany's biggest companies and the world's most successful chemical and drug firms without the embarrassing legacy of the cartel's name (though to judge by the example of Siemens and others, the link with the camps would not necessarily have proved much of a disadvantage). But forty per cent of IG Farben was in the Soviet Zone and was nationalised without compensation. A "shell company" set up by the Allies therefore remained alive in the west, quoted on the Frankfurt stock exchange, just in case the chance ever came to repossess the rest of IG Farben. The day after the Berlin Wall opened, its shares started to climb steeply as various speculators (including London merchant banks with strong Jewish connections) bought into IG Farben AG i.A. (the last two initials stand for *in Abwicklung*, in dissolution). The company lodged restitution claims for the east German plants by the deadline of 13 October 1990. Since Soviet property seizures before the founding of the GDR are specifically excluded from restitution under the union treaty, the claims do not at first sight seem promising; but if that takeover and the subsequent handover to the GDR were done without formal paperwork, as may well be the case with some plants, the speculators could be in with a chance. There will be not a few fervently hoping they choke on it.

Buna, which employed 18,000 until the end of 1990, still makes artificial rubber among other things. It switched from oil to lignite as the raw material from which to extract the makings of the synthetics. It thus rendered twice over to the GDR the service it had performed for Nazi Germany: reducing imports of raw materials by saving on petroleum as well as on rubber. But the substitution of lignite for oil added enormously to the menacing miasma of pollution over the noxious River Saale, which has the misfortune to run through an area once rich in minerals, a coincidence which accounts for the local concentration of chemical works. Buna, a vast complex of plants which has begun to clean itself up, cannot compete with western technology or prices for its range of products and could cost DM3 billion to modernise. The same goes for the two massive chemical plants outside Merseburg, Leuna I and Leuna II, owned for the time being, like all the others, by the ubiquitous Treuhand.

Buna has designed itself a new company flag. The main colour is green, which is either shameless, cheeky or optimistic according to taste. Leuna's is white, which is merely impractical. Its headquarters building has emerged from an ancient carapace of grime and worse as a delicate lilac affair, already turning grubby again. All these places are linked with Halle by a long-distance, narrow-gauge tram service for the workers, which may have the most uneven tracks in the world.

Schkopau, not much more than a village, has an old centre, a totally neglected walled town complete with round tower and ancient church, languishing at the side of the road like an abandoned Trabi. Anywhere else and they would have been up in arms trying to preserve and restore it. Over the road back to Halle there hung a grubby white banner saying, "Halle and Merseburg – no chemicals, no future!" So desolate and foul is this landscape, living up to everything I had heard and read (and briefly seen from the train on Unification Day), that the visitor is immediately convinced that the converse, no future with chemicals either, must also be true: damned if they don't and damned if they do. It all seemed very hard on the local people who had no say in the quality of their lives before 1990.

It remained to explore Halle itself, despite everything an interesting place because it lies in a hollow and therefore has streets at different levels. With 240,000 residents it has 50,000 fewer than Magdeburg, but has much more of its old character left. Once you have coped with chaotic road signs and some of Europe's worst-organised roundabouts and found the centre, it turns out to be a lively, thronged place, even on a bitter day. There are a few good buildings round the small and very busy Marktplatz with its statue of Handel, but round the centre the housing is in a shocking state, even by GDR standards, and there are many gaps where buildings have fallen or been pulled down. I can remember London looking like this when I first saw it as a small boy just after the war. Up the road Halle-Neustadt (new town) is a huge high-rise worker settlement of the customary bleakness, though not all the architecture is bad.

I expected, correctly, better things of the Altmark in the opposite direction from Dessau, to which I drove next day along deserted, tree-lined roads. I was bound for this region's largest town, Stendal, idly wondering the while whether it had named (and misspelt) itself after the great French author of *Le rouge et le noir*, and if so why. It turned out to be the other way round. The novelist, born Henri Beyle (1783–1842), an officer of dragoons in the Napoleonic wars, came to admire Stendal's best-known citizen, the archaeologist and art-historian Johann Joachim Winckelmann (1717–1768), effectively the inventor of both his chosen intellectual disciplines, so much that he adopted the name of his hero's home town as his *nom de plume* in 1817. Winckelmann's birthplace is now a museum dedicated to him; and Stendal had an 'h' in it until the last century: QED. Stendal also acquired a nuclear plant before the *Wende*, with two 1,000-megawatt reactors under construction. Work was stopped well before they were put to use – but only after an investment of nearly half a billion marks.

I was not surprised to find myself the only visitor to the Altmark Museum, which was in a former nunnery cloister and unheated, except for the office in the hall where the young woman on duty was comfortably ensconced. She told me she was a trained librarian who had been transferred to the museum, which was financed by the town council for the time being, though with misgivings about the cost. Engagingly shy and modest though she was, she made it clear she had not been expecting a visit from a wandering scribe from England that day, or indeed any other. Her museum was intrinsically interesting for what it revealed of local history, but it was nothing special for Germany, where these local *Heimat* museums are much more numerous and elaborate than most of their British counterparts. At least this town and its remarkably peaceful rural surroundings served as a corrective: Saxony-Anhalt's pollution is uniquely catastrophic, but not unconfined. This was uplifting on the eve of my last full day in the former GDR, when I planned to visit Bitterfeld.

Driving to Bitterfeld on the B184 from Dessau, a distance of twenty-five kilometres, you reach Wolfen first, a town slightly larger which is part of the same outlandish conurbation. From here you see what appear to be three different but vast chemical works in quick succession, pipes crossing and recrossing the road, nameless vapours rising, houses cowering amid the incomprehensible spread of metal and concrete in all directions. This is the devil's kitchen of the GDR, made notorious in 1989 by frightening articles in *Der Spiegel* magazine and elsewhere and previously starkly depicted, very thinly disguised, by Monika Maron, the east German novelist, in her *roman à clef*, *Flugasche* (flying ash), before she went into exile. In fact the majority of the chemical installations are in Wolfen, which is completely overshadowed by them. Halle is big enough not to seem physically overborne by its chemical works, and those to the south are in otherwise open country.

The Wolfen end of Bitterfeld, however, offers an extreme example of how industry literally swallowed up a town and how people's lives were completely overshadowed and threatened by their environment. The seemingly separate plants are all joined together by the pipelines and belong to one giant works, now called Chemie-AG Bitterfeld-Wolfen, which makes viscose fibres and other products. As if that were not enough there is also the separate Mitteldeutsche Braunkohle AG, which turned lignite from the colossal opencast pit on the edge of Bitterfeld into energy, pouring sulphur dioxide into the atmosphere in the process. On the B100 from Bitterfeld to Halle there is the most almighty hole in the ground, the biggest I have ever seen, about a kilometre square and at least twenty metres deep – an all but exhausted sunken desert of a brown coal pit with a blackened church teetering on its edge. This hole at least may become an artificial lake.

Even Bitterfeld had its pedestrian zone and had made its town centre legally impenetrable to strangers. So I parked on the outer edge of the centre, on the other side of the road from a frozen, pus-coloured stream beyond which a little open-air market was doing some business in the welcome but icy sunshine. On making my way to the Kirchplatz, the small central square on which the modest but dignified Wilhelmine *Rathaus* and principal church stand, I was pleasantly surprised to see a green and white house which, with its gracefully curved gable, would not have looked out of place in Amsterdam or Cape Town. Even here some careful restoration work had been done, though not much. There was a little local museum – with a special exhibition of old toys made of lead, which was just what the town needed to round off its deadly cocktail of pollutants: what innocent had thought of carrying lead to Bitterfeld?

Applying for the last time at the *Rathaus* my procedure of turning up unannounced, I was sent without fuss or protocol to the mayor's office on the first floor. Waiting for me was a slight, pale-faced woman of thirty or so with a fashionable, auburn pageboy haircut, informally but neatly dressed in pale trousers and dark-blue polo-neck top. Frau Ilka Trautmann, assistant to the mayor (Frau Edelgard Kauf, CDU, who was away that day), told me that citizens' movements had formed in Bitterfeld before the *Wende*, and they had begun to complain about the appalling environment before *Der Spiegel* got round to exposing it.

"We knew it was no place to take a *Kur*," she said, "but we had no means of knowing how terribly bad our situation was." The works had done analyses, but never told anyone the results. Then the dreadful details all came out at once when *Spiegel* and the round table and the New Forum caused an uproar. Private individuals started to dig around for hard information and shocked the public with what they discovered. The level of air pollution and the drinking water were analysed first. Experts were working on the earth itself in various places, finding out how deep to dig in order to reach uncontaminated soil. The Modrow government, the GDR's last but one, set up a special commission to look into the worst-polluted areas, with particular attention to Bitterfeld. There was an independent investigation and the chemical works were approached directly for information. So was the brown coal plant, which drew on many opencast mines in the area. One result was the closure of nearly thirty sections of Chemie-AG, which made economic sense as well, as they had no chance in the new trading conditions after the *Wende*. There was even some extra central government money, DM53 million for the region, of which Bitterfeld received DM9,257,000. "We were able to clean up a stream and five children's playgrounds, repair a few buildings, renew some drinking-water pipes and so on. It wasn't much, but it was a start." It was also the first improvement since anyone could remember, even if it was only scratching at the surface of the problems. "We have an endless shopping list of things that need doing, but that is new too. Nobody ever drew up such a thing before," said Frau Trautmann.

Bitterfeld's population of about 20,000 has been falling, but since that of Wolfen (40,000) has been rising there has been no substantial flight from the area, although as so often in the ex-GDR, young adults were noticeable by their absence. The enormous adverse publicity in Germany and abroad about Bitterfeld was double-edged; it prompted the commission, some closures, a bit of money and official recognition of the problem. But it burdened the town with an image which is going to be very hard to soften – just when it desperately needs investment and so many other more promising places are competing for slices of a limited cake. There is a real danger that people will write it off altogether. BASF had sent a team from Bavaria to have a look round but, if it did anything, it would only take bits of the local plant, Frau Trautmann thought. Total closure would mean near-total unemployment. Chemie-AG had already cut its workforce from 15,000 to 8,000 by putting 7,000 workers on "short time" – they would lose their jobs in due course. A complete shutdown of all the offending factories in the region would mean a loss of up to 20,000 jobs in an area where 130,000 people live. Chemie-AG had been in IG Farben, but went back to long before the industrial revolution. It had not been specially built up by the GDR, but had always been big, though it came to produce an inordinately large part of the GDR's national income with its electro-chemicals and man-made fibres.

"The price paid by the local population has been very high," said Frau Trautmann. "People suffer from hair and skin diseases here, they have weak lungs and lots have chronic bronchitis; many children are sickly." It was quite clear the workers were never properly protected from the dangerous materials they had to work with. Children did not reach the average height of the rest of the country and life expectancy was measurably shorter, by a year or two, as statistics proved. Pollution undoubtedly contributes to the distinctly shorter life expectancy in the GDR compared with the old FRG.

"We are hamstrung by the administrative chaos accompanying the reorganisation of all levels of regional government and the new laws from the west, to say nothing of the lack of finance. We have had to borrow money to keep the town going; eventually we will have an enormous debt." Would all these problems lead to unrest, I asked? "I know some people say that, but I don't believe it," said Frau Trautmann. "But I also know we haven't touched bottom yet. What I don't know is how far down we are going to have to go before things improve – as they must and will."

I thanked her for the powerful coffee which had fuelled our conversation until lunchtime. For the first and last time in my travels round the GDR, Frau Trautmann thanked me for stealing her morning. She apologised for the fact that her suffering home town had not yet got around to producing a glossy brochure about itself as she rummaged in a cupboard for something I could take back with me as a memento. She came up with a history of prewar airship and seaplane construction in the town, a pamphlet about the local railways – and finally a triangular pennant bearing the town's coat of arms (complete with price-tag for ninety pfennigs). How extraordinary, how heartening that the most touching moment of all my time in the former German Democratic Republic should come at what might otherwise have been the bitter end, in Bitterfeld.

Throughout those months I had been making visits of various lengths to Berlin, at the beginning and end of each instalment of my tour. I was about to pass through again briefly to do my final errands before returning home to start writing. I have therefore held back my impressions and gleanings from that exhilarating, restless city until now.

– VII –

EAST BERLIN

*Divided shop window – contrasts – big city – Mitte – Marx and
Engels – Unter den Linden – Museum Island – Pergamon – GDR
sport – Prenzlauer Berg – Treptow – Soviet memorial – Köpenick –
Bärbel Bohley, dissident – from SED to PDS – gravy train – real
trains – Stasi HQ – Stasi undead? – ominous murder – the
Treuhand – another paid optimist – property problem II – wrong
principle – how much a capital? – nostalgia*

– VII –

East Berlin

As Germany was divided, so was its capital Berlin. The sectors of the three western Allies, America, Britain and France, together formed West Berlin, a brightly-lit shop window for capitalist democracy on a political island in a GDR-Communist sea, with a population of two million. Because the Allies retained sovereignty over their sectors, West Berlin functioned as West Germany's eleventh *Land*, but was effectively limited to observer status in the Bundestag. Fifty per cent of the enclave's revenue came in subsidies from Bonn, which also paid the running costs of the three Allied garrisons, allowed residents to pay half the West German going rate of income tax and practically bribed industry to move there. All this was to help keep the place going, a precedent not lost on the struggling residents of the ex-GDR, whose need is very much greater. The Soviet sector, with nearly half the total area of Greater Berlin and a population of 1.2 million, was the capital of the German Democratic Republic, as the SED regime never tired of reminding the world. Road signs to and within it referred to "Berlin – *(die) Hauptstadt der DDR*". Many saw this as a symptom of insecurity: the British, after all, see no need to say "London – capital of the UK". This repetitive usage led one of my wife's wittier students to ask who was this Belinda Hauptstadt everybody was talking about.

The SED did all it could afford by way of restoring or maintaining the grandeur of East Berlin, which included the *Bezirk* (meaning "borough" in this context) called Mitte, the heart of Greater Berlin encompassing Unter den Linden, local equivalent of The Mall or the Champs Elysées, Alexanderplatz, the central square, and most of the monumental buildings. As these were restored or added to piecemeal over the GDR years, depending on the availability of funds (a task still far short of completion), East Berlin looked different on each visit. It also looked different in its entirety from West Berlin with its bright lights, its raffish night-life and its "we never close" atmosphere. Despite the destruction of seventy per cent of the whole city by Anglo-American bombing and Soviet artillery, East Berlin perforce left many streets, even whole districts, standing (or crumbling) in their original state, complete with ancient cobbles, rusting stations and grubby façades. Residential central Berlin is in the main an inner city of large, five or six-storey apartment blocks with shops at ground-floor level. One obvious difference between west and east is the relative absence of shops in the latter; another is, of course, the enormous gap between the physical condition of the buildings in east and west. There is not much to choose in terms of bleakness between the huge high-rise developments in the two parts. The east has kept some of its trams, the west not.

What is not clear from a map is the scale of the place. A detailed plan will show street numbers, leading the foreigner to calculate that a walk from, say, number 60 to number 160 involves passing no more than fifty evenly numbered individual premises. But the numbers relate to plots of ground, each of which usually has a frontage big enough for several shops, so that your short stroll doubles, trebles or quadruples itself. Unter den Linden (under the limes) is broad enough to accommodate a dozen lanes of traffic (and with hardly any crossings is decidedly hostile to ped-estrians). The main squares – Alexanderplatz, Potsdamer-Platz, Marx-Engels-Platz – are simply enormous. The distances between s-bahn stops are rather larger than those between London Underground or New York Subway stations, for example; those between u-bahn halts are about the same. And within the city boundaries, east and west, north and south, are enormous tracts of forest and lake "stolen" from Brandenburg.

The Alexanderplatz (previously Ochsenplatz, the city's old cattle market) was renamed in honour of Tsar Alexander I and the Russo-Prussian alliance against Napoleon. It is now a bitterly cold place in winter and metaphorically so all year round, a concrete field across which no less than twenty-seven tram routes used to run before the war, but which is now reserved for the pedestrians who never fill it. The futuristic world clock showing times round the globe must have been a sick joke for the inhabitants of east Berlin when getting out of their part of the divided city was so difficult. The modern red and white "showpiece" department store, Centrum, used to be a dreary place with little variety of goods on display; now it is busy, untidy and thronged with bargain-hunters going through the down-market clothes and other goods delivered in large quantities from the west. The store is run by a chain represented in every west German city. Its main rival has taken over the running of the once equally depressing Haus der Mode, the women's clothing store. Other inglorious modern buildings include the Reisebüro travel agency (which will probably not put up a plaque to commemorate my frequent visits), the Haus der Presse, Haus der Elektroindustrie (home of the Treuhand) and the Hotel Stadt Berlin. Let us not forget, too, the tallest building in all Germany, the ineffably tedious television tower – which offers a fabulous view from its top all the better for not including the television tower . . .

To the west, the neighbouring Marx-Engels-Platz and Forum (once the Lustgarten – pleasance or pleasure garden) is also very large indeed, but rather less forbidding, even though the dark and surprisingly modest memorial sculpture of the ideological terrible twins stands out for being all alone. Its low, square plinth bore the best graffiti I saw on my visits, one on each side: "We're sorry; See you at the labour exchange; It'll be better next time; We're not guilty." Also in and around this great open space are the "Red *Rathaus*" (a reference to its bricks, not its politics), Berlin's city hall and seat of the now defunct East Berlin *Magistrat* (council), to be taken over by the new Greater Berlin *Senat* (government); the Roman Catholic Cathedral (1905, copied from the Italian Renaissance); the very modern, white and copper-coloured Palace of the Republic, where the Volkskammer used to sit; a smart new hotel; and a couple of ghastly former GDR-government buildings. What is missing from here is the Royal Palace, torn down for ideological reasons in 1950 – except for the balcony from which the Communist Karl Liebknecht declared a republic in November 1918, which has been incorporated into an otherwise featureless modern block. Opposite the Red *Rathaus* is the pedestrianised Nikolai quarter, heart of medieval Berlin, excellently rebuilt with a few restored old buildings flanked by self-effacing apartment houses whose yellow stucco recaptures something of the past without copying it. Some appropriately dressed, deadly earnest lunatics were running a "medieval" Christmas fair there, complete with blacksmith's stall, dyspeptic horses, ancient crafts, weird music and reassuringly modern beer and sausages. If the British take their pleasures sadly, the Germans take them seriously.

Running west from Marx and Engels to Pariser-Platz with the Brandenburg Gate is Unter den Linden, where Lili Marlene waited for her young man. This grandest of boulevards is lined with portentous buildings such as the State Opera, the State Library, the Humboldt University, the Museum of German History (former arsenal), a couple of palaces and the New Guardhouse containing the memorial to the victims of Fascism and war. In front of that the People's Army used to mount a goose-steeping guard whose mechanical gait came from Prussia, was copied by Russia, retained by the Red Army and recopied by the GDR from the silly walk of the KGB troops guarding Lenin's Tomb in Moscow. The dominant architect for this area was the neoclassicist Karl Friedrich Schinkel (1781–1841). Parallel to and south of Unter den Linden is Französische-Strasse (French street) which has a splendid matched pair of cathedrals, one called French for the Huguenots, the other German for the Evangelical Lutherans, on either side of the Platz der Akademie, with Frederick the Great's attractive Schauspielhaus (playhouse) set between them.

To the north of the Marx-Engels-Platz is a complex known as the Museum Island, between the River Spree and the Spree Canal. Here are the National Gallery, and museums called the Old (said to be Schinkel's finest effort), the Bode, the New (still a bombed-out ruin) – and the Pergamon Museum, one of the greatest in the world. It is named after its principal exhibit, the altar (second century BC) of the ancient Greek city of Pergamum in north-west Anatolia, an edifice magnificently rebuilt from its own stones and statues, and filled out with imitation pillars, which takes up more than 1,200 square metres of floor-space. It was one of the wonders of the ancient world and is a unique survivor into the modern age. In the next hall is the highly impressive market gate from the Greco-Roman city of Miletus (second century AD), which is thirty metres wide and seventeen high; in some ways it is even more imposing than the altar because much more of the original is extant.

When you have digested these, you walk deeper into the building and behold Nebuchadnezzar II's Ishtar Gate of ancient Babylon (sixth century BC) at the end of a reconstructed processional way lined in glazed blue tiles with white and gold-coloured bas-reliefs showing bulls, lions and sacred dragons. Not much of the original is there, but the reconstruction is one of the most brilliant exhibits anywhere, absolutely stunning the first time and merely breathtaking on return visits (one always seems to forget how big it is). Compared with plunder like this, even the Elgin Marbles in the British Museum begin to look like archaeological small change. One wonders how the German diggers would have brought their loot home but for the invention of the steamship.

The principal "culprit" behind the classical collections was Heinrich Schliemann (1822–90), the businessman turned archaeologist born at Neubukow in Mecklenburg, who found Homer's Troy and also dug at Mycenae and Tiryns. At the Old Museum I saw a temporary special exhibition marking the centenary of his death, making clear the extent and importance of his work, and showing how he went about it as well as what he brought back. In fact, the Levant had better look out: a Pergamon Patrons' Association was founded after the *Wende* to fill the gaps in the collections . . . Plans are also afoot to reunite Germany's and Berlin's divided cultural collections by rationalising exhibitions and exchanging exhibits. The results should be spectacular indeed.

Upstairs at the Pergamon are great collections of east Asiatic and Islamic art, the latter including the main gate and part of a tower from a desert fort in Jordan. At a distance the sandstone looks porous; on closer inspection it proves to be covered in minutely detailed decorative carving. This was a gift from the last Sultan of Turkey to the last Kaiser of Germany.

After the frivolities of ancient culture it was high time to get down to something serious, and nothing was taken more seriously in the GDR than sport, where the regime set out to excel by all means short of war. It was the only sphere of activity for which east Germany was better known than wall-building. So I went to see Volker Kluge, who writes about sport for *Junge Welt* magazine, used to be chief press officer of the GDR National Olympic Committee and was busy gathering first-hand information from past and present stars with a view to writing the definitive history of GDR sport.

After the Russians shut down all German sporting bodies in 1945, the East Germans had to start again from scratch in 1945 at municipal level, via the FDJ (the youth movement) and factory organisations. The first man in charge of this programme was none other than Erich Honecker. Then the German Sports Committee was formed in the Soviet zone in 1948, supported by the FDJ and the FDGB (trade union federation). The West Germans formed a National Olympic Committee in 1949 and the East Germans in 1951; but the latter was subordinated to the former by the International Olympic Committee (IOC). This so enraged Walter Ulbricht, the GDR leader, that East Germany did not take part in the 1952 Olympics. Ulbricht fully recognised the potential of successful sports stars as "diplomats in training-suits". Parity was achieved in 1955 when the IOC provisionally recognised two NOCs; but East and West Germany still had a single Olympic team, the last vestige of German unity. This arrangement lasted ten years. The GDR entered a separate squad for the first time in 1968; it was soon outperforming every nation in the world in terms of medals per million population.

The regime started building up sport across the country by encouraging all children and young people to take part through generous provision of time, money and facilities. Soviet advice was sought on training; a "university" was set up for trainers and special schools for promising youngsters, where intensive training was combined with reduced daily study over a longer period at school. A fine-meshed net of talent-spotters trawled the whole country looking for potential stars in sports clubs, the youth organisations and the schools. Swimming-pools were built all over the country. "I doubt whether there has ever been anything quite as intense, not even in the Soviet Union, where they had the same system, but not our discipline," Herr Kluge said. The tragic Munich Olympiad, marred by the Palestinian massacre of Israeli athletes, was treated in advance as a huge national challenge by the GDR in 1972, the year in which it shed its diplomatic pariah status, thanks to East-West and inter-German détente. The East Germans came third in the medals table after the two superpowers, an astounding achievement for a nation with barely one fifteenth of the population of either. In 1976 they went one better, passing the United States – a mixed blessing because now the regime would not accept anything less than second place in the world. By this time, Kluge said, athletics and a narrow range of other sports were hogging the GDR's sports budget and other games went to the wall, including soccer and basketball, hockey and "bourgeois" equestrian sports. Particularly satisfying for the SED was the large gap in performance between the two Germanys.

"Only in the mid-eighties was it recognised officially that you couldn't just concentrate on performance sport to the total neglect of sport as exercise, as a social event, to say nothing of fun. The tremendous pressure to find winners was encouraged and intensified by democratic centralism, with its totally over-centralised leadership."

What about the use of drugs, something for which just two GDR athletes were caught, though rumours were rife because of their consistently freakish performances? "Of course drugs were used. Very few knew officially, but the whole thing was elaborate and systematic, under the central control of doctors. The GDR was one of the very few countries to have a centralised medical service for sport, a large collective with the usual democratic-centralist pyramid structure." This was beginning to sound like another great contribution from the German medical profession to the lowering of moral standards. How was it done, I asked?

"Drugs were in general use, but they were so tightly controlled that they could not be detected. We were so distrusted internationally because of our amazing performance that we could not afford to be caught: it would have been a political and diplomatic as well as a sporting disaster which the SED could not afford." None of this altered the fact that the system as a whole worked, in that it enabled the best talent to come to the top. No talent was wasted. Drugs were administered sparingly in optimum conditions to raise peak performance even higher. The doctors experimented to the limits of legality and they kept each other informed about the effects of drugs and how to prevent detection.

"That is an important point, because elsewhere individual doctors or trainers have put athletes on drugs in total secrecy, which made mistakes – and discovery – much more likely," Herr Kluge pointed out. "In the GDR there was a shared body of knowledge. These sports doctors were treating healthy people, working with trainers and not against them, for a common political goal. They knew the risks and stopped short of practices that would have damaged the athletes." In other words the east Germans interpreted the ban on drugs in terms of the eleventh commandment: thou shalt not be found out. "The drug abuse business was a bit like the Stasi. Most people had nothing to do with either for nearly the whole of the time!" Herr Kluge said.

After the *Wende* the west German sports organisations began to absorb their east German counterparts, starting with the Olympic Committee. Kluge thought the western federal and the eastern centralised system would prove irreconcilable. "We all know what that means: we will have to adapt to theirs, and that means performance will go down. We used to have 592 track and field trainers here; now we can probably afford only sixty. There is bound to be a serious shortage of funds compared with what was spent before, but perhaps it will be more evenly spent on sport for the people rather than sport to win. I would have liked to see some of the better aspects of the GDR system, such as the special schools, kept on in modified form, but I'm not optimistic."

There is much more to east Berlin than the imposing, representational Mitte on which so much of the G D R's meagre treasure was spent. *Die Szene*, the "in" place after the reunification of Berlin began, was a district called Prenzlauer Berg. This was proving as powerful a magnet to students, squatters, the restless, the anarchistic *Autonomen*, the young and poor, the radical and all manner of misfits whom less tolerant Germans lump together under the label *Chaoten* – chaots, devotees of chaos. Before the Wall opened the principal concentration of this western urban phenomenon was to be found in the West Berlin district of Kreuzberg, right up against the wall. Prenzlauer Berg offered the same Bohemian atmosphere for much less money. Even here the *Wessis* were moving in on the *Ossis* to save a few marks.

Berg means "hill" but there isn't a real one for miles. Berlin is very nearly flat. One street, the Husemannstrasse, shows what the Prenzlauer Berg could and, in the opinion of the middle class, should be. Western-based coach tours of east Berlin still pass this way to look at two long blocks on either side of this street, restored to the highest standard. It probably never looked like this in real life. On the eastern side there are a couple of modest museums, on working life in Berlin at the turn of the century (special exhibition on "the culture and lifestyle of the proletariat") and on hairdressing down the ages. There were also some twee shops on the ground floors of apartment houses, often with a typically drab Berlin *Hinterhof* (backyard) visible through the main entrance. The old Konsum collective still seemed to be running the consumer-goods shops. There was a high-class junk shop, a seamstress, a grocery, a greengrocer, a knife-grinder, a carriage hire business for weddings and a couple of inviting, old-fashioned café-restaurants. I was so early that cafés and museums alike were closed, saving me the trouble of sampling either.

The surrounding area had many gloomy shops propping up filthy apartment buildings covered in crumbling grey stucco. The building fabric was falling off in lumps – you could see the debris on the pavement, and that was in the streets where no work was being done. The only colour was provided by the inhabitants, who included a fair proportion of ordinary, elderly Berliners among the casually dressed young people picking their way over the smashed pavement to cross the cobbled street. This is fairly typical, and it will take billions to regenerate the tired, neglected and depressed exterior of most of east Berlin, a truly colossal task which will spill over into the next century.

Later that morning, when I realised I was on the wrong train, I broke my journey at the inner suburb of Treptow and walked through the big park to see whether the grimmest monument in Berlin was drawing any visitors these days. The Soviet Union's memorial to its dead in the Second World War takes the form of a sunken field with large tombs on either side, a raised monumental sculpture at the far end, and at the entrance a commemorative gateway made of highly polished slabs of dark red marble. Thereby, I am told, hangs a tale. When the Red Army was searching Berlin after capturing it, troops came to a railway marshalling yard. In a siding they found a couple of waggons loaded with red marble. On investigation they discovered that the Wehrmacht, thoroughgoing, forward-looking organisation that it was, had assembled this valuable material in 1941. Its purpose? To construct the German victory memorial in Moscow! Fortunately an almighty effort by Marshal Zhukov's tanks stopped the German advance in the western outer suburbs of the Soviet capital and the waggons stayed put, giving the Red Army its opportunity to find an alternative use for the material.

While it seemed that the parties of western tourists, whom the SED regime more or less obliged to visit the memorial as part of any coach tour of east Berlin, were no longer coming, there was a surprising number of individuals looking at the site. It is much more imposing than the other Soviet memorial in the centre of Berlin, near the Brandenburg Gate but just inside the old British sector, which was guarded for so many years by Soviet soldiers, who had to be guarded against the occasional demonstration by Berlin police, who were ultimately guarded in turn by British redcaps.

Having joined the right train, I went all the way out to Köpenick, the outer suburb at the south-eastern corner of Berlin which I had never seen before. Once again I had allowed myself to be fooled by the map, which seemed to suggest that the s-bahn station called Köpenick was just a short distance north of the centre of this old town turned suburb (in 1920). It was a two-kilometre trudge, to which I did not object in principle, being a considerable walker; but it was bitingly cold, I had already had a nice walk, thank you, in Treptow Park, and my ankles were threatened by the state of the pavements. Even so it was well worth the modest effort. Köpenick is special for at least three reasons: its intrinsic historical and physical attraction, its setting amid water and forest – and its immortal "Captain".

In 1906 a shoemaker called Wilhelm Voigt got hold of an Army captain's uniform, marched into the brand-new *Rathaus* at Köpenick at the head of ten bemused soldiers, "arrested" the mayor, took charge of the town treasury and withdrew into the distance with 4,000 Reichsmarks, rather a lot of money in those days. The coup caused much delight locally for making the stuffed shirts of the officer class and the petty municipal bureaucracy look thoroughly silly. Even Kaiser Wilhelm II was said to have been privately amused by the episode (which is saying something for Queen Victoria's pompous grandson) and to have consented to a pardon when the money was returned. The tale gained national and international currency, however, when Carl Zuckmayer, the playwright from the Rhineland (where Prussians have traditionally been mocked, especially at carnival), turned it into a delightful comedy in 1931 (also filmed twice). Zuckmayer spoke out against the Nazis in Austria, where he lived from 1926, his works were banned by them and he escaped to America in 1939, returning as an official of the US Military Government after the war.

My modest lunch at the *Rathauskeller* cost a good deal less than 4,000 marks and set me up nicely for inspecting the town. The main attraction is the *Schloss*, which stands on its own island. It was built for the Great Elector by Ruudiger van Langevelt, a Dutch architect, just after the Thirty Years' War, in restrained baroque style with splendid interiors. Köpenick stands at the confluence of the Dahme and Spree rivers – hence the island – and was a Slav fort before it became a German one, and then, from the sixteenth century, an electoral hunting lodge. On its island with forest all around (before the town intruded) it must have been an ideal setting for such a retreat. The area has been inhabited since the Middle Stone Age and was given its town charter in 1232. It now constitutes *Bezirk* number sixteen of Berlin and spreads to the north and south of the *Schloss*, which houses an impressive Museum of European Craftsmanship. Opposite the *Schloss* is a matching chapel, justly known as "the pearl of Köpenick". To the east is a generous area of rolling, wooded country, part of the Berlin Forest, and the very large Lake Müggelsee with its popular bathing beach. It would be good to come back one summer.

I went back to the Prenzlauer Berg on another afternoon, one I had been looking forward to with great interest for some days. It was a milestone on my journey to be able to telephone somebody, thanks to the good offices of a mutual friend, and make an appointment for several days ahead. Much more significant than this civilised arrangement was the person with whom I had been fortunate enough to make it: the artist Bärbel Bohley, key figure in the New Forum, which, above all other citizens' initiatives, had posed the moral challenge to the SED regime that it had proved unable to suppress, let alone answer. Frau Bohley's delicate features and earnest mien became familiar through the world's television sets during the dramatic events of late 1989 and 1990. She lived with her grown-up son in an apartment house which from the outside looked ready to fall down, as its next-door neighbour (completely missing) had presumably done. The street was a stylish terrace built in the second half of the last century. It should have been majestic but had been allowed to rot to such an extent that it had been condemned in 1963 – yet remained standing for want of an alternative. As so often in east Germany, the exterior gave no clue to the quality and comfort of the interior, which overflowed with books.

We talked across a coffee-table in an airy front room with a high ceiling, big windows making the most of the fading winter light, and off-white walls, the whole sparsely but tastefully furnished. The coffee was strong and Frau Bohley smoked a lot during our two-hour conversation. She is short and surprisingly broad-boned (her face alone, with its wide mouth and cheekbones and its spare flesh, as seen on television, had prepared me for someone rather more wraithlike) and talks nervously – at any rate with a complete stranger from another country.

After opposing the old regime, I asked, ending the introductory exchanges, did Frau Bohley consider herself in opposition to the new?

"I suppose I have stayed in opposition ever since the western parties came over here and took over the political landscape. Our role was made clear by that. In a way I am quite happy about the election results in so far as they have made the situation clear, and I certainly don't think people are silly for voting the way they did." The Federal election of 2 December 1990 had been the fourth in nine months, and there was no chance that the citizens' movements would get a mass vote. The vote for the CDU did not mean that the people were content with everything: Kohl's promises had been all too easy to grasp and the CDU had seemed consistent through its promises.

"The question is whether they are going to be able to stick to them, which I never believed they could. The SPD should have run a different campaign. They should have opposed the unification treaties, they should have demanded a different kind of treaty, but they were obviously scared of being seen to oppose union as such. They didn't follow a consistent course with their Yes in the Bundesrat and their No in the Bundestag, they couldn't offer the continuity the people wanted, so they lost badly. So did the PDS [successor party to the SED]: with all their resources you'd think they would have done better than the eleven per cent they got here. As for the citizens' movements, I think they were too preoccupied with possible alliances; we are not Greens and we should not be lumped together with them in the public mind," said Frau Bohley. Everything had happened much too quickly politically and economically, yet the biggest decisions had been put off and were being taken too late.

What about the remarkable overall similarity between the broad results in west and east?

"This was partly *Anpassung* and partly the German conformist mentality. People over here were always well informed about what was going on over there," Frau Bohley replied. She preferred, she said, not to engage in yet another analysis of the past year or so: "I'm more interested in the present and the future." She was certain, however, that if the SPD had happened to be in power in the west when the *Wende* came in the east, the SPD would have won the general election. December 2 had been a repeat of March 3, the first and last free Volkskammer election, when the people had voted for those then in power. "I regret most of all that we had too little time to think. I believe a lot of things are going to go very badly wrong in the next year or two, and that people will regret the speed of the initial events before union actually came."

That the new dispensation was far from perfect in its approach to human rights had already been disturbingly demonstrated, she felt. Jews who had come to the GDR from the Soviet Union before Unification Day on October 3 were having a hard time under the western laws which took effect then; different members of the same family were being given different conditions of residence, for example, so that it was going to be difficult for them to stay together.

"Squatters are a new phenomenon here, but they are being given the West Berlin treatment, with the police storming in. Here bishops and city councillors tried to mediate between the police and the squatters as they did in 1989, but they were ignored. The low-flying police helicopters, which we had never experienced before, scared old people living near the squats: to them it sounded like the last days of the war. For that reason I think the SPD-led government in West Berlin thoroughly deserved its defeat on December 2."

Frau Bohley also regretted the passing of the round tables as instruments of mediation between ordinary citizens and the authorities, whatever the nature of the latter. "They are still very much needed. They were concerned with social problems, not politics or elections. Who knows, when government policy collapses under the weight of the problems over here, they may make a comeback. We need to be patient and to remain ready to help when a lot of issues come to a head, as I fear they must. Bonn has shown too little imagination. They have no idea of what it's like here and they haven't looked far enough ahead. What happens when we have colossal unemployment, as we're going to, and the benefit runs out, for example? And people can't possibly afford to pay western-style economic rents for all the rotten property. Their biggest mistake in Bonn is to think that all problems can be solved by their approach and their approach alone."

Bärbel Bohley recalled that nobody believed the Berlin Wall would come down in their lifetimes – until it actually came down overnight. "If they wanted change, as most did, I'm sure, then they wanted a changed, a reformed, a better GDR. If only the whole process had been more orderly and less headlong, so that we in the east could have made a bigger contribution to settling our own future." As things stood, she foresaw, *inter alia*, problems with the differences between western and eastern qualifications and the different training of social workers, which meant that eastern ones were unemployable under western regulations. Agriculture was heading for a major crisis because under the collective-farm system, people had become specialised and were not capable of running a mixed farm – always assuming they could find the capital to buy one.

"They have been extremely arrogant in the west in how they have moved in and tackled the problems here. We were thrown straight into the European Community without time to prepare or adjust, which makes us second-class citizens of the EC as well as Germany. In that sense we are still behind a wall. One tiny example of the way the new people behave: for two days I thought something was wrong with my telephone. Every time I picked it up it sounded wrong. Then I learned that they had simply altered the dialling tone; but they never bothered to tell us!"

There had been enormous changes of much greater importance in all areas of life, demanding commensurate adjustments. People who had sworn to defend the Communist system were either facing dismissal or else having overnight to swear to support a democratic one, which was poor psychology, she thought. "A lot of people from here took refuge in West Germany in the old days, and the general understanding is that it took them a couple of years as individuals to adjust to the very different way of life. Now the entire GDR has had to 'flee the republic' and is being forced to adjust, whether it wants to or not. It wasn't necessary. There was no need for it to happen like this."

Western firms had marched in, taken over enterprises in the east, sacked the workers and even captured some of the GDR's former markets in eastern Europe with produce made in the west. Events since unity had shown that there were a lot of huge problems in the east which could not be swept under the carpet or made light of. Some of them could only be solved in a much wider framework than united Germany. "We need to help the rest of eastern Europe and unite the entire Continent. We mustn't end up with a boundary between rich and poor, whether it's where the inter-German border used to be or on the Oder-Neisse frontier with Poland."

A moral gulf had to be overcome as well, something people in the west completely failed to appreciate: the lack of a true sense of right and wrong in the east. "Not only did people have to lie or at least dissimulate all the time; they also lived in a state which offered no legal security because the rule of law didn't apply. So people had no respect for the state or the law, which was very demoralising. They also used to rely on the solidarity of their own circle of trusted friends and family, and that is disappearing because the system which made it necessary for survival is disappearing. But it could actually make a comeback if the accumulation of problems leads to confrontation, as I fear it will . . ."

Why had Frau Bohley not stood on behalf of Bündnis 90, the citizens' movement alliance which had joined hands with the eastern Greens and just managed to win seats in the new Bundestag? (It won more than five per cent of the total vote in the ex-GDR; the Federal Constitutional Court, to its credit, overruled the established Bonn parties which had voted in the Bundestag to make the "five percent hurdle" apply to the total vote across the united country: this would have eliminated both the alliance and the Communist PDS.) Should she not have taken the chance of going to Bonn and arguing her case there?

"I'm a painter and I haven't done much work lately. Besides, I didn't like the idea of being in Bonn. I don't like the way the new deputies from here have grabbed all the privileges built up by the western system. I also thought there was not enough democracy in Bündnis 90 when it came to choosing candidates, or in the electoral law. I didn't like the alliance with the Greens; I would have wanted to be independent, and it's virtually impossible to get elected as an independent to the Bundestag. I don't think the CDU or the SPD, still less the PDS, represent the true interests of the people of the GDR, and I think the voters will soon realise this. I suppose I am not very trusting of parliament; I think the deputies are too far removed from the people."

I detected a touch of arrogance or *Besserwisserei* here, this knowing better than her allies or the people or their elected representatives. Or was it the impatient idealism of an obviously intelligent and also genuinely concerned person, whose moral courage and independence of mind were beyond question? She was certainly not planning to opt out: "There is going to be a lot to do in a new, democratic opposition outside parliament. I think my place is here in some kind of constructive opposition, in Berlin where I know my way about. I have come to know a lot of people in the past year, right across the political spectrum, and I hope I can use any influence I've got across the parties, which I'm now free to do."

As I prepared to leave after two hours, I had the impression that she was a bit of a loner by nature and also more than a little depressed. She firmly denied the bitterness ascribed to her by other observers, but there could be no denying her disappointment with the way things had turned out. "I have to admit that the events of 1989 and 1990 probably couldn't have gone much differently in the circumstances, but I'm still very sorry they didn't."

The PDS, the Party of Democratic Socialism, the heir and successor of the SED mentioned by Frau Bohley, is thought to have spent the tidy sum of DM60 million in order to obtain its 11% of the total vote in its former east German fief, or 2.4% of the all-German turnout. Considering that the SED's pre-*Wende* membership of 2.4 million fell to 300,000 afterwards, this is an achievement bordering on the amazing. The leader of the PDS, Gregor Gysi, is both clever and personable, not slow on his feet and good at interviews. The party's advertising campaign for the December 1990 election was slicker than any other and full of cheek: "Left is lively" said the posters, showing a highly fashionable young woman poking out her tongue; "the other Germany" was promised (or threatened) if the PDS won. Not only were more than forty years of misrule thus treated just like the Nazi period in the GDR, as the work of unrelated aliens; an almighty scandal about misappropriation of SED funds which broke in the final stages of the campaign was shrugged off too. The SED regime behaved like a Third World dictator as it went into its precipitous decline, stashing away untold sums of money in the Soviet Union, Norway, the Netherlands and Switzerland, to name but four. The shining examples of the Duvalier and Marcos regimes (and the Nazis) were followed by the outgoing *Bonzen* of the GDR, a fact which was brought to light when a former SED functionary walked into an Oslo bank and coolly tried to cash a cheque for DM70 million, and another was arrested for trying to salt away DM107 million in Moscow.

These developments doubtless came as a great relief to the Berlin police, who had raided the PDS headquarters in the Karl-Liebknecht-Haus in east Berlin without a search warrant early in October 1990. At around the same time the Bonn police raided the headquarters of the Green Party and seized copies of a leaflet urging Bundeswehr personnel to refuse to serve in the Persian Gulf. This "incitement to mutiny" against an order which had not been issued at the time was apparently deemed to justify a raid (albeit with a warrant) on the offices of a party then represented, by the will of the people, in the Bundestag (as was the PDS). The action was repeated, but still well before Bonn decided to send a squadron of aircraft to Turkey in distant support of the American-led coalition against President Saddam Hussein of Iraq. Herr Gysi protested vociferously against this high-handed (and undoubtedly questionable) behaviour, which he likened to the Nazis' favoured ploy of the *Nacht und Nebel* (night and fog) *Aktion*. The heavy-handed raid was defended under a regulation permitting a search without a warrant if the imminent danger can reasonably be held to exist that evidence of crime would otherwise disappear. But it was not only the Communists who saw the raid as a dangerous precedent for future action against small opposition parties in parliament. The Bavarian government set its security agents to eavesdrop on local PDS offices for a while, on the grounds that the party was "anti-constitutional".

After the arrests "justifying" the Berlin police raid *ex post facto*, Herr Gysi came close to resigning, but managed to resist the temptation and fought the election to the end. By mid-November the PDS claimed to have put ninety-five per cent of its inherited property and assets in the hands of the Treuhand (the eastern CDU and eastern Liberals did the same with all theirs). Secret talks began between PDS and SPD about the restitution of assets taken from the eastern SPD when it and the Communist KPD were forcibly merged into the SED. An independent commission for the investigation of assets held by GDR parties was trying to determine who owned what and what should happen to it. There were reasonable suspicions in Bonn, Berlin and elsewhere that the SED had stashed away countless millions, perhaps billions, of marks which rightfully belonged to the people who had endured its totalitarian rule. Judging by the decline of the PDS's share of the vote over the four elections in the GDR from March to December 1990 (by roughly fifty per cent), it can be expected to disappear from federal and probably state legislatures in short order. While the hunt for hidden SED funds remains entirely justifiable, indeed essential, Bonn would be well advised otherwise to let nature take its course and refrain from harassment of the PDS, which could so easily become counter-productive.

If the old SED gravy-train had ground to a halt, the real ones operated by the Deutsche Reichsbahn were still running over the decaying network of the intensely used GDR railway network. I went to see the Reichsbahn at its new headquarters, part of the old Stasi complex in the inner suburb of Lichtenberg, where I met Claudia Ruttmann of the public affairs department. It was just after the first shutdown of the network since 1953, in protest against low pay, poor working conditions and rumours of mass dismissals. Frau Ruttmann, commanding close attention by speaking very softly, said that the DR planned to reduce its swollen labour-force of 240,000 – the same number as employed on the railways in west Germany – by 68,000 (twenty-eight per cent) over five years, by natural wastage. Meanwhile the DR was to work with the Deutsche Bundesbahn (DB) in the west over the next two years to prepare for unification of the two networks.

"We need a complete technical reorganisation and most personnel will need retraining. And we are not used to the kind of worker mobility taken for granted by the DB," she said. The DR had a lot of people aged up to seventy-five on the payroll eking out their pensions, as was customary in the big GDR undertakings: rent and essentials were cheap, but everything else was expensive on the prevailing low wages. On the other hand, while the DB had gigantic debts and had never made a profit, the DR was entirely free of debt until the *Wende*. This can safely be attributed to low pay, Communist accounting methods which took no notice of economic "reality" as understood in the West – and the GDR's intelligent policy of legally enforced, maximum preference for rail over road for freight – another abandoned *Ossi* idea which deserved closer examination by Bonn. Fares would, however, be subject to *Anpassung* and "harmonisation". I took this to mean that DR prices, which went up sharply on 1 January 1991, would soon rise to DB's daunting level. Until the New Year, the DR charged passengers eight pfennigs a kilometre on long hauls second class and eleven in first, while the DB demanded twenty-two and thirty-three respectively. That and the huge appetite for western cars was bound to hit passenger traffic.

"The DR's future depends on the level of economic activity in the ex-GDR. If there is little work going on, we shall be in serious trouble. It has been estimated that we need an investment of DM100 billion over the next ten years to catch up, compared with DM120 billion for the roads," said Frau Ruttmann. But in the GDR the railways carried twice as much goods as the DB on half the amount of track (14,000 kilometres), handling eighty per cent of goods traffic. After the *Wende* the proportion fell by half in a matter of months as the new freedom of choice led people to prefer the roads, which appeared quicker and more flexible, but soon proved unable to cope with the resulting increase in heavy lorries. "We were not quick in the old days, true, but we were utterly reliable." The DR was deriving no benefit from the huge increase in consumer goods coming from west to east, and at the same time was suffering from the collapse of its brown coal traffic, a pillar of its former business, for environmental reasons. "The special trains carrying winter food aid to the Soviet Union are the only new business we've had, and that, of course, won't last," Frau Ruttmann said. One main reason for the GDR's heavy reliance on the railway had been to save money on roads.

Experiments were in hand from before the *Wende* with trailer-trains, an American idea whereby containers were equipped with both road and rail wheels. They could thus travel on the railway as far as possible, retract their rail bogeys and lower their road wheels for attachment to a truck for the first and last stages of their journey. This sounded like the perfect solution to the nuisance of transfer from road to rail and back to road which had led so many hauliers to save time and trouble by doing the whole journey on the road, to the ever-increasing detriment of the environment and the railways. "One of our advantages is going to be the fact that the roads here are so bad!" To compete against aircraft and new or rebuilt autobahns, fast new track on stretches such as from Berlin to

Bonn would be built in the next few years. In view of how long it took to build roads and airports, DR might even get its blow in first. A principal reason for the comparatively large workforce was that it, too, operated its own system of autarky to overcome the chronic shortages and poor infrastructure. DR built its own rolling stock, ran its own catering (the miserable Mitropa) and did all its own maintenance; only some of the locomotives came from elsewhere. Now extraneous sections such as Mitropa were being hived off.

DR's new offices are in the Ruschestrasse, which crosses the Normannenstrasse to the north of the Frankfurter Allee running due east from the city centre. I had already been to the Normannenstrasse to look at the national headquarters of the Stasi, an undistinguished, long, low-rise block made of polished slabs of mustard-coloured stone with dictatorship-copper windows, tinted this colour to frustrate the inquisitive at least as much as to keep out the sun. Through the heavy steel grille of the fortified gate one could see that this was merely the foremost block of a complex of buildings. Across the street, protruding from the surrounding houses a block or so away, was a building festooned with aerials, obviously a Stasi communications centre. What I had not realised, as I wandered through the supermarket which had established itself on the ground floor of the copper-coloured block, was the true scale of the complex of which this had merely been the nerve centre and main entrance. It became clear to me only when I went to the DR and had to look for building number fifteen, entrance G. The Stasi had occupied an oblong site on more than two square kilometres, with dozens of buildings of all shapes and sizes, constructed to a considerably higher specification than the homes and workplaces of the people they spied upon with their 100,000 staff and half a million informers. All the entrances to this complex had heavy defences; the crowds which burst in during the *Wende* must have had help, both to get in and to find where the files were kept.

The legacy of distrust and fear left behind by this creepy organisation is going to take some time to extirpate. There are probably whole battalions of undiscovered Stasi spies planted in west Germany by General Markus Wolf, the Stasi spymaster who took refuge in the Soviet Union after the Wall opened and for whose arrest a warrant was issued by the Federal Attorney-General. There are fears that some of these may have gone over to working for the KGB, which is still highly active in Germany despite the

Kremlin's blessing for unification. Some Stasi agents were still at work after union, as was shown by the fact that their most highly paid known spy, a plant in the Office for the Protection of the Constitution (West German counter-intelligence), confessed to having met his "control" in east Berlin two days *after* unification (if only to say *Auf Wiedersehen?*).

The disappearance of Stasi files and their embarrassing reappearance in such incidents as the smearing of Lothar de Maizière and later of a senior journalist of *Der Spiegel* (promptly if inconclusively subjected to the investigative streamroller of his own paper after being "exposed" in another) does suggest a residual Stasi underground. There is also evidence that senior eastern policemen, by definition ex-SED and close Stasi collaborators, have been sabotaging the work of the Joint Criminal Bureau of the five new *Länder* (temporary eastern equivalent of the Federal Criminal Bureau in Wiesbaden) and other agencies investigating the excesses of the old regime. General Erich Mielke, the octogenarian GDR Minister for State Security and *ex officio* head of the Stasi, went soft in the head (or appeared to) while in detention in Berlin awaiting trial for human rights infringements, issuing orders down an unconnected telephone to phantom formations of secret police, as I learned from a private source. Mielke had even kept a file on Erich Honecker himself; its contents too were revealed, showing the erstwhile head of Party and state to have oversold his anti-Fascist "heroism" as a Nazi detainee and to have betrayed a fellow resister. One wonders whether this dossier was ever used to bring pressure to bear on Honecker in the years before the *Wende* and if so, to what end. There could have been no other reason (apart from self-preservation) for Mielke to have kept such a record.

The hunt for Stasi agents and informers continued into 1991; fears that the process of weeding out the worst offenders would be uneven, uncertain and therefore unfair in many cases seemed to be justified as eastern office-bearers sought to sweep the whole sinister legacy under the carpet while western ignoramuses tried to stoke up a witch-hunt. There is surely no way of performing such a distasteful task to universal or even general satisfaction. But it had to be done.

That the hydra-headed Stasi organisation was not yet dead, despite multiple administrative decapitations and many arrests, was suggested *inter alia* by a detailed report in *Der Spiegel* (as usual). The Hamburg magazine said in March 1991 that some operatives calling themselves the "Red Fist" had gone underground to continue the fight against those engaged in dismantling GDR institutions. This is reminiscent of Operation "Werewolf" whereby bitter-enders were meant to carry on guerrilla warfare after the defeat of the Nazis. Sabotage, arson and death threats were soon ascribed to the Red Fist. It is reasonable to assume that many missing Stasi files are in the hands of its former agents, for use at appropriate moments: some have already been used to cause maximum embarrassment as the stuff of sensational revelations.

At the end of March 1991 five ex-Stasi senior officials including a deputy minister, purportedly exposed by a television investigation, were detained for alleged involvement in training terrorists of the "Baader-Meinhof group", which styled itself the Red Army Faction (RAF) and shocked West Germany in the Seventies with a series of murders of leading figures in the public service and the "military-industrial complex". A convicted RAF terrorist had given details of this cynical GDR exercise in destabilisation in a press interview some months earlier; shortly after unification west German security officials rounded up ten suspected RAF members who had been living in hiding in east Berlin. Stasi involvement, alleged by several Bonn politicians, was not excluded by the police as a possibility when the RAF admitted responsibility for the shocking assassination, at his home in Düsseldorf on Easter Monday 1991, of Detlev Carsten Rohwedder, the chairman of the Treuhandanstalt. He had received anonymous death threats and a Treuhand branch office in Berlin was firebombed shortly before his death.

By that time the Treuhand, which started life as the world's largest holding company and soon became the world's busiest asset-stripper, had also become the principal scapegoat for the collapse of the economy in the former GDR. "Treuhand out!" was one of the most frequently heard cries in the new wave of demonstrations which arose in east Germany when the winter began to wane. Some of his political masters in the ruling coalition in Bonn grew uneasy about Rohwedder's strategy in disposing of the more than 8,000 ex-VEBs or state-owned businesses. These had been entrusted to the Treuhand on 1 March 1990, when it was founded by the last SED government under Hans Modrow. Its original task was simply to turn the VEBs into western-style joint stock or private limited companies. When I called at its offices on the "Alex" in January 1991 it had privatised some 700 firms and also shut down several of the very largest GDR enterprises with the loss of hundreds of thousands of jobs.

It was only under the treaty of monetary union which came into force on 1 July 1990 that the Treuhand's role changed from conversion to privatisation and *Sanierung* (rehabilitation). Its status is that of a public institution or corporation under the supervision of the Federal Ministers of Finance and Economics. By that date the de Maizière government was in charge; the idea of switching to doctrinaire privatisation came from Bonn. It set up a branch in east Berlin and each of the fourteen other *Bezirke* of the former GDR. Western managers took the top jobs in each place; east Germans recruited from the old command economy took the secondary and tertiary posts, which made a lot of east Germans suspicious and unhappy. In overall charge was Herr Rohwedder, SPD member, economic state secretary in Helmut Schmidt's administration and then for ten years chairman of Hoesch, the west German steel company which he saved from bankruptcy and led to new levels of prosperity – a man much admired by Helmut Kohl, who prevailed on him to convert his short-term commitment to the Treuhand into a long one. It turned out to be for a lifetime, cut tragically short by a fanatical gunman.

A few companies could be privatised almost at once and some others after a relatively straightforward rehabilitation, but most only after lengthy slimming and surgery, much of it drastic or even terminal. Each ex-VEB was told to prepare a scheme for its own reorganisation and privatisation, including an opening balance of assets and liabilities expressed in D-marks, and send it to the Treuhand by February 1991. Once this stage was complete and the Treuhand had gone through the flood of paper thus generated, decisions were expected on a substantial number of bank-ruptcies of the weakest companies – a good thousand, Treuhand sources thought, but nobody could do anything but guess. Of the 400 firms which had been examined by the time I called, about fifty, one in eight, had been closed as unviable. During the waiting period, workers with little or nothing to do were being put on what was politely termed "short-time working" on up to ninety per cent of their pay until 30 June 1991 at the latest. After that, at the end of the first year of economic union, workers lost their last protection from dismissal. This was widely expected to be the low point – or the start of the worst period of adjustment – for the whole of the ex-GDR economy and society. The only questions were, how low and how long? The forecasts grew worse and worse as the economic problems mounted before the deadline. Workers who did not take early retirement, retraining or new jobs would then have to fall back on unemployment benefit.

Each Treuhand branch has an advisory council with local government, business, union and other representatives. The head office is run by an administrative council which has senior representatives of the *Länder* governments on it. The Treuhand controlled the fate of six million people out of the twelve million who had been on the GDR's bloated payrolls (the real workforce was about nine million, of which the VEBs employed half). At the turn of the year, some 700,000 were officially out of work and two million more on "short time"; predictions of fifty per cent unemployment in mid-1991 were already commonplace before winter ended. One sensible idea from Bonn was to re-enlist retired western managers and executives temporarily to help east German concerns to adapt to the social market economy. Some 250 to 300 western managers were helping to root out and replace the old-boy networks of the previous regime (the in word for this was *Seilschaft*, literally a group of people on the same rope, as in mountaineering). Some old SED bosses had built up contacts in west Germany before the *Wende*, something which also had to be watched.

Dr Schneider, the busy press spokesman of the Treuhand, had the jacket sleeves of his expensive double-breasted suit rolled up, his tie at half-mast and a strong American cigarette protruding from under his bushy blond moustache when I called (by appointment for a change). The worst problems for the trust corporation were, as he saw them, the organisation of the Treuhand itself and its work, still far from finalised, and the question of who owned what in the ex-GDR. "How can you sell a business or persuade anyone to invest in it when you don't know who owns the land? Fortunately there is protection for property whose restitution would cost jobs," he said.

In addition to privatising (or closing) the VEBs, the Treuhand had set up a separate company for the privatisation of trade, whose task was to dismantle the HO (Handelsorganisation, trade organisation) and Konsum (the consumer cooperative) into 11,000 or so component shops, restaurants and other small businesses. The Treuhand's budget until the end of 1991 for all its activities stood at DM25 billion at the end of 1990; any money it made from sales was to be added to this, such as the DM1.5 billion it had got for 200 companies. As early as Easter 1991, however, a deficit of DM7 billion was forecast. The Treuhand's assets had an estimated paper value of DM600 billion in the form of over 8,000 undertakings with a total of 40,000 plants, plus 45,000 small businesses, 1.8 million hectares of farmland and 1.9 million of forest. The trust would have no objection if cooperatives, whether in farming or shopping, continued as such under the new dispensation. It also owned all the property once held by the Stasi, which might be worth DM20 or even

DM40 billion, the former holdings of the SED, the bloc parties and the old state or Party mass organisations. "All in all the Treuhand owns eighty per cent of the world's eleventh industrial power, which makes us the world's biggest holding company. Our ambition is to become the smallest."

One VEB in four was likely to be handed over to local government, as was much of the land. Nearly two million individual items were, however, the subjects of the one million property claims lodged by 13 October 1990, and it would take ten to fifteen years for all the legal questions to be resolved. "But we can't wait that long. Paragraph 41 of the treaty of union says we can act as owners if the fate of a piece of property is vital to the interests of the economy.

"We are not interested in speculative but only in genuinely entre-preneurial investment. We do not necessarily take the best monetary offer, but we are looking at the bidder's plans for investment, develop-ment and jobs as well, with a view to the best interests of the economy – even if that means we have to chip in ourselves," Dr Schneider said. Unfortunately there was seldom more than one bidder in play – if any. The total accumulated debt of the Treuhand's holdings amounted to the pretty sum of DM110 billion, which the organisation was having to service. "Naturally new investors don't want to take on old debts or environmental problems and we do what we can to help out, even to the extent of contributing the odd million. If a business with a paper value of DM50 million owes 30 million and has an ecological problem which will cost 20 million to clear up, we might sell the whole thing for DM1!"

Why should investors come to east Germany? Dr Schneider pointed out that it was in the European Community, which was lowering its internal trade barriers at the end of 1992; that ninety-five per cent of its exports had gone to the old Soviet bloc, which meant there was enormous knowledge of eastern Europe on hand, to be exploited when current uncertainties in and around the Soviet Union ended; and that the standard of education was high, with a lot of knowledge of Russian. "All that most workers here need is a few months retraining and then they'll be ready. There are two workers here for each real job available, which suggests peak unemployment of 4.5 million; but in the medium term I would expect 2.5 million new jobs in service industries. I don't think more than one in eight of the old VEBs will actually have to be liquidated; certainly not the one in three predicted in some quarters." (This optimis-tic assessment of course took no account of the likelihood that nearly every privatised company would have to shed jobs even if it survived otherwise intact.)

Dr Schneider expected to see most economic problems solved or well on the way to solution within five years. "Some assets like the shipyards in Rostock and the steelworks at Eisenhüttenstadt will probably never be sold because they are in the wrong industries. But we will make an attempt to sell the lot. We want to encourage management buyouts and we are also trying to get the Community to invest, but there is a general shortage of capital. Of the foreign investors, the French have shown the most interest, but the Americans and the Italians have been in touch too. Our main problems are serious, yes, but they are mostly short- and partly medium-term. There has never been a corporation more keen to wind itself up and go out of business than the Treuhandanstalt."

The whole question of who owned what in the former GDR had come up yet again during my visit to the Treuhand, after so many people I met elsewhere had mentioned it as the principal obstacle to new investment and a prosperous future for the new *Länder*. I therefore determined that before I left Berlin and the former GDR I would try to find out more about this minefield of a problem, even though nobody had a full overview of it as claims had been lodged at municipal level.

My invaluable guide on this occasion was Herr Puhst of the Finance Department in east Berlin. He told me that there were 150,000 to 200,000 cases (each of which might include more than one claim) affecting assets of all kinds in east Berlin, not just ground and buildings. There were between 70 and 80,000 claims on land, 30–40,000 on mortgages not paid off under the old regime and about 60,000 bank, post office or building society accounts and other items. "This is a very crude estimate. For instance, a person might be claiming for a house, the furniture that had been in it, the precious vase that stood on the furniture and so on. The claims came in by the sackload, and we are busy putting them all in a computer, which is taking an awful lot of time, but it's the only way we will be able to handle it all."

Herr Puhst suggested as a notional example that one person living in west Germany after leaving his former east Berlin home without GDR government permission might have a claim on a piece of land in his native Rostock. Not knowing precisely where to send in his claim, he might have written to Rostock, to Berlin because he lived there, to the mayors of both cities, to the last GDR government and the present all-German one. East Berlin was by far the worst affected ara, so much so that it was hard to find a piece of land there which was unencumbered. If a plot was owned by the local authorities continuously from before 1933 the city government could immediately use it for new investment or other socially beneficial purposes.

"The overall legal position is still not clear," said Herr Puhst. "But I think the basic philosophy must be that an old injustice should not be corrected by a new one, especially when it comes to people's homes. A dispossessed owner must, of course, be compensated, but someone who rented his property in good faith should not be evicted, certainly not if the owner does not need or want to move into the place as his residence. In other cases the only humane solution is monetary compensation. The Federal Government will have to sort out at what level this is paid. Nor should a tenant be affected by a change of owner over his head: the tenancy agreement should remain in force. I see the questions of ownership and of rental agreements as fundamentally separate."

Herr Puhst thought people who demonstrated against the prospect of mass evictions had acted prematurely because there was no such threat. But he understood their point of view. There was general insecurity and uncertainty about the future, whether about work or housing. Everybody knew the subsidies were coming off in 1991. "What is getting through to everybody now is that they have lost the cocooning from cradle to grave that they used to have under the old system, which was often very constricting, but sometimes it was reassuring too. Yet a system which held rents down to fifty marks a month or less in a place like Berlin was bound to come a cropper at some stage."

He thought the land claims would be the hardest to settle; claims for bank accounts and the like should be settled routinely in a year or so. But the property issues could drag on for ten or twenty years. Owners might have a right to land, but certainly not to the buildings or services put on it since they lost it; in such cases compensation was the only solution. "The Swiss family which owns the ground on which the east Berlin television tower stands will get compensation, not the tower. But this won't be possible until we know at what rate compensation is to be paid. That will depend on new legislation. Property speculators are talking about prices of DM14,000 per square metre in Berlin-Mitte, which is more than land costs now in the Kurfürstendamm [west Berlin's smartest thoroughfare]. I can recall when such land cost DM10 per metre! Such talk is madness."

The treaty documentation made it clear that land urgently needed for preserving old or creating new jobs or for the construction of new housing would not be returned; compensation would be paid. Judiciously used, Puhst said, this could be a loophole for solving some urgent economic and social questions. It amounted to dispossession by compulsory purchase and ought to be used circumspectly, he thought, and there was indeed much hesitation before using it. "Otherwise we shall be accused of behaving just like the SED." The draft Berlin city law taking advantage of this provision had been back and forth twice between officials and legislators, and only the third draft had been accepted because of the sensitivity of the issue. Lower limits on the number of jobs involved – 100 – and the level of investment had been set to make sure dispossession was not imposed for trivial or capricious reasons. Since the first city-wide election, coinciding with the Federal one on December 2, had made the CDU the largest party in Berlin instead of the SPD, the new CDU-led "grand coalition" with the SPD was bound to look at the matter again.

In fact, almost everybody with whom I discussed this issue in depth all over eastern Germany took the view that fair monetary compensation should replace restitution as the guiding principle in the settlement of all property claims and that this should be enacted as soon as possible as a Federal law. Only then would tenants and small businesses feel secure, investors confident and local authorities free to make optimum use of land standing idle. On reflection, failure to make this common-sense amendment looks insensitive, cruel and extremely shortsighted.

Article two of the Unification Treaty says: "Capital of Germany is Berlin." A debate raged from the moment the text was released in August 1990. It all depends on what is meant by the word "capital". Berlin was the Prussian capital, and Prussia as the biggest and strongest German state acted as the locomotive of unification in 1871. Berlin therefore logically became the capital, in the broadest sense, of the Second Reich, and the Third, and the Weimar Republic in between, the whole of the period during which modern Germany was united, from 1871 to 1945. Now Germany is united again and Berlin has been restored, only symbolically so far, to its old status and the role for which it was created. The real issue now lies between Bonn and Berlin as legislative and administrative capital. A report prepared by consultants at the behest of Bonn city council claimed in February 1991 that it would cost DM50 billion or more to make the switch, and 100,000 people would have to move house to a place with a desperate housing crisis. Say we halve this worst-case estimate; it still seemed insane even to think of it when the cost of unification had already gone into orbit.

Foreigners, whose business it essentially is not, have argued that Berlin is unsuitable because it is the place from which all Germany's foreign wars were launched. If that argument is valid, then surely unification should not have been allowed either. If there is a psychological cum political and diplomatic argument against Berlin it has less to do with the past than with the future. To my mind a move there would indicate a shift (yet again) of German attention eastward, to the alarm of the Poles, the annoyance of the Soviet Union and the anxiety of the West. A decision to stay in Bonn, for all but symbolic national acts like the opening of parliament in the Reichstag building, would be a reassuring sign of enduring commitment to the West, to the European Community and the Nato Alliance (whatever form that may take in the future). For Chancellor Kohl and most other German politicians of all colours, German unification is but the prelude to European unification, of which Germany, the Continent's strongest economy, would like to be the locomotive.

There are many aspects to a capital city, of which the "metropolis" concept is probably the most important. New York will always remain the American metropolis and financial capital, and Amsterdam the Dutch, no matter what goes on in Washington or The Hague. In South Africa, which is no more federal than the Netherlands, Cape Town is both the metropolis and the legislative, Pretoria the administrative, Bloemfontein the judicial and Johannesburg the financial capital, and Durban the principal port. In West Germany before union Bonn was the legislative and administrative capital, Frankfurt the financial, Karlsruhe the judicial and Hamburg the main port. Other Federal Government functions are spread across the country from the central driver and vehicle registry in Flensburg to the patent office in Munich. Berlin is monumental in every sense and is already the metropolis of union and the cultural capital, unique and not inconsiderable national functions inseparable from the identity of united Germany. As an admirer of the city for a quarter of a century and as someone who has always welcomed any chance to go there, I venture to suggest that this seems exactly right. Anything more would only add to the very considerable headaches arising from the reunification, within German unification, of its symbolic capital.

On 12 January 1991 there occurred the seventy-second anniversary of the assassinations of Karl Liebknecht and Rosa Luxemburg, far-left Socialist leaders of the Spartacist revolt, which was an attempt to turn Germany into a Soviet republic. They were murdered by cavalry officers and their bodies thrown into the Landwehr Canal in central Berlin. This anniversary was a traditional occasion for a massive SED rally in east Berlin, attended by the *Politbüro* and the entire Party leadership. It was, therefore, more than merely astounding that an estimated 80–100,000 people turned out in bitterly cold weather to attend the first commemoration of this event to be organised by the PDS, as an unofficial demonstration after the revolution which brought down the SED regime. Obviously this was not a display of sentimentality for the universally loathed Communist administration. So what was it – a sign of regret that Socialism was given no chance to reform itself, that the GDR was not allowed to seek a "third way"? In any event, reports of the death of Socialist sentiment in the former German Democratic Republic seem decidedly premature. As hardship spread and protests mounted across the territory of Germany's failed Communist experiment under its new CDU management, this nostalgic manifestation looked like a most intriguing portent. The only question is, of what . . .

EPILOGUE

Bonn's megablunder – incomprehension – migration goes on – protest revived – German Question answered? – Silesia – Poland mishandled – funny old freedom

Epilogue

East Germany was the least unsuccessful example of the now totally discredited, Soviet-Communist socio-economic model. When the Marxist-Leninist chickens began to come home to roost in 1989, seventy-two years after the Russian Revolution, all eastern Europe was affected. Of the ten countries involved, the German Democratic Republic seemed best placed by far to make the transition to a democratic, social market economy with the least pain. While all the others had to make do with such internal resources as they could muster, plus unpredictable favours from the European Community, the United States or nobody at all, the GDR was adopted by its fellow Germans, shareholders in Europe's strongest economy, and was spared the effort of making its own way in a world transformed by the dissolution of the Soviet bloc. Was it not uniquely fortunate in having the bulging coffers of West Germany plc to draw upon?

The short answer is No. Initially Bonn refused to open its coffers wider than a crack, relying on free enterprise and minimum governmental pump-priming to work the same wonders in the new German east as Ludwig Erhard's economic miracle, sparked by Marshall Aid, had begun to do in the west forty years earlier. But this was a false analogy. The plight of the east in 1990 was completely different from that of the German west in 1950, when the whole of Europe, including Germany's neighbours and former conquests, was just beginning to recover from the Second World War. East Germany's immediate and voracious demand for consumer goods could be met comfortably from spare western productive capacity. There was a strong and sustained boom in western Germany at the expense of east Germany's hopelessly uncompetitive economy – out of date, debt-ridden and choking on its own pollution. The profits and tax revenues thus gained stayed overwhelmingly in the west, which therefore sidestepped the recession affecting other western countries. Meanwhile asset-strippers, carpetbaggers, flying traders and smooth salesmen of the superfluous were given the run of the former GDR, where so many of the market-unwise population were readily persuaded to part with their savings. At the same time the Treuhand was only too keen to rationalise their jobs out of existence in order to rid itself of otherwise unsaleable assets. When Bonn began to realise the scale of the disaster it had unleashed, it opened the coffers in panicky fits and starts, throwing out handfuls of money and slamming the lid down again until the next time it was moved to make a handout.

The truly shocking, the mind-boggling, gobsmacking blunder of the conservative-liberal coalition in Bonn was its total failure to draw up any kind of a plan for the integration of the GDR into the Federal Republic. Its doctrinaire error was to believe that Marxist-Leninist planning had been bad, nay fatal, for the GDR; therefore all planning was bad. The Kohl government, above all the Chancellor himself, handled the political aspects of German unification with consummate skill, backed by a combination of flexibility, opportunism and sheer luck (otherwise known as Mikhail Gorbachev). But it wasted a whole year, from the announcement in February 1990 of the first free election in the GDR to the promulgation of Federal tax increases in February 1991, before beginning to get to grips with the economic and financial catastrophe in the east. And it was but a beginning; the tax increases were only for the year starting 1 July 1991 and would yield only DM37 billion (whereas modernising the ex-GDR's hospitals alone could cost DM30 billion).

Prior to that Bonn had relied on the free market and on unprecedented government borrowing – DM70 billion in 1991 alone, more or less doubling Bonn's total indebtedness at a stroke and incurring formidable burdens in interest and repayment, which will constrain future aid to the east. Early tax increases would have been much more economical, sparing government and tax-payer interest payments and probably forestalling rises in interest rates. The only concessions to the already obvious need for more revenue before the election were to raise social security contributions, which hit the lowest-paid hardest (including the east Germans), and to force the Federal Post to raise telephone charges, which was a sadistic insult to the ex-GDR, where the service was of Albanian standards. It was very noticeable how Bonn's leading politicians, who had been virtually commuting between west and east during the 1990 general election campaign, stayed away as the economic winter bit hard and deep in 1991. Despite the considerable best efforts of Doctors Biedenkopf and Stolpe plus the west German media to convey the burgeoning horror in the east, the observer was left with the impression that Bonn either could not or would not see the scale of the problem, apparently hoping that it would go away.

Seldom, if ever, accused of giving any government the benefit of the doubt, I nevertheless incline to the view that Bonn's complacent-to-comatose early response was due less to conspiracy than to cock-up. Dr Kohl's record (and frequent success) in sitting out crises until they "go away" is irrefutable; there is no reason to doubt that the *laissez faire* Chancellor, his political lightweight of a Finance Minister, Theo Waigel, both CDU-CSU, and their free-enterprise liberal coalition partners from the FDP actually did believe at the beginning that the free market would be the making rather than the breaking of the ex-GDR. Doubtless they were encouraged in this belief by the readiness of the last (CDU) government of the GDR to say Yes to almost everything Bonn's CDU-led government suggested, thus exposing their constituents to the hurricanes of the economic winter correctly forecast by the opposition SPD and countless independent experts and observers in east and west. Dr Kohl's promises that nobody would suffer and no taxes would be raised for union may even have been pious hopes or Micawberism rather than the calculated lies in the interest of electoral victory of which he was widely accused when the truth began to dawn.

However, I am morally certain that there were those in his camp who saw it coming very clearly indeed and said nothing because it would have annoyed the Chancellor, alarmed the voters and helped the SPD. The east Germans were let down by the eastern CDU, which did nothing to protect them, and knowingly or unknowingly deceived by the western CDU, which did nothing to prepare them. But the freshly united party made a huge and unrepeatable profit from its spectacular political unification coup before the economic bills started to come in. Dr Kohl achieved a brief apotheosis and won his place in the history books as Chancellor of union; but the pages of history remain open and there is still time for them to record the ruination of his government and his reputation as a result of the bungling of unification. His crushing defeat in Rhineland-Palatinate in April 1991 already gave back control of the Bundesrat (upper house) to the SPD.

Meanwhile the former GDR, already a "wild east" for the new criminal class and the dwindling police force, threatened to become a "deep east" as more and more of its younger people commuted – or migrated – in their tens of thousands to the west for work. Half the people aged between eighteen and twenty-six left Schwedt in Brandenburg to find work in the west. The birth-rate fell measurably in big cities such as Leipzig, while the suicide rate went up (by nine per cent in Potsdam) and millions tackling or facing unemployment began to develop the feeling that they had been sold down the Elbe. Bus, tram and train fares, gas and electricity went up by a factor of three or more, and rents were poised to go through the leaking roof: tenants of an apartment house in Bärbel Bohley's street were warned of a twenty-five-fold increase to finance renovations, by no means a unique manifestation of the free play of market forces. Whole cities faced bankruptcy and a collapse in public services. The health service was in a similar state.

Within weeks or months of union, railway workers and truck drivers had staged damaging warning strikes, police had resigned in thousands or demonstrated massively for better pay and conditions, 35,000 shipbuilders took over Rostock to protest against the threat of dismissal, the first factory strikes and sit-ins in despairing defence of disappearing jobs had taken place, and agriculture seemed set to gag on its own unwanted produce. Weekly demonstrations resumed in Leipzig, Erfurt and elsewhere. More sadly still, they were soon called off because the people had lost the will to protest. All this before 30 June 1991, when those still in work in eastern Germany lost the last vestige of special protection from redundancy unless they had managed to register for a retraining course. At times the forecasts of fifty per cent unemployment, worse than anything in the Slump, looked a shade optimistic. To have to cope with such an economic typhoon seemed bad enough; for it to coincide with the deliberate demolition, replacement or upheaval of every public institution seemed almost calculated to cause a collective breakdown. All this for the want of a plan.

Did unification finally answer the German Question? Was and is there a definitive political and diplomatic gain to show for the economic black hole rapidly developing on the territory of the former GDR? The answer to this question about a Question lies in Poland. It was deeply depressing to see in Germany's (and Europe's) finest intellectual magazine, *Die Zeit*

Epilogue

of Hamburg, in the very week of unification, a special supplement on the residual German minority in Polish Silesia. This may number a third of a million, though the "German Friendship Circle", newly permitted in the region by democratising Poland, postulated a total of 800,000 people of German origin; there might be a million in all Poland (total population about 40 million). The true figure will never be clear because those with German connections may not have German names and quite commonly lack the language, which was effectively banned by the defunct Polish Communist regime. But could this minority develop into the kind of destabilising "critical mass" that ethnic Germans had become in the Bohemian-Czech Sudetenland, in Danzig and Polonised West Prussia between the wars? If the Poles continue as they began, keeping cool, being fair and not objecting to local cultural revivalism, the answer is probably not: there are not enough Germans concentrated anywhere in Poland to pose such a threat.

But that does not mean the end of all anxiety for the Poles. Chancellor Kohl, for one, is not good on the Polish problem, which he does not fully understand he has. Mishandled, it could still become a minefield comparable with Bonn's ever-hypersensitive relationship with Israel (or Britain's uncomprehending relations with Ireland), and for not dissimilar reasons. Not long after coming to power in 1982, Kohl gave an interview to *Die Zeit* in which he said that the legal issues arising out of the truncation and division of Germany remained open in the absence of a formal settlement of the Second World War – this a dozen years after Bonn had solemnly recognised all borders in Europe in its "eastern treaties" with Warsaw and Moscow, as it did again under the Helsinki accords in 1975. Somehow the Poles were not mollified by Kohl's subsequent protestations that Bonn would never seek to recover Silesia unilaterally or break its treaty obligations, still less allow a war to start from German soil again for any reason.

As the German unification bandwagon began to roll, the Poles requested a formal and final all-German recognition of the Oder-Neisse line as Germany's permanent eastern frontier. So did the Soviet Union, the United States and Bonn's European allies, amid increasing consternation over the silence from Bonn. Kohl stalled for internal political reasons with his general election in mind. When Poland got its wish, it was granted with such ill grace that the Poles undoubtedly continued to regard German unity as a standing threat to them.

The internal political reasons on Kohl's mind were the millions of

261

voters, mostly CDU, who came to west Germany from Poland and points east of the Oder-Neisse line. These are represented in the powerful League of Expellees. Kohl was the first Chancellor to attend the League's annual congress, a milestone in the history of a body which enjoyed enormous clout in Bonn from the beginnings of the Federal Republic. Other chancellors had wisely kept their distance, though none tried to put a stop to Bonn's annual subsidy to League funds, sanctioned by the Bundestag, where expellee deputies were prominent. The League had for forty years helped to keep alive the irredentist hope of German *re*unification, which is to say the reconstitution of Germany as it was in 1937, including East Pomerania, Silesia and East Prussia. There was nothing to the right of the League's position except the lunatic fringe demanding the borders of 1914. So long as unification (the union of the two German states which had arisen after 1945) remained unrealised, the League held out the hope of reunification *à la mode de* 1937 to those in Silesia who still wanted to be Germans without the hassle of having to move to Germany; they would prefer Germany to move to them. Only on union in 1990 was it clear to these people that Bonn was going to leave them outside the new Germany. The League continues to minister to their aspirations; Bonn continues to "sub" the League (to the tune of DM12,372,423 in 1990). To her credit, Rita Süssmuth, CDU President (speaker) of the Bundestag, publicly said this was wrong on a visit to Warsaw early in 1991.

As for the Poles themselves, Bonn showed no sign after union, or even after the first all-German election, of developing the requisite sensitivity towards them so manifestly lacking beforehand. When Kohl met Prime Minister Tadeusz Mazowiecki at Frankfurt-on-Oder in November, he stalled on aid and visas; everybody knew the Germans had agreed to the meeting to boost Mazowiecki's chances for the presidency against the (in Bonn's eyes) "unpredictable" Lech Walesa, who nevertheless and predictably won hands down. When Jan Krzystof Bielicki, the new Polish Prime Minister, visited Bonn in March, Kohl stalled on aid and visas, and promised no more than sympathy to the new Polish Government in its efforts to reduce Poland's horrendous foreign debt. Although Poland removed visa restrictions on 1 January 1991, Germany did not do so until April 8. When it did, the first Poles to arrive were subjected to disgraceful abuse, threats and barracking by racists and extreme right-wing demonstrators. Although Bonn promised in November 1990 to start ratification of treaties recognising the border and instituting general intergovernmental cooperation "as soon as possible", there was no sign of it when Mr Bielicki left. The best Dr Kohl could offer was a possible tabling of the treaties by the end of June; no promises, mind. Meanwhile another issue was waiting in the wings: the passage of the Soviet troops from eastern Germany across Poland back to their homeland, which Poland regarded as a problem it did not need.

Relations with Warsaw will never come right unless Bonn elevates them to the same level of priority as its very successful relationship with touchy France, its key neighbour in the west. This was based on an understanding that three huge wars launched from Germany in seventy years had to be made good; but it was also eased by German admiration for most things French, which goes back to Prussian days, if not earlier, and almost amounts to an inferiority complex. In the case of Poland, *pro rata* the nation most badly damaged by the Second World War, there is a German historical tradition of disdain amounting to widespread superiority feelings or, not to put to fine a point on it, racism. I have heard and seen the evidence that it is still alive today in Berlin when it was swarming with Poles just before unification day. This is going to be much harder to overcome, but, if the united Germans want security on their eastern frontier, they must not allow it to become either a fence to keep out the Poles or the boundary between rich and poor in Europe as a whole. We have lived to see a French president and a German chancellor holding hands at Verdun; shall we see a chancellor and a Polish leader doing the same at Gliwice (formerly Gleiwitz), where the Second World War began? Or are the resurgent neo-Nazis in the east to be allowed to set the tone?

Marion Countess Dönhoff, distinguished *doyenne* of German journalism and a senior editor of *Die Zeit* (which has an all too rare "feel" for German-Polish relations), reported early in March 1991 to her paper that the Poles were coping much better with adapting to the free market which was proving such a trauma for the east Germans. This was in spite of the especially daunting problems Poland had to face, such as a freeze on tiny wages and gigantic price rises, huge external and internal debts, lack of capital, backward agriculture, antiquated industry and all the rest. But Poland is a proud nation with its own defined borders (Bonn permitting), behind which it can shelter while it brings its own house in order. Despite great hardships unmatched in eastern Germany, the Poles, undiminished by years of political struggle which led the way to the liberation of eastern

Europe as a whole, seemed to be regenerating their even more down-at-heel country with a resolution few believed they possessed. They appeared to be psychologically prepared to see the process through, virtually regardless of the sacrifices. East Germany was never a nation and has ceased to be a state; it has nothing behind which it can shelter to prevent itself being swallowed up by the untrammelled free market, as represented by west Germany and the European Community.

How ironic in the straitened circumstances on either side of the Oder-Neisse line that it should have been the disciplined east Germans with their rich western cousins who could not cope, and the poor, chaotic Poles with no D-marks and few friends who showed such determination to help themselves – and to do it in their own way. But it is precisely that which was denied to the hapless denizens of Thuringia, Saxony, Brandenburg, Mecklenburg-West Pomerania, Saxony-Anhalt and east Berlin: the chance to rescue themselves in their own way. Dazzled by the D-mark, dunned by carpetbaggers, deceived by their new leaders and devastated by a rampant free market, they live on the wrong side of the tracks left behind by the old fortified boundary, in a Federal German occupation zone.

Freedom was never like this.

Acknowledgements

I should like to offer my warmest thanks to all those east German people who helped me with information so unstintingly. They did so in almost every case, despite my rapidly adopted tactic of turning up unannounced.

I should also like to express my gratitude to Ion Trewin, Editorial Director of Hodder & Stoughton, for his enthusiasm about the underlying idea, which grew out of our unplanned lunch at the Frankfurt Book Fair; to my old friend Wolfgang Bergsdorf; to Margit Hosseini of the German Embassy in London, for information and advice; to Michael Shaw and Marion Cookson at Curtis Brown, my literary agents; to the staff of Twickers World travel agency in Twickenham, who solved many unnecessary but real logistical problems; to Andrew Frost for contacts; to Desmond Cecil for the loan of books; and to my wife, for tolerance of long absences and a very pleasant surprise birthday-party in Berlin, when she was in the midst of showing her students a state in dissolution and I was trying to find hotel rooms in east Germany with similar designs upon my readers.

I consulted many guide books, histories and works of reference. Those planning to see east Germany for themselves will be well advised to make use of the only book of its kind in English, *Guide to East Germany* by Stephen Baister and Chris Patrick (Bradt Publications, Chalfont St Peter, Bucks, 1990; distributed in the USA by Hunter Publishing, Edison, NJ). The most comprehensive German-language guide I found is *Baedekers Allianz Reiseführer DDR* (Karl Baedeker Verlag, Stuttgart, fifth edition, 1990).

CENTRAL EUROPE

SWEDEN

DENMARK

BALTIC SEA

NORTH SEA

USSR

ENGLAND

Hamburg

Berlin
EAST
GERMANY

POLAND

Warsaw

London

NETHERLANDS

BELGIUM

LUX.

Brussels

Bonn

WEST
GERMANY

Prague

CZECHOSLOVAKIA

Paris

Vienna

Budapest

FRANCE

SWITZERLAND

AUSTRIA

HUNGARY

ROMANIA

0   300 Km

Zagreb

Milan

ITALY

YUGOSLAVIA

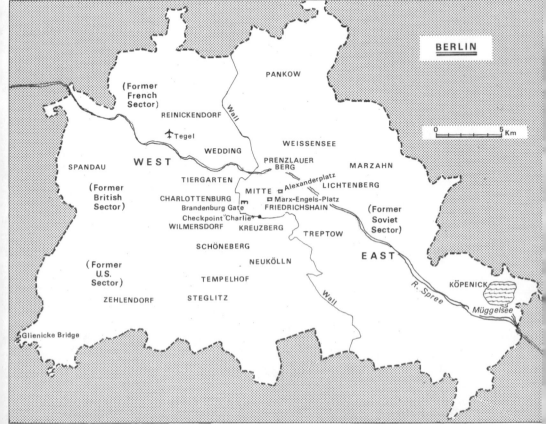

BERLIN

PANKOW

(Former
French
Sector)

REINICKENDORF

Wall

WEISSENSEE

MARZAHN

Tegel

WEDDING

SPANDAU

WEST

PRENZLAUER
BERG

0   5 Km

TIERGARTEN

Alexanderplatz

LICHTENBERG

(Former
British
Sector)

CHARLOTTENBURG

MITTE

Marx-Engels-Platz

Brandenburg Gate

FRIEDRICHSHAIN

(Former
Soviet
Sector)

Checkpoint 'Charlie'

WILMERSDORF

KREUZBERG

TREPTOW

EAST

SCHÖNEBERG

NEUKÖLLN

(Former
U.S.
Sector)

TEMPELHOF

R. Spree

KÖPENICK

ZEHLENDORF

STEGLITZ

Wall

Müggelsee

Glienicke Bridge